Liberation Theology and Praxis in Contemporary Latin America

Liberation Theology and Praxis in Contemporary Latin America: As It Was in the Beginning?

Edited by
Pablo Bradbury and Niall H. D. Geraghty

Available to purchase in print or download
for free at https://uolpress.co.uk

First published 2025 by
University of London Press
Senate House, Malet St, London WC1E 7HU

© the Authors 2025

The rights of Pablo Bradbury and Niall H. D. Geraghty to be identified as authors of this Work has been asserted in accordance with sections 77 and 78 of the Copyright, Designs and Patents Act 1988.

This book is published under a Creative Commons Attribution-NonCommercial-NoDerivatives 4.0 International (CC BY-NC-ND 4.0) license.

Any third-party material reproduced in the book is not covered by the book's Creative Commons licence, unless indicated otherwise in the image or text's credit line. To reuse third-party material not published under the same licence as the book you will need to obtain permission from the copyright holder.

A CIP catalogue record for this book is
available from The British Library.

ISBN 978-1-915249-59-3 (hardback)
ISBN 978-1-915249-61-6 (paperback)
ISBN 978-1-915249-64-7 (.epub)
ISBN 978-1-915249-63-0 (.pdf)
ISBN 978-1-915249-62-3 (.html)

DOI https://doi.org/10.14296/hflc8361

Cover image: Pablo Roberto Suárez, *Martirologio y gloria de los santos anónimos*. Photography by Viviana Gil courtesy of the *Museo de Arte Moderno de Buenos Aires* (Buenos Aires Museum of Modern Art).

Cover design for University of London Press by Hayley Warnham.
Book design by Nigel French.
Text set by Westchester Publishing Services UK in Meta Serif and Meta, designed by Erik Spiekermann.

Contents

Notes on contributors	vii
Foreword: Theology in the footsteps of the martyrs	xi
Acknowledgements	xix
Introduction: As it was in the beginning? Pablo Bradbury and Niall H. D. Geraghty	1
1. Conflict and ecclesiology: Obedience, institutionality and people of God in the Movement of Priests for the Third World Pablo Bradbury	23
2. Legacies of the 'bridge man': Catholic accompaniment, inter-class relations and the classification of surplus in Montevideo Patrick O'Hare	53
3. Orlando Fals Borda's participatory action research: At and beyond the crossroads of Camilo Torres's neo-socialism and liberation theology Juan Mario Díaz-Arévalo	83
4. The impact of liberation theology in the Latin American built environment Fernando Luiz Lara	113
5. When liberation theology met human rights Anna Grimaldi	131
6. 'Women, the key to liberation?': A feminist theology of liberation at the Catholic women's conference at Puebla Natalie Gasparowicz	159
7. Towards the possibility of an ecofeminist political theology: The case of the *Con-spirando* collective Ely Orrego Torres	179
Afterword. Contemporary witnesses to life and liberation: The persistent and evolving reality of Latin American martyrdom Elizabeth O'Donnell Gandolfo	199
Index	213

Notes on contributors

Pablo Bradbury holds a PhD in History from the University of Liverpool, writing his thesis on the emergence and mobilisation of liberation Christianity in Argentina, and particularly its political responses to state terrorism. His research more broadly focuses on left-wing political cultures and social movements in Latin America's Cold War, exploring religion, international solidarity and strategies towards state repression. He currently teaches at the University of Greenwich.

Juan Mario Díaz-Arévalo is an interdisciplinary researcher, with much of his work focusing on the interlocking challenges of conflict, violence and social injustice through the practice of participatory action research. He is a research fellow at the Department of Politics and International Relations, University of Sheffield. He completed a BPhil in Philosophy and Letters and a BA in Theology, followed by an MA in Latin American Literature. In 2017, he completed his PhD in History at the University of Roehampton, London. He is currently working on an intellectual history of sociologist Orlando Fals Borda.

Natalie Gasparowicz received her PhD from Duke University (USA). Her dissertation explores Catholic debates over sex, marriage and pleasure, following the creation of the newly invented birth control pill, in late twentieth-century Mexico. She is a recipient of the Fulbright-Hays Doctoral Dissertation Research Abroad fellowship and the American Catholic Historical Association's John Tracy Ellis Dissertation Award.

Niall H. D. Geraghty is Associate Professor in Latin American Cultural Studies at University College London. Niall's first book was *The Polyphonic Machine: Capitalism, Political Violence, and Resistance in Contemporary Argentine Literature* (University of Pittsburgh Press, 2019). He has published articles and book chapters on literature and film from Latin America, with a particular interest in memory, urban culture and religion in the region. He is currently working on a project involving a radical re-examination of the work of Argentine artist León Ferrari (1920–2013), which also explores the interrelations between politics and religion in twentieth-century Argentina, and the potential correlations between contemporary philosophy and liberation theology.

Anna Grimaldi is a lecturer in international development at the University of Leeds. In 2023, she published her first book, *Brazil and the Transnational Human Rights Movement, 1964–1985* (Anthem Press). Currently, her work focuses on the pedagogy of Cold War Latin American History, including a recent project to study the far right in the region. Her work is inspired by solidarity in its myriad forms.

Fernando Luiz Lara is a Professor of Architecture at the Weitzman School of Design, University of Pennsylvania. His recent publications includes edited volumes on *Spatial Concepts for Decolonizing the Americas* (Cambridge Scholars, 2022) and *Decolonizing the Spatial History of the Americas* (Texas Center for American Architecture and Design, 2021), and the books *Street Matters: A Critical History of Twentieth-Century Urban Policy in Brazil* (with Ana Paula Koury, University of Pittsburgh, 2022), *Excepcionalidad del Modernismo Brasileño* (Romano Guerra, 2019) and *Modern Architecture in Latin America: Art, Technology and Utopia* (with Luis Carranza, Texas Press, 2015).

Elizabeth O'Donnell Gandolfo is the Earley Associate Professor of Catholic and Latin American Studies and Associate Dean for Academic Affairs at Wake Forest University School of Divinity. A constructive feminist theologian rooted in the Catholic tradition, her teaching and research places Christian theology in conversation with human resilience and resistance to vulnerability and violence, especially in contexts of social injustice and ecological degradation. Gandolfo's most recent publications include *Ecomartyrdom in the Americas: Living and Dying for Our Common Home* (Orbis, 2023) and the co-authored book *Re-membering the Reign of God: The Decolonial Witness of El Salvador's Church of the Poor* (Lexington, 2022).

Patrick O'Hare is a Senior Researcher and UKRI Future Leaders Fellow at the University of St Andrews. He received his PhD in Social Anthropology (Cambridge, 2017) and has held research positions at the Universities of Cambridge, Manchester and Surrey, conducting research in Uruguay, Mexico, Argentina and the UK on themes relating to labour, waste, recycling and plastics. He is the author of *Rubbish Belongs to the Poor: Hygienic Enclosure and the Waste Commons* (Pluto Press, 2022), co-author of *Taking Form, Making Worlds: Cartonera Publishers in Latin America* (Texas University Press, 2022) and co-editor of *Circular Economies in an Unequal World* (Bloomsbury, 2024).

Ely Orrego Torres was born and raised in Chile and is a PhD candidate in Political Science at Northwestern University (Evanston, Illinois). Currently, she is a visiting PhD student at the Centre de Recherches Internationales (CERI) at Sciences Po-Paris. She was a Northwestern Buffett Global Impacts Graduate Fellow, a Social Science Research Council Religion, Spirituality, and Democratic Renewal Fellow (SSRC-Fetzer Institute) and a Mellon Cluster Fellow in Critical Theory. Previously, she earned a BA in Political Science from the Pontifical Catholic University of Chile and an MA in Philosophy and Contemporary Thought from Diego Portales University. Her research agenda intertwines political theory and international relations to address questions on religion and politics in the global context.

Martha Zechmeister CJ was born in 1956 in Austria and studied theology in Vienna, where she completed her doctoral thesis in 1985 and habilitation thesis in 1997. She was Professor of Fundamental Theology at the University of Passau, Germany, from 1999 to 2008. Since 2008, she has been Professor of Systematic Theology at the Universidad Centroamericana José Simeón Cañas, San Salvador (El Salvador), and since 2012 has directed the master's programme in Latin American Theology. She is also responsible for the 'Casa Dean Brackley', a residence of scholarship students from extremely poor areas. Her main research interests include political theology, Latin American liberation theology and Ignatian spirituality.

Foreword: Theology in the footsteps of the martyrs

Martha Zechmeister CJ

Allow me to begin very simply.[1] Jon Sobrino, my colleague here at the *Universidad Centroamericana José Simeón Cañas* (UCA), has repeatedly stressed how crucial it is to make us aware of the place from which we do theology: the *ubi*. My place is El Salvador, and in November 2020 my university celebrated the thirty-first anniversary of the martyrdom of its rector Ignacio Ellacuría with five of his Jesuit brothers and two women companions. What liberation theology means to me, I cannot separate from this place and this history.

The legacy of the martyrs commits us

In the immediate vicinity of my office and the lecture halls of the Department of Theology of my university is the Rose Garden, the place where our companions were killed. This place makes it truly clear to me what it means to do theology. For me it is holy ground, and like all of El Salvador it is sanctified by the blood of its martyrs, among them Óscar Romero and Rutilio Grande. In them and through them the drama of Jesus became present, current historical reality, as Ignacio Ellacuría would say. The martyrs of El Salvador, like Jesus, placed themselves unconditionally at the side of the victims, unmasking those who have the power to kill. In doing so, they provoked the fury of the perpetrators and were finally destroyed by those to whom they pointed. Salvadoran martyrs are the real presence of the mystery of Jesus' crucifixion and resurrection, the central mystery of our faith.

This mystery, which they have consistently lived and sealed with their blood, is matched by the theological language that they wielded with extraordinary power. Rutilio Grande, Óscar Romero and Ignacio Ellacuría marked a new way of proclaiming the Good News and denouncing sin in a way that the Salvadoran Church had not known before. This new way of speaking firmly rejects theological and pastoral 'docetism', empty words to which the 'flesh' of historical reality does not correspond. In this new language, 'the living and effective Word of God incarnates, sharper than any two-edged sword' (Heb 4:12). It creates reality: it is 'liberating and redeeming like Jesus's language' (Bonhoeffer 2010, 390), to put it in the words of Dietrich Bonhoeffer.

The central concept of this way of doing theology is the notion of the 'crucified people'. In it, the suffering of people who were exposed to every kind of cruelty during the civil war is boldly identified with the redemptive suffering of Jesus on the cross. The people thus addressed understood and 'canonized' this way of speaking spontaneously and immediately: 'They speak of us'. The language of Rutilio, Romero and Ellacuría reached the hearts of the most vulnerable, the victims, without hesitation, giving them ultimate theological dignity and making them subjects of their own history.

The risk of squandering this legacy

This legacy is precious because it has cost the lives of so many good people. But there are many ways to squander it. As great as the joy of the beatification and canonisation of Óscar Romero may be, it has also brought with it the danger of squandering this legacy through its inflationary exploitation and its instrumentalisation for ecclesiastical and political interests. It is scandalous when the Salvadoran president acts in his official residence in front of a huge painting of Óscar Romero, thereby concealing the government's murderous 'security policy'. The 'extraordinary measures' proposed by the president and approved by the country's legislature legalise the repression of the marginalised sections of the population and open the door to all kinds of aberrations such as torture, disappearances and 'extrajudicial executions', the lynching of marginalised young people suspected of being gang members.

To do theology from the perspective of the victims is to continue the theology of the martyrs and to be committed to the principles that guided them. The fundamental of these principles is 'honesty with what is real'. This kind of theology denies ignorance and indifference to that part of reality which harms the victims; and secondly, recognises as the most important theological task the proclamation of the 'God of life' – in resistance against all 'idols of death'. Such a theology proclaims with all available human and spiritual energies the glory of God in the struggle for the lives of the weakest and the victims.

To do this, real intellectual rigour is needed, but the task is never just an intellectual one. To do theology in the footsteps of the martyrs requires that we become followers of their practice, which is neither more nor less than the practice of Jesus. Anyone who wants to do theology in the tradition of an Óscar Romero and an Ignacio Ellacuría is committed to do what they have done. Using the metaphor of Dietrich Bonhoeffer, the great martyr of the German Lutheran Church in the Nazi era, we are called to block the spokes of the wheel with our whole existence: the barbaric instrument of medieval torture and execution symbolizes the contemporary machinery from lethal mechanisms that constantly smashes its victims.

Ignacio Ellacuría gives us the decisive clue as to what it means to actualize this theology: 'Actualise does not mean primarily updating it, at least in the sense that this expression means that it corresponds to the fashion of the times. Actualise means, rather, giving it actual reality' (Actualizarlo no significa primariamente ponerlo al día, al menos en el sentido que esta expresión puede tener de estar a la moda de los tiempos. Actualizarlo significa, más bien, dar realidad actual) (1990, 398). The theoretical-scientific effort to know the philosophical-theological concepts of the generation of martyrs also requires that we 'give actual reality' to their practice here and now. The decisive hermeneutic key that opens the access to the thinking of the martyrs is to attune ourselves with their action. Intellectual effort becomes blind if it is not illuminated by the martyr practice, and that means the practice of Jesus. Theological fruitfulness can only come from this way of acting.

Ellacuría gives us a second indication of what is essential for this kind of theology. When the Second Vatican Council urges us to explore the signs of the times, Ellacuría insists that, among the 'signs of the times' to be scrutinised, there is a principal one: 'This sign is *always* the historically crucified people, who associate with their *permanent* presence the *always different* historical form of their crucifixion' (este signo es siempre el pueblo históricamente crucificado, que une a su permanencia la siempre distinta forma histórica de su crucifixión) (1981, 58. My emphasis). It is a sad paradox: the most current and urgent challenge of all time is always the crucified people. That 'always' has nothing to do with an eternal metaphysical truth but confronts us with the ongoing scandalous reality of the crucified people in history. Any possibility of getting used to this scandal, of adapting to the inevitable, is cynicism. And the 'always the same' is in sharp contrast to the variety of the always new forms of crucifixion of human beings: the sin of the world is highly creative!

Consequently, it is not enough to notice the permanent existence of the crucified people, but it is always necessary to mobilise all available intellectual energies to analyse in detail the dynamics and vicious circles of structural sin. It takes courage and sharpness of mind to get to the bottom of this, to investigate thoroughly what the powers and mechanisms are that bring death to so many people.

The method of doing theology in the footsteps of the martyrs

Every serious theology begins with an act of contemplation, with the mysticism of open eyes. It begins with the courage to look carefully, not to close one's eyes to these realities that provoke the natural instinct to look in the other direction as quickly as possible. It begins with resisting the temptation of 'not seeing' the reality of the victims of current violence, which seems to be the fierce denial of a good and merciful God. This 'seeing', this act of contemplation, is an act in which we allow ourselves to be penetrated by the pain of the victims. As Johann Baptist Metz would put it: 'People who use "God" in the way Jesus does accept the violation of their own personal preconceived certainties by the misfortune of others' (1999, 230).

The fact that the language of Óscar Romero and Ignacio Ellacuría was so powerful that it immediately reached the hearts of the victims is mainly due to their ability to 'see'. Without this act of contemplation as the beginning of every theological task, the language of theology easily degenerates into a bigoted word. We can also corrupt the most sacred words of this tradition as a 'crucified people' through inflationist abuse or through verbosity. Theological language only has value and significance if, again and again, it is born of pain, of feeling with the victims down to the marrow of our bones. In Simone Weil's words, to do theology begins with an 'act of attention' that allows the 'affliction of others to enter into our flesh and soul' (1973, 20).

To 'see' is the first step. However, if one follows the classical triple step 'see – judge – act' as the theological method, a fatal misunderstanding of the next step, 'judge', is possible. It can never be understood in the following way: first you see and then you subject what you see to the judgement of the theologian. Rather, the second step, in the words of Ignacio Ellacuría, is to 'carry reality'; that is, to assume the weight of that reality.

You might ask yourself: why is it so hard, so difficult, to listen to the victims, to let them talk, to give them real attention and not steal it to address issues that seem more important to us academically? Obviously, it is hard to bear, to bear and not to escape. It requires great courage to act counterculturally, even against what seems appropriate for academic work, so that the weight of the victims' reality falls on us. The scheme of 'see – judge', 'hear – interpret' must be transformed into 'see – take the weight', 'hear – and give space in our hearts to what we hear'.

A theology born in this way does not pretend to be the spokesperson for the victims, the 'voice of the voiceless', but it listens to the voice of victims. No one wants to hear it, not even the governments, because that would give the impression that everything is going well in the country. But often, the victims are not heard either by the churches or by other institutions in society. An elementary demand and a first step in stopping violence is to create spaces where victims find the place to be heard, where they can transform themselves from objects of cynical interest into sons and daughters of God and can begin their costly journey towards healing and reconciliation. Without salvation for the victims there is no salvation for anyone.

In Ignacio Ellacuría's triple step of 'taking charge' of reality, 'carrying' reality, and 'being responsible' for reality ('hacerse cargo' de la realidad, 'cargar' con la realidad y 'encargarse' de la realidad) (2000, 208), Jon Sobrino adds a fourth: 'letting ourselves be carried by reality' (2008, 2). This means that listening to the victims is not an altruistic act by the people who do it. People who really open themselves to the victims, receive life through them. The paradox applies, where life is threatened, where death seems omnipresent, in the same place life vibrates in a density as in few other spaces. Grace seems to burst in with preference into these places of death. There blossoms the 'primordial holiness' of which Jon Sobrino speaks, the goodness and generosity of the human heart in an immediacy and purity as is sought in vain elsewhere. Only by kneeling before this mystery of life is there hope for us too.

To conclude

Liberation theology seems to be an anachronism, a relic from a vanished, utopia-pregnant time. Too much tied to socialist projects, which have long since been refuted by history and have betrayed the hopes of the poor; it seems questionable if it can be a productive offer in the dramatic crises of our times.

What I certainly do not want to tempt with these considerations is to remain nostalgically attached to a glorified past, or to want to make liberation theology a 'school' that stereotypically reproduces the concepts of the 1960s and 1970s. That would be a mockery of this tradition. To repeat its language monotonously contradicts its very own claim. Rather, we are called upon to understand and decipher our time with all our intellectual strength and creativity. To really get involved with it will throw many of our supposed certainties overboard. The theological word that our time demands is never already given but is only reborn from this struggle.

For what stands at the origin of liberation theology is precisely the definitive farewell to any kind of timeless doctrine, to any kind of speaking that pretends to stand above the respective concrete historical moment and to apply unchanged beyond it. The breakthrough of liberation theology marks the radical turn from a theology as metaphysical doctrine to the temporalisation of the speech about God – to the God who becomes an instruction for action in the concrete historical situation. And most deeply connected with it is the dangerous memory of the historical Jesus, of his concrete life, in his socio-political context.

It is worthwhile reminding us for a moment that what this Jesus of Nazareth did in concrete terms has hardly played a role in the 2,000 years of the history of theology: that he took care that people got enough to eat; that he took care of their illnesses; that he offered closeness and community to those who were outcasts for decent society. All that hardly occurs in the 'Christian teaching' up to the Second Vatican Council, and in no way does it become structure-forming for theology or even find its way into the Christian Credo. It seems to be insignificant: Jesus, the Christ, was conceived, born, suffered, died and rose from the dead. But what constitutes his life, and his concrete practice, does not seem to be relevant for the 'orthodox doctrine'.

Latin American liberation theology has made a radical conversion to the concrete Jesus of Nazareth. It really thinks the incarnation to its end: God is present in what this Jesus concretely does and lives. And to be a Christian means in consequence to do what he has done. The practice of Jesus becomes the instruction for all church activities. To 'de-spiritualise' the Gospel and to let it become concrete and bodily experienceable, a 'joyful message' to the people threatened by the powers of death. This is the lasting imperative that starts from liberation theology.

Notes

1. This foreword is adapted from Martha Zechmeister's keynote address, titled 'The Productive Asynchronicity of Liberation Theology: Theology in the Footsteps of the Martyrs', at the November 2020 conference 'As It Was in the Beginning? Liberation Theology and Praxis in Contemporary Latin America', Institute of Latin American Studies, School of Advanced Studies, University of London.

References

Bonhoeffer, Dietrich. 'Thoughts on the Day of Baptism of Dietrich Wilhelm Rüdiger Bethge, May 1944'. In *Dietrich Bonhoeffer Works, Volume 8: Letters and Papers from Prison*, edited by John W. Gruchy, 383–90. Minneapolis: National Book Network, 2010.

Ellacuría, Ignacio. 'Discernir el signo de los tiempos', *Diakonía* 17 (1981): 57–9.

Ellacuría, Ignacio. 'Utopía y profetismo'. In *Mysterium liberationis. Conceptos fundamentales de la teología de la liberación I*, edited by Ignacio Ellacuría and Jon Sobrino, 393–442. Madrid: Editorial Trotta, 1990.

Ellacuría, Ignacio. 'Hacia una fundamentación del método teológico latinoamericano'. In *Escritos teológicos I*, 187–218. San Salvador: UCA Editores, 2000.

Metz, Johann Baptist. 'In the Pluralism of Religious and Cultural Worlds: Notes Toward a Theological and Political Program', translated by John Downey and Heiko Wiggers, *CrossCurrents* 49, no. 2 (1999): 227–36.

Sobrino, Jon. *No Salvation Outside the Poor: Prophetic-Utopian Essays*. Maryknoll: Orbis Books, 2008.

Weil, Simone. *Waiting on God*. Translated by Emma Craufurd. New York: Harper & Row, 1973.

Acknowledgements

There are a large number of people whom the editors wish to thank for their support in producing this volume. The book itself emerged from a conference with the same name held in November 2020, and the editors would like to thank all participants whose contributions shaped this book. The event was hosted by the Centre for Latin American and Caribbean Studies (then the Institute of Latin American Studies), King's College London (KCL) and University College London (UCL), with the generous support of the Leverhulme Trust. Special thanks go to Vinicius de Carvalho (KCL) for co-organising the original event and providing invaluable guidance while planning the publication, to Olga Jiménez for all her help organising the conference, and to Linda Newson (CLACS) for her support throughout. The keynote speakers at the original event were Martha Zechmeister CJ, who provides the foreword to this volume and, arguably the pre-eminent historian of liberation theology, Enrique Dussel, who sadly passed away in 2023. The editors thank both for their presentations and their larger bodies of work which were a source of continual inspiration while working on the book. At the University of London Press, special thanks go to Emma Gallon, Julie Willis and Jamie Bowman for their advice and guidance during the publication process, while the anonymous reviewers provided valuable and insightful feedback. The editors also wish to convey their personal thanks to the family of Pablo Roberto Suárez for allowing them to use his artwork *Martirologio y gloria de los santos anónimos* as the book's cover, and to the staff of the Museo de Arte Moderno de Buenos Aires, especially Julieta Aguiar and Viviana Gil, for their assistance in obtaining this permission and the image. In addition, Pablo Bradbury wishes to thank Andrew Redden for his encouragement and insight and Francisca Torres Cortés for always being helpful and supportive, and Niall H. D. Geraghty wishes to thank Adriana Laura Massidda for her continual support, advice and intellectual engagement with the project, and the Leverhulme Trust for funding the research project from which the original conference and this book emerged. Finally, the editors would like to extend their gratitude to the authors of these chapters for their contributions, as well as their patience and enthusiasm for the volume.

Introduction: As it was in the beginning?

Pablo Bradbury and Niall H. D. Geraghty

It is now more than fifty years since liberation theology emerged from Latin America with a prophetic vision for the Catholic Church that would alter its social mission, as well as its relationship with the laity, with other religions and with the world. With the benefit of historical hindsight, however, it can seem that the first wave and the high watermark for the discourse were one and the same. If, amidst the febrile revolutionary atmosphere of 1968, the second meeting of the Consejo Episcopal Latinoamericano (Latin American Bishops Conference, CELAM) in Medellín proclaimed the influence of liberation theologians on the institutional Church, the publication of Gustavo Gutiérrez's seminal *Teología de la liberación: Perspectivas* in 1971 seemed to cement its importance. What was being proposed was not merely a new theological movement but, in Gutiérrez's famous words, a 'new way of doing theology' (Gutiérrez 1988, 12).

Such bold claims seemed matched by a wave of clerical innovations and a groundswell of radicalism across the continent whose ethic and aesthetic brought together both revolutionary Marxists and Catholic militants. By the CELAM meeting in Puebla in 1979, however, the tide had seemingly turned. Key liberation theologians who had done so much to shape Medellín were sidelined from Puebla, the result of a concerted effort by an unsympathetic Latin American episcopal leadership. Exiled to a convent a few blocks from the conference proceedings, a large group of liberation theologians managed to interact with participating bishops and influence the tightly guarded discussions indirectly, however, resulting in a mixed final document demonstrative of the divergent theological interests and influences of different members of the Church (Smith 1991, 209–21).

Although key figures sought to claim Puebla and its final document as a victory for liberation theology, in retrospect it appeared to be confirmation of its declining status in the institutional Church, and its proponents were increasingly on the defensive. Pope John Paul II (1979) himself looked with suspicion toward the idea of a Church 'taking concrete form in the poor' as being ideologically conditioned, warning that any 'magisteria other than the Church's Magisterium' was 'ecclesially unacceptable'. His very public rebuke of Ernesto Cardenal in 1983 for assuming office in the revolutionary Sandinista government, and the subsequent prohibition imposed on Cardenal administering the sacraments, seemed to cement an emboldened institutional backlash against liberation theology's political articulation. In 1985, Leonardo Boff was instructed to observe a period of obsequious silence following the publication of his book *Igreja: Carisma e poder* (1981), and the Congregation for the Doctrine of the Faith issued its (in)famous 'Instructions' on the theology in 1984 and 1986. In one of the most shocking setbacks in El Salvador, a country that had already witnessed the murder of Archbishop Óscar Romero after delivering a sermon calling on the armed forces to stop carrying out government repression, a group of renowned Jesuit liberationists were massacred at the *Universidad Centroamericana José Simeón Cañas* (UCA) in 1989. Considering these reactions against liberation theology collectively seems to sketch out a picture of decline, of a theology subdued by institutional discipline and smashed by violent repression. By linking such events with broader historical trends, it is with good reason that Luis Martínez Andrade comments that: 'With the fall of the Berlin Wall, the disintegration of the socialist bloc, the declaration of the "end of history" and the verbiage on the inevitable victory of the free market, some thinkers – such as Jozef Stanislaw Tischner – declared that liberation theology was mortally wounded' (2015, 109). However, by returning to the central question of praxis – that is, the lived experiences and spiritual and embodied practices of all those engaged in social action in the region – this book seeks to challenge the narrative that suggests that liberation theology had reached its twilight by the end of the 1970s. Instead, across the chapters it contains, it will be shown that this theological and socio-religious movement cannot be reduced to a single grand narrative or confined to an easy linear periodisation.

Global perceptions of liberation theology often rely on rather generalised frameworks and spectacular events, and, in that regard, there can be no doubt that recent events have rekindled interest in the movement. While it is too early to tell if (or, perhaps, too optimistic to presume that) the conflict between liberation theology and the Vatican has been fully resolved (Løland 2021), the election of Pope Francis certainly seemed to augur a more sympathetic reproachment from the Holy See. Since his investiture in the diocese of Rome, Francis oversaw the canonisation of Archbishop Romero and the beatification of Argentina's Enrique Angelelli (another prelate close to the movement and assassinated by a military regime), as he also granted Ernesto Cardenal absolution from his censorship. Moreover, the critique of capitalism in his encyclical *Evangelii Gaudium* (2013), and his turn to ecological concerns in *Laudato Si'* (2015), echoed the economic and environmental focus of theologians such as Gutiérrez and Boff. Indeed, it would also seem that the Amazon Synod of 2019 and the clamour for reform of the Curia confirm the importance of liberationist approaches to ecology and radical ecclesiology. Similarly, secular social movements such as those against feminicide and for the decriminalisation of abortion have precipitated considerable advances in women's theology in Latin America, not least by such movements as Católicos por el Derecho a Decidir (Catholics for the Right to Choose), while building on the base constructed by early liberation theologians.

What we want to propose, however, is that such developments may not signal a *return* of liberation theology but rather indicate that its impact reached deep into and altered the religious and social life of the continent, albeit in multiple forms and iterations. Thus, this book seeks to re-evaluate the history and legacy of liberation theology by examining religious praxis in the region from the 1960s to the present day. To cite but one example, in the book's Foreword, Martha Zechmeister looks back to the murder of the liberation theologians in El Salvador and calls for future theologians to take up the challenge of 'doing theology in the footsteps of the martyrs'. For her part, in the book's Afterword, Elizabeth O'Donnell Gandolfo responds by reminding us of the contemporary martyrdom of environmental and human rights defenders across Latin America to reinforce the immediacy, urgency and importance of liberation theology today. And across the intervening chapters, a picture emerges of liberationist Christianity (the term employed by Michael Löwy to denote a wider network and praxis in addition to a well-known theological production) that is at once more diverse and internally conflicted, more widely resonant outside ecclesial confines and more interconnected over time than often allowed (Löwy 1996). That is to say, a vision of liberationist Christianity that is more vibrant and alive than generally recognised.

A variety of scholarly analyses have sought to capture the historical evolution of liberation theology, offering interpretations and syntheses of the myriad changes occurring across a diverse continent since the 1960s. For example, Iván Petrella's thesis maintained that liberation theology suffered essentially from the end of history consensus that characterised the end of the Cold War in 1989, citing the abandonment of the historical project (originally socialism) as its crucial weakness from the 1990s (Petrella 2016). Liberation theology was born in the 1960s at a time of Church renewal and socio-economic ferment, as many sought more radical solutions in the context of the exhaustion of developmentalist projects and the so-called institutionalised violence of capitalism and dependency. Certainly, in many cases, socialist revolution offered a vision that allowed liberationists to move from the purely prophetic dimension to a transformational project inspired partly in the example of the Cuban Revolution. No doubt, the US's Cold War triumph and the neoliberal hegemony post-1989 limited liberation theology's disruptive energy, and it simultaneously appeared unable to retain the capacity to attach itself coherently to a positive political project. But we might question the simplicity of this narrative that folds a complex region into a rather simple historical sequence. For example, in many places, it was arguably the intensification of polarising Cold War dynamics – rather than their end – coupled with the proliferation of repressive anti-communist military regimes of the 1970s, that disarticulated and disoriented the wider organisational networks of the movement, bringing with it a shift away from discourses of socialist revolution. The *Cristianos por el Socialismo* (Christians for Socialism) movement in Chile, for instance, represented one of the more politically bold initiatives, resonating internationally in the midst of Salvador Allende's socialist government, until it dissolved faced with the crushing repression of General Augusto Pinochet's regime from September 1973 (Amorós 2005).

In a related note, Christian Smith, in his insightful work on liberation theology as a continental social movement, claimed, paradoxically, that violent repression in the 1970s and 1980s actually *rescued* a movement perturbed by, and on the defensive because of, a conservative reaction from the Church's hierarchical leadership, enabling it confidently to reattach itself to the downtrodden (1991, 192–8). Nevertheless, the dissemination of liberation theological discourses across Latin America did not necessarily translate to organisational vitality, which varied between countries. Neither, it might be said, did the association with victims of state violence result in liberationists cohering around a positive and concrete political project. In fact, the impact of state terrorism on the wider liberationist Christian movement was uneven: while in Brazil, the base ecclesial movements offered a critical space for protest against a hardening military dictatorship in the early 1970s, in other places martial rule annihilated the radical initiatives of liberationists. In Chile, the famous Vicaría de la Solidaridad (Vicariate of Solidarity) may have emerged as a thorn in the side of Pinochet's regime, but it was less straightforwardly tied to liberation theology than was *Cristianos por el Socialismo*. At a similar conjuncture, mounting repression in mid-1970s Argentina devastated the (albeit already divided) *Movimiento de Sacerdotes para el Tercer Mundo* (MSTM; Movement of Priests for the Third World). Thus, the cult of martyrdom and the discourses of 'captivity' that characterised liberation theology in the years of lead in Argentina may well, as Smith affirms, have given the movement a greater claim to identification with the suffering and persecuted, particularly as the institutional Church came to be seen as a vital strand of what is often referred to as a *dictadura cívico-eclesiástico-militar* (civil-ecclesiastical-military dictatorship) due to its close collaboration with the military (1991, 201).[1] However, this surely produced shifts towards a more narrowly prophetic function of denunciation and affirmation of a discourse of human rights, as it signalled a move away from the concrete historical project of social and political revolution.

A second, connected observation about liberation theology's evolution relates to the move from integral narratives of social revolution to an increasing engagement with other forms of marginalisation and subjugation, especially regarding questions of identity and other cleavages not strictly limited to the figure of the poor. As the cycle of revolutionary mobilisation abated in the 1970s, beaten back by vicious anti-communist forces and crippled by the exhaustion of popular movements, and as neoliberal hegemony appeared unrivalled in the 1990s, the 'liberation' in liberation theology assumed new meanings. For David Tombs (2002), this represented the expansion of the movement, which in the 1980s and 1990s started to engage with other dimensions of oppression. In a similar key, Mario I. Aguilar (2007, 12), employing Karl Mannheim's theory of generations, claimed that liberation theology became a 'diversified subject', as new waves of intellectuals responded to changing social contexts. Such analyses emphasise the multiple perspectives taken up by inheritors of the movement's legacy, seemingly shifting the focus away from a sense of universality in the liberation of the poor to more particular questions of indigeneity, ethnicity, race, gender and ecology.

Diego Irarrázaval, for instance, in the 1990s, explored the theology of inculturation and the syncretic forms of Christianity generated by Indigenous peoples, offering a framework that could contain the diverse cultural expressions of Christianity in the continent (Irarrázaval 2000).[2] Responding particularly to local and Indigenous movements for land and rights, this emphasis coincided with a series of reflections, in and leading up to 1992, on 500 years of colonialism in the Americas and the complex consequences of evangelisation. Gutiérrez himself had identified 'the racial question' as a major challenge, calling the anniversary an 'occasion for an examination of conscience regarding the immense human cost historically connected with that evangelisation – I mean the destruction of individuals and cultures' (Gutiérrez 1988, xxii). Leonardo Boff's *Nova evangelização: perspectiva dos oprimidos* (1990) is one such examination which simultaneously strives radically to reconceptualise evangelisation due to this very legacy. However, the engagement with race and ethnicity was not simply a reflection of colonialism in Latin America but also the result of a wider global interaction with experience elsewhere, including the diverse manifestations of faith in Africa and interfaith dialogues in Asia. In previous years, Latin American liberation theologians, particularly following the 'Theology in the Americas' conference in Detroit (1975), had also begun to pay more attention to Black theologians in the United States who had emerged simultaneously in the 1960s, rooted in the historical experience of racial oppression of African Americans (Torres and Eagleson 1976). However, although this has often been portrayed as a new development generated by the meeting in 1975, attentiveness to the broad and varied histories of liberation theology might point us towards earlier interactions, especially through the World Council of Churches (WCC). The WCC, which elected its first Black general secretary in 1972, offered a shared space for Christians from the Global North and the Global South. Indeed, in the wake of dramatic processes of decolonisation and revolutionary effervescence, the 1960s was a formative period for a new global ecumenism that foregrounded racially oppressed and Third-World voices. Protestants (especially from Brazil and the Southern Cone), in the context of a Latin American evangelical 'boom' characterised by 'revolution, liberation and exile', participated fully in this process, and, for them, 1975, as the year of another significant WCC assembly in Nairobi, was more of a culmination of this dialogue rather than a starting point (Schilling 2018).

If the 1970s have been understood as a launchpad for engaging with questions of racial oppression, the 1980s have been perceived as a period of emergent feminist challenges, a development that assumed a variety of forms (Tombs 2002, 256–70). For some, this involved highlighting the gendered dimensions of, and commitment among, women religious in liberationist Christian struggles, even if not always strictly assuming a feminist paradigm.[3] The sharp writings of thinkers such as Ivone Gebara (1999) and Marcella Althaus-Reid (2000), on the other hand, pushed feminist and queer theology to the forefront of theological debates, and their analyses mounted scathing criticisms of liberation theology while remaining at least partially within its tradition. For instance, Althaus-Reid pointedly reproached Enrique Dussel as developing a straightforwardly homophobic framework (2006, 10–13). Thus, the engagement with gender, feminism and sexuality was not just a significant development within liberation theology but a major critique. However, as with race and ethnicity, we must be careful about the extent to which we declare such developments in the 1980s to be totally novel or as deriving from a single source.

One notable feature of the final document from the CELAM meeting in Puebla was the specific recognition of the *condición doblemente oprimida y marginada* (doubly oppressed and marginalised condition) of women in Latin America (CELAM 1979, §1135n297). While it is inescapable that gender had been overlooked in the most influential publications of the movement in the 1960s and 1970s, the marginalisation of women and the reproduction of patriarchal structures and narratives had not passed unnoticed. For example, one contribution of Claudia Touris's recent work on the *tercermundista* 'constellation' is that it captures a component of liberationist Christian history in Argentina during the 1960s and 1970s – the agency of women religious – hitherto almost entirely ignored by scholarly and popular histories, which focus mostly on the mobilisation of priests (2021, 353–429). Although not explicitly a feminist rendering of the movement, *tercermundista* nuns were deeply concerned about the role and situation of women, and Touris finds in the discourse and practice of these women religious an unresolved tension between different models of women's involvement in the public sphere, one centred on the personage of Marianne (the embodiment of the values of the French Revolution) and one on María.[4] Such research bluntly reveals the reproduction of gendered hierarchies and clerical masculinity in early liberation theology, as well as the inadequacies of our understandings of the wider liberationist movement: although nuns made up three-quarters of religious in Argentina, the MSTM was the fulcrum of liberationist Christianity in the country and has been the subject of most research on the phenomenon.

More broadly, there is no question that women made up much of the grassroots membership of wider liberationist movements across Latin America. Ana María Bidegaín (1989) made similar points, indeed, about the importance of women's participation in the wider life of liberationist Christianity, particularly Catholic Action and the youth branches crucial to the movement's emergence in the 1950s and 1960s. Bidegaín and Althaus-Reid, both participants in liberationist circles, each recalled how grassroots networks often suffered from hostility to questions of gender emancipation. If Bidegaín sustained, however, that Latin American feminist theology only began to be publicly sketched out later in the 1980s, Althaus-Reid (2000) claimed that even these theological discourses sometimes reproduced *machista* assumptions about sexuality and gender, reinforcing traditionalist concepts of complementarity rather than disrupting hierarchical gender constructions. Thus, at the turn of the twenty-first century, Althaus-Reid played a key role in taking liberation theology into new territory, advancing a radicalisation of such themes by developing a queer and 'indecent' theology. As regards this current volume, in keeping with its aims, it contributes to our understanding of feminist liberation theology in two ways. First, Natalie Gasparowicz returns to 1979 and the CELAM conference in Puebla to recover the history of the off-site event Mujeres para el Diálogo (Women for Dialogue), arguing that it constitutes a key moment in the development of new perspectives on gender and sexuality within liberation theology. Second, Ely Orrego Torres examines new ecofeminist theologies that have emerged from previous liberationist discourse, expanding its remit in order to respond to the contemporary climate crisis. Where Gasparowicz thus re-examines the praxis and agency of women in the late 1970s, Orrego Torres focuses instead on the praxis of contemporary social movements that have emerged from this tradition, notably the Chilean collective *Con-spirando*.

As previously noted, another feature of liberation theology's evolution was the apparent engagement with discourses of human rights, which began to supplant 'revolution' as the key watchword for activist collectives and social movements across Latin America. At a basic level, this may be understood as a defensive move, responding to the massive violations of basic rights and the state violence against left-wing movements in the 1970s and 1980s. In much of Latin America, hopes of revolution faded as military and paramilitary forces persecuted those defined as enemies by the national security doctrine, and the global human rights movement came to be seen as a critical ally against such violence. Some have noted that liberation theology was initially suspicious of the human rights paradigm that emerged as a global force especially in the 1970s, understanding it as reflecting a bourgeois liberalism that sidelined the deeper questions of socio-economic inequalities and legitimising the structural violence that characterised Latin America (Engler 2000). After a period of avoidance and critique, however, liberation theologians from the late 1970s undertook a nuanced theological appropriation of human rights.

Once again, however, recent research has challenged an easy periodisation. In fact, various liberation theologians of the first generation, heavily influenced by the invocation of dignity and human rights in papal encyclicals *Pacem en Terris* (John XXIII, 1963) and *Populorum Progressio* (Paul VI 1967), affirmed that neocolonialism violated basic human rights (Lantigua 2020). It is certainly the case that influential figures remained suspicious of the Carter administration's attempt to advance human rights as the moral core of a politics that lambasted violent dictatorships but reproduced neoliberalism. Analytically, many remained suspicious of the utopian claims to universality of such a discourse advanced from the Global North in a world marked by dependency, institutionalised violence and structural sin. However, many liberationists also employed human rights language and discourse as a weapon against the patchwork of regimes imposing state terror across Latin America, encountering strategic allies among certain international institutions and networks critical of repressive authoritarian regimes.

The assumption of some iteration of human rights politics was indeed a more general development among the wider left from the 1970s and 1980s. A qualitative shift from the radical transformation of society via supporting revolutionary capture of the state to the more defensive posture centring on protection of life and liberty from the state and other powerful actors could be identified among some liberationist sectors (Bradbury 2023, 194–220). And the denunciation of human rights violations would often assume a prophetic tone, somewhat in line with much previous liberationist discourse. But liberationists also attempted to make their own contribution to human rights, foregrounding the poor and collective rights, destabilising an apparently legalistic and apolitical paradigm. And one might even posit an interconnection between this critical politics of human rights and the move toward group-based struggles, such as those of race, ethnicity and gender. In other words, whereas integral affirmations of liberation as revolution and the poor as the authentic historical subject often enabled a folding and flattening out of identity-based oppressions, the critical alternative view of human rights generated an inevitable follow-up question: rights for whom?

One may also wonder whether the human rights paradigm had some connection to emerging ecological concerns. In recent years, after all, a range of political movements have raised the possibility of the rights of nature, even succeeding in enshrining them in law (if with relatively little practical success in halting ecological destruction). Indeed, it is particularly notable that it was the Inter-American Court of Human Rights which issued an opinion affirming the autonomous right to a healthy environment in 2017.[5] Ecological issues, in fact, increasingly became a dimension of struggle in some liberationist circles and followed many of the same patterns of critique. The most well-known example of this in terms of intellectual production came from Leonardo Boff, who emphasised the fundamental link between human suffering and the destruction of the earth. Of course, the assumption of ecological concerns mounted a profound critique of dominant models of development. At the same time, Boff's outline of the 'planetary community' extended the elimination of false dualisms – so prominent in Gutiérrez's work, rejecting the clean separation of temporal and the spiritual planes – to condemn the anthropocentrism of modernity that rendered nature a mere resource for humanity. Boff affirmed that this had to be broadened to include all creation, in an analysis that not only condemned the ecological destruction driven by global accumulation but also advanced a non-anthropocentric Christology that linked the crucifixion of Jesus with the divinisation and liberation of all beings in the universe (1997, 110–14). While Boff may have been the most prominent proponent of this ecological liberation theology, there are striking comparisons with Ernesto Cardenal's mystical poetry (and poetry in prose) written throughout his life which provided a vision of God's love as the unifying driving force of all creation throughout the universe and the fount of human liberation (or salvation history, as Gutiérrez would name it) on earth.

This emerging ecological cosmology redefined the epistemological focus from the colonial periphery to a planetary perspective (and even interplanetary, in the case of Cardenal), bringing to mind the tension between contextualism and universality. It is true that Gutiérrez's early writings reproduced certain elements of the utilitarianism that Boff denounced, when he affirmed that humankind 'is destined to dominate the earth' and 'fulfills itself only by transforming nature and thus entering into relationships with other persons' (Gutiérrez 1988, 165). Nevertheless, Gutiérrez's emphasis on the intimate interrelation between, or rather unity of, creation and salvation, which collectively constitute God's active role in history, was essentially more fully developed by liberationist engagements with ecology in theology (such as those developed by Boff) and mysticism (as in Cardenal). For Boff in the 1990s, liberation theology had now to support 'a new covenant between human beings and other beings, a new gentleness toward what is created, and the fashioning of an ethic and mystique of kinship with the entire cosmic community' (1997, 112). More recently, of course, Pope Francis thrust the environment to the centre of his public agenda, tying it closely to social and political justice and emphasising the disproportionate impact of environmental destruction on the poor in his encyclical *Laudato Si'* (2015), and reaffirming its central importance to his papacy in the Apostolic Exhortation *Laudate Deum* (2023). This has strong theological associations too: even if the pope refrained from going as far as Boff in his rejection of anthropocentrism, his identification with Saint Francis of Assisi foregrounded a prioritisation of the vulnerable, a love of creation and an 'integral ecology', with which we might draw parallels with Gutiérrez, Boff and Cardenal (Francis 2015).[6]

A final observation about liberation theology's evolution is the apparent move away from clericalism. The very methodology of the movement has frequently appeared to elevate (at least rhetorically) lay actors, emphasising the agency and self-liberation of the poor and even the evangelisation of the Church by the oppressed – a theme later restated in Francis' *Evangelii Gaudium* (Francis 2013; Gutiérrez 1990). However, while recognising that liberationist Christianity has been much too varied a phenomenon to cast simple generalisations about its clerical-centric character, many of the major first-generation liberation theologians and key figures were members of the clergy, rooted in academic settings or reflecting on pastoral practice. The relationship between a social movement stressing grassroots mobilisation and proximity to a hierarchical Catholic Church has generated debates and disputes, with much of this focusing on popular religiosity and ecclesiological organisation. For some, the ecclesial base communities (*Comunidades Eclesiales de Base*, CEBs), an innovation originally introduced by the hierarchy to respond to shortages of priests but which in the 1970s became associated with liberation theology, were models for decentring clergymen and emphasising the self-organisation of lay Catholics (Hebblethwaite 1994).[7] For his part, Boff took this to a radical conclusion when he located the true vitality of the Church as born of the faith of the people, highlighting the CEBs as authentically communitarian in contrast to the alienating hierarchical structures of the institutional Church – a move that ran directly counter to John Paul II's 1979 address in Puebla (Boff 1984; John Paul II 1979). Boff's formulation, identifying a communitarian Church in dialectical tension with a Church institution, may at first appear analogous to the notion popular in New Christendom ecclesiology of the *corpus mysticum* (the mystical body of Christ, held to be interior and invisible) in contradistinction to the juridical Church (Cavanaugh 1998, 205–52). Liberationist ecclesiological perceptions of the popular or communitarian Church, however, rejected the separation of spiritual and temporal planes, instead critiquing a politico-juridical institution tied up with the oppressive social structures of capitalist society and imperialism. The CEBs, for Boff, were the authentic communitarian counterpoint to a bureaucratising tendency.

In addition to an institutional-popular tension within liberationist ecclesiology, we should also raise liberation theology's presence outside the Catholic Church as such. On the one hand, despite Catholicism's dominance (albeit diminishing in recent years) over religious identity in Latin America, Protestant spaces and churches incubated similar and connected movements and discourses. Although the dominant histories and major milestones of liberation theology tend to contain the phenomenon as a Catholic development, a point which also relates to the clericalism associated with the movement as priests' groups such as ONIS (*Oficina Nacional de Información Social*, Peru), Golconda (Colombia) and the MSTM

(Argentina) served as major reference points for liberationist practices and mobilisation. Nonetheless, a significant number of the major theologians and figureheads were Protestants,[8] and liberationist initiatives often found stronger support in the ecumenical world, for which reason in the 1980s and 1990s ecumenism became a central theme for liberation theology across the region. This was particularly promoted through initiatives such as the Ecumenical Association of Third World Theologians (EATWOT) established in 1976. Although more recently the explosion of charismatic evangelical and Pentecostal church communities has often been associated with reactionary politics, ecumenical movements have frequently been at the forefront of liberation theology's new developments across such issues as human rights, gender and anti-racism.[9]

Recent years have also witnessed further appeals for liberation theology to transgress and supersede its earlier clericalism (raising questions over the Church's relationship to the theology) and to advance the movement's insights and dynamism outside of the religious sphere altogether. Such is the case, for instance, with Iván Petrella's 'liberation theology undercover' (2017), which affirms that the movement's 'preferential option for the poor' should be reproduced in public policy, planning and the wider professional sectors. For Petrella (2017, 332–3), liberation theology's key insights include an epistemological shift – which anchored thinking to the reality of deprivation and marginalisation – and the identification of the body as the locus of salvation, reflected for instance in the renowned health practices of Paul Farmer. In this way, the critical reflection on praxis can be turned to challenge the 'idolatries that need to be unmasked' and, we might extrapolate, the reproduction of structural sin (Petrella 2017, 337). Such a rendering of the movement's insights outside strictly religious communities chimes with the participation of many liberationists in the professionalisation of social action, especially from the 1980s, which generated a plethora of NGOs, associations and organisations (Catoggio 2016, 203–10). And it incites further reflection on the scope of the Church from a liberationist perspective, as well as liberation theology's relation to both secularisation and the secular sphere.

This volume offers new insights and research that cut across and connect the themes discussed above. Running through the contribution is the fundamental question of *praxis* as an integral and necessary part of theology from the liberationist perspective. The book begins with Martha Zechmeister CJ's reflections on the martyrdom of Ignacio Ellacuría and seven colleagues at the *Universidad Centroamericana José Simeón Cañas*, reaffirming the centrality of place and context in liberation theology. She affirms the liberationist call to attend to concrete experience, foregrounding the perspective of the victims and the oppressed as the fundamental subject of theology. Liberation theology's insight, Zechmeister argues, is precisely this temporality, offering a starting point for praxis as situated action.

A variety of the contributions touch upon or confront directly ecclesiological themes and the clerical-centric character of liberation theology. Pablo Bradbury's research on the Movement of Third World Priests in Argentina in the 1960s and 1970s analyses some of the early ecclesiological debates, centred on the institutional-popular tension later echoed in writings such as Boff's *Ecclesiogenesis*. Bradbury argues that the notion of the Church as people of God, rooted in the conciliar document *Lumen Gentium*, became entangled in the vexed intra-ecclesial conflicts between liberationists and their critics. Motivated by a post-conciliar atmosphere of innovation, the legitimising force of the 1967 'Manifesto of Third World Bishops' that advocated a form of socialism and popular mobilisation against an authoritarian dictatorship girded by the ecclesial leadership, priests experimenting with participatory pastoral praxis and politicised discourses clashed with traditionalist sectors. Borrowing analytical tools from social movement theory and anthropology, Bradbury claims that such disputes were understood in terms of containment within or transgression of an institutional Church, and they were visualised partly in terms of a negotiation between horizontalism and verticalism. Within this framework, the bitter disagreements in the mid-1970s within the MSTM over celibacy and the acceptance of married priests in the movement can be better comprehended as fundamentally ecclesiological and rooted to some extent in structurally determined stances towards apostolic obedience.

Rich in thick description, Patrick O'Hare observes similar tensions between hierarchies and social cleavages in his ethnographic account of pastoral and religious-inspired social work in contemporary Uruguay. Exploring the praxis of *acompañamiento* – rooted in the preferential option for the poor – in the context of the COVIFU (*Cooperativa de Vivienda de Familias Unidas*) housing cooperative, O'Hare shows how ecclesial spaces shaped by liberation theology can mediate between upper and lower classes. Although frequently cast as a manifestation of revolutionary politics within Christian spaces, liberation theology contained little consensus over the precise social meaning of the preferential option for the poor – and was often ambivalent about an unqualified attachment to social revolution and class politics. O'Hare's chapter speaks to a manifestation of the movement arguably more in tune with a form of class reconciliation associated with much of Catholic Social Doctrine. He pays close attention to the influence of Padre Cacho, noting how such ecclesial spaces provide affluent Uruguayans a form of access to the poor and a channel to enact charitable practice. However, the *acompañamiento* of the priests and nuns of the Church community manifests here not as conventional charity but a praxis imbued with an integral commitment to share the life of the marginalised, mixed with popular education and participatory democratic themes. The ecclesial actors in this way both act out the liberationist principles of living with and empowering the poor while acting as a bridge to enable cross-class engagement.

Such contributions capture attempts by ecclesial actors informed by liberation theology to overcome what they understand as alienating frameworks and traditionalist structures. In a similar way, Juan Mario Díaz-Arévalo's essential chapter emphasises the role that nascent liberation theology in the 1960s played in attempts to move beyond functionalist social science. Díaz-Arévalo teases out the cross-fertilisation of ideas and forms of practices between the influential 'guerrilla-priest' Camilo Torres and the prominent (and Presbyterian) sociologist Orlando Fals Borda – representing, respectively, the belligerent and civic-resistance intellectual tendencies of the origins of Participatory Action Research (PAR). Díaz-Arévalo's close examination of Fals Borda's break with functionalist social research centres on 'subversion' as a framework of social analysis, with Torres occupying the role of path-breaking archetype of resistance to social injustice that reveals the contradictions within a social order and sheds light on new utopian values. In doing this, Díaz-Arévalo captures one aspect of liberation theology's wider impact in Latin America, which we can see echoed in Petrella's appeal to undercover theology, as the specific participatory and immersive form of commitment to the poor is extended beyond the religious sphere. Indeed, the chapter reveals how the practical-theoretical elements of liberation theology – insertion into the conflictive social process, the objective to facilitate communal self-empowerment and the commitment to the struggle of the oppressed – shaped Fals Borda's PAR. As such, the well-trodden debates over the role of the social sciences in liberation theology are reversed, demonstrating the mutual impact of liberation theology in the social sciences.

In a similar vein, Fernando Luis Lara also emphasises the wider impact of liberation theology's participatory nucleus through an analysis of architectural practices developed across Latin America. Drawing on decolonial literature examining the ontological effects of the colonisation of the Americas, Luis Lara emphasises that the emergence of abstraction as an architectural approach tacks closely to the conquest. Nonetheless, his central provocation is that Latin American architectural insights in recent decades have subverted such methods of abstraction, reclaiming a relational approach inspired by liberationist hermeneutics. Parallel to developments in Anglo-architectural scholarship in the 1950s and 1960s focusing on self-help, in Brazil, Uruguay, Mexico and other parts of the continent a new generation of architects emerged with a more participatory focus. Luis Lara suggests that the architectural models of relational engagement in opposition to abstraction share common roots with the participatory and contextual emphases of liberation theology, both of which decentre the dominant colonial subject. In doing so, following Enrique Dussel and other thinkers on the coloniality of power, he refocuses our attention on liberation theology's relationship with the ontology and epistemology of the longer process of colonisation, in addition to placing the movement within a wider shift in praxis that cuts across both religious and secular spheres.

Díaz-Arévalo's and Luis Lara's contributions read together thus present an interesting counterpoint to Petrella's 'liberation theology undercover'. It is notable in this regard that Petrella directly discusses architecture as one sphere of intellectual and practical development that would benefit from liberationist insights. Notable, too, is the fact that Petrella's article is rather more pedagogical than historical and takes a contemporary architectural organisation in Rwanda that set out 'to design and build a hospital based on liberation theology's principles' as case study. According to Petrella, this organisation recognised 'that a finished hospital, beautifully designed, that contributes to the dignity of the patient, can be empowering. But the process of building the hospital, the involvement of the community, its history and skills, also dignifies and empowers' (Petrella 2017, 334). Nonetheless, his article is composed with a certain naivety, citing little of the extensive literature on participatory co-design and vernacular architecture, especially that developed over the course of the twentieth century in Latin America. It is precisely this absence which Luis Lara addresses, thus suggesting (as Díaz-Arévalo also does) that the application of liberation theology's insights in the social sciences and professional vocations may not merely be a possible project for the future but rather that its epistemological break was, from the beginning, something enacted in dialogue with intellectuals, students, popular movements and local communities across Latin American society, and that this history must be recovered.

Whereas Díaz-Arévalo and Luis Lara look at the reverberations of liberation theology's insights in social science and the arts, Anna Grimaldi revisits the ambivalent relationship between the theological movement and the international human rights movement. Challenging previous periodisations of liberationist engagements with Western human rights that locate a positive assumption of human rights later in the 1970s, Grimaldi highlights an earlier dialogue located on a transnational plane in the 1960s in the context of Brazil's authoritarian military dictatorship. She posits a reciprocal exchange shaped by structural and contingent factors: a global Catholic network with the Young Christian Workers (*Jenunesse Ouvriere Chretiènne*, JOC) in Europe as its pivot; the 'incidental exile' of liberation theology, as Brazilians fleeing persecution brought with them nascent liberationist ideas; and the resonance that certain high-profile figures, particularly Dom Hélder Câmara, attained in Western European media. What emerges here is a dialectical relationship: from Brazil, the critical stance toward a global economy marked by capitalist dependency and the identification of Christ with the oppressed and suffering of the existing world; and, from Europe, the human rights paradigm that offered an internationally recognised lexicon, opened access to institutions and offered a global audience. The result was an early example of a framework of human rights not reduced to individual rights but which incorporated values of solidarity and equality and, partly through shining a spotlight on the plight of Indigenous populations, recognised the coloniality of power.

If Grimaldi's account forces us to rethink liberation theology's complex relationship with human rights, Natalie Gasparowicz revises our understanding of the feminist challenge, identifying the little-studied Catholic Women's Conference running parallel to the CELAM meeting in 1979 as a turning point for diverging feminist liberation theologies. She analyses materials produced by *Mujeres para el Diálogo* (MPD) that placed women as a historical subject at the centre of struggles for liberation, even while refraining from explicit identification with feminism. Perhaps the most contentious issue here was that of reproductive rights, particularly the birth control pill and abortion, which confronted the liberationist focus on the body and material suffering. Here, Gasparowicz perceives a tension between, on the one hand, family planning programmes as a form of population control imposed on dependent regions that do not address the root causes of gendered dynamics of poverty and, on the other, birth control methods as a powerful tool that enable women to control their own bodies. Nonetheless, her close reading of a key MPD pamphlet circulated among CELAM's participants in Puebla notes that the question of abortion was left untouched, and claims that the issue is defined implicitly 'more as a tragedy rather than a right'. The question of abortion occupied highly contentious terrain, a cornerstone for the feminist movement more widely but anathema to the Catholic Church. The MPD meeting at Puebla may have witnessed differing opinions and the leading figures may have tread carefully to avoid a major confrontation. Nonetheless, Gasparowicz identifies the event as formative, investing an emergent Christian feminism with a political character providing a launchpad for elaborations that increasingly enshrined contraceptive and abortion rights as pillars of liberation.

While Gasparowicz examines a formative historical experience for feminist liberation theology, Ely Orrego Torres's chapter picks up more recent developments in ecofeminism, interrogating its potential to reformulate political theology and to challenge anthropocentrism and androcentrism. Orrego Torres affirms that the Schmittian concept of political theology, that all modern conceptions of the state are secularised theological ideas, does not merely reduce theology to dominance and violence but also imbues it with possibilities of redemption and liberation. Thus, in similar ways to liberation theology, ecofeminist theology is held to disrupt and subvert the notion of the sovereign and concepts of authority and hierarchy (both social hierarchies and those between humans and non-humans). In contrast to Gasparowicz, however, Orrego Torres is concerned with tracing the ways in which this new ecofeminist theology emerged yet also critiqued and diverged from the liberation theology tradition, whose preference for the poor is seen as purely socio-economic. Ecofeminist theology, she argues, following Ivone Gebara and others, centres on the ways in which women and nature constitute the subjects of subjugation in the vision beginning in Genesis. This is not merely abstract theorising, as Orrego Torres explores the influential example of *Con-spirando*, a prefigurative movement that seeks to subvert hierarchical and patriarchal forms, re-signifying Christian rites with reference to ecological cycles.

Ending with this chapter presents a challenge to the 'pluralisation' narrative of David Tombs and Mario I. Aguilar. Are developments such as ecofeminist theologies elaborations of a liberation theological root or do they represent something apart? Do the later developments that are explored in this volume represent an extension of the original core of liberation theology, a critical reflection on praxis and an option for the oppressed, or are they sufficiently distinct to be considered separate phenomena? How much differentiation can we allow within liberation theology without the term losing its meaning? Certainly, a number of key themes run through the book's contributions, of which three are central. First, the relationship between praxis or situated realities – the specific forms of violence, social organisation and political contingencies – and theological, theoretical or artistic production. Second, the destabilisation of hierarchies, whether that be in terms of ecclesial structure, between the secular and the spiritual, between classes and gender, or between the human and the non-human. And finally, the appeal to participatory forms and the self-realisation of liberation of the oppressed, attempting to move beyond paradigms of passivity and objectivity, whether in terms of agency manifests in terms of gender, class, community, social research or architectural production. With these in mind, themes present even in the nascent stages of the movement, we can pose the question as to whether liberation theology is as it was in the beginning. Thus, with perfect circularity, our book closes as it began with a theological reflection on martyrdom in Latin America. In this instance, and as previously intimated, Elizabeth O'Donnell Gandolfo responds to Zechmeister's challenge to produce theology in the footsteps of the liberationist martyrs of the past, by reflecting theologically on the martyrdom of environmental and human rights defenders of the present. O'Donnell Gandolfo's insistence 'that martyrdom in Latin America was not and is not a thing of the past, but rather a very real and present experience' reminds us that, its objectives as yet unrealised, liberation theology remains as vital for society, as it is dangerous for those committed to its praxis, as it ever was in Latin America.

Notes

1. For a detailed study of the relationship between the Church and the dictatorship, see Mignone (1986).
2. See also Suess (1990).
3. We could, for instance, point to Pamela Hussey's (1989) observations on the role of nuns during the violence in El Salvador.
4. In this analysis, Marianne alludes to the French revolutionary symbolism of freedom depicted as a woman, representing a model of full participation in public life, whereas María refers to 'the spiritual, woman-mother, submissive chaste and selfless' (357).
5. For discussion of the same, see Tigre and Urzola (2021).
6. Given our previous discussion of gender, it is interesting to note that, in this latest publication, Pope Francis cites recent work by the feminist scholar Donna Haraway on the interconnection of species.
7. Of course, this was also inflected with gender dynamics, given the predominance of women in CEBs.
8. Among the first generation of liberation theologians, Rubem Alves and José Míguez Bonino stand out, while more recently, Marcella Althaus-Reid (who studied with Míguez Bonino) was one of the most visible theologians emerging from the liberationist tradition.
9. The political involvement and alignment of evangelical Christianity has been, according to Freston (2008), more varied, multifaceted and fluid than sometimes assumed. On the links between liberation theology, ecumenism and human rights in 1970s Argentina, see Bradbury (2023).

References

Aguilar, Mario I. *The History and Politics of Latin American Theology. Volume I*. London: SCM Press, 2007.

Althaus-Reid, Marcella. *Indecent Theology: Theological Perversions in Sex, Gender and Politics*. London: Routledge, 2000.

Althaus-Reid, Marcella. '"Let Them Talk . . . !" Doing Liberation Theology from Latin American Closets'. In *Liberation Theology and Sexuality*, edited by Marcella Althaus-Reid, 5–18. Aldershot: Ashgate, 2006.

Amorós, Mario. 'La Iglesia que nace del pueblo: Relevancia histórica del movimiento Cristianos por el Socialismo'. In *Cuando hicimos historia. La experiencia de la Unidad Popular*, edited by Julio Pinto Vallejos, 107–26. Santiago de Chile: LOM, 2005.

Bidegaín, Ana María. 'Women and the Theology of Liberation'. In *The Future of Liberation Theology. Essays in Honor of Gustavo Gutiérrez*, edited by Otto Maduro, 105–21. Maryknoll: Orbis Books, 1989.

Boff, Leonardo. *Igreja: Carisma e poder*. Petrópolis: Vozes, 1981.

Boff, Leonardo. *Eclesiogénesis. Las comunidades de base reinventan a la Iglesia*. Santander: Editorial Sal Terrae, 1984.

Boff, Leonardo. *Nova evangelização: Perspectiva dos oprimidos*. Fortaleza, CE: Vozes, 1990.

Boff, Leonardo. *Cry of the Earth, Cry of the Poor*. Maryknoll: Orbis Books, 1997.

Bradbury, Pablo. *Liberationist Christianity in Argentina, 1930–1983: Faith and Revolution*. London: Támesis Press, 2023.

Catoggio, María Soledad. *Los desaparecidos de la iglesia. El clero contestatario frente a la dictadura*. Buenos Aires: Siglo Veintiuno Editores, 2016.

Cavanaugh, William. *Torture and Eucharist: Theology, Politics, and the Body of Christ*. Malden: Blackwells, 1998.

Congregation for the Doctrine of the Faith. 'Instruction on Certain Aspects of the "Theology of Liberation"'. 6 August 1984. https://www.vatican.va/roman_curia/congregations/cfaith/documents/rc_con_cfaith_doc_19840806_theology-liberation_en.html. Accessed 18 October 2024.

Congregation for the Doctrine of the Faith. 'Instruction on Christian Freedom and Liberation'. 22 March 1986. https://www.vatican.va/roman_curia/congregations/cfaith/documents/rc_con_cfaith_doc_19860322_freedom-liberation_en.html. Accessed 18 October 2024.

CELAM. 'Documento de Puebla III Conferencia General del Episcopado Latinoamericano'. 1979. https://www.celam.org/documentos/Documento_Conclusivo_Puebla.pdf. Accessed 18 October 2024.

Engler, Mark. 'Toward the "Rights of the Poor": Human Rights in Liberation Theology', *Journal of Religious Ethics* 28, no. 3 (2000): 339–65.

Freston, Paul, ed. *Evangelical Christianity and Democracy in Latin America*. Oxford: Oxford University Press, 2008.

Gebara, Ivone. *Longing for Running Water: Ecofeminism and Liberation*. Minneapolis: Fortress Press, 1999.

Gutiérrez, Gustavo. *Teología de la liberación: Perspectivas*. Lima: CEP, 1971.

Gutiérrez, Gustavo. *A Theology of Liberation: History, Politics, and Salvation*. Fifteenth anniversary edition with a new introduction by the author. Maryknoll: Orbis Books, 1988.

Gutiérrez, Gustavo. 'Pobres y opción fundamental'. In *Mysterium liberationis. Conceptos fundamentales de la teología de la liberación. Tomo I*, edited by Ignacio Ellacuría and Jon Sobrino, 303–22. Madrid: Editorial Trotta, 1990.

Hebblethwaite, Margaret. *Base Communities: An Introduction*. Mahwah: Paulist Press, 1994.

Hussey, Pamela. *Free from Fear: Women in El Salvador's Church*. London: CIIR, 1989.

Inter-American Court of Human Rights. 'Advisory Opinion OC-23/17 of November 15, 2017. Requested by the Republic of Colombia, "The environment and Human Rights"'. https://www.corteidh.or.cr/docs/opiniones/seriea_23_ing.pdf. Accessed 18 October 2024.

Irarrázaval, Diego. *Inculturation: New Dawn of the Church in Latin America*. Maryknoll: Orbis Books, 2000.

Lantigua, David M. 'Neoliberalism, Human Rights, and the Theology of Liberation in Latin America'. In *Christianity and Human Rights Reconsidered*, edited by Sarah Shortall and Daniel Steinmetz-Jenkins, 238–60. Cambridge: Cambridge University Press, 2020.

Løland, Ole Jakob. 'The Solved Conflict: Pope Francis and Liberation Theology', *International Journal of Latin American Religions* 5 (2021): 287–314.

Löwy, Michael. *War of Gods: Religion and Politics in Latin America*. London: Verso, 1996.

Martínez Andrade, Luis. *Religion without Redemption: Social Contradictions and Awakened Dreams in Latin America*. London: Pluto Press, 2015.

Mignone, Emilio F. *Iglesia y dictadura. El papel de la iglesia a la luz de sus relaciones con el regimen militar*. Buenos Aires: Ediciones del Pensamiento Nacional, 1986.

Petrella, Iván. *The Future of Liberation Theology: An Argument and Manifesto*. Abingdon: Routledge, 2016.

Petrella, Iván. 'Liberation Theology Undercover', *Political Theology* 18, no. 4 (2017): 325–39.
Pope Francis. *Evangelii Gaudium*. 24 November 2013. https://www.vatican.va/content/francesco/en/apost_exhortations/documents/papa-francesco_esortazione-ap_20131124_evangelii-gaudium.html. Accessed 18 October 2024.
Pope Francis. *Laudato Si'*. 24 May 2015. https://www.vatican.va/content/francesco/en/encyclicals/documents/papa-francesco_20150524_enciclica-laudato-si.html. Accessed 18 October 2024.
Pope Francis. *Laudate Deum*. 4 October 2023. https://www.vatican.va/content/francesco/en/apost_exhortations/documents/20231004-laudate-deum.html. Accessed 18 October 2024.
Pope John XXIII. *Pacem in Terris: On Establishing Universal Peace in Truth, Justice, Charity, and Liberty*. 1963. https://www.vatican.va/content/john-xxiii/en/encyclicals/documents/hf_j-xxiii_enc_11041963_pacem.html. Accessed 18 October 2024.
Pope John Paul II. 'Address of His Holiness John Paul II'. Puebla (Mexico), 28 January 1979. https://www.vatican.va/content/john-paul-ii/en/speeches/1979/january/documents/hf_jp-ii_spe_19790128_messico-puebla-episc-latam.html. Accessed 18 October 2024.
Pope Paul VI. *Populorum Progressio: On the Development of Peoples*. 1967. https://www.vatican.va/content/paul-vi/en/encyclicals/documents/hf_p-vi_enc_26031967_populorum.html. Accessed 18 October 2024.
Schilling, Annegreth. 'Between Context and Conflict: The "Boom" of Latin American Protestantism in the Ecumenical Movement (1955–75)', *Journal of Global History* 13, no. 2 (2018): 274–93.
Smith, Christian. *The Emergence of Liberation Theology: Radical Religion and Social Movement Theory*. Chicago: University of Chicago Press, 1991.
Suess, Paulo. 'Inculturación'. In *Mysterium liberationis. Conceptos fundamentales de la teología de la liberación. Tomo II*, edited by Ignacio Ellacuría and Jon Sobrino, 377–422. Madrid: Editorial Trotta, 1990.
Tigre, Maria Antonia, and Natalia Urzola. 'The 2017 Inter-American Court's Advisory Opinion: Changing the Paradigm for International Environmental Law in the Anthropocene', *Journal of Human Rights and the Environment* 12, no. 1 (2021): 24–50.
Tombs, David. *Latin American Liberation Theology*. Leiden: Brill, 2002.
Torres, Sergio, and John Eagleson, eds. *Theology in the Americas*. Maryknoll: Orbis Books, 1976.
Touris, Claudia. *La constelación tercermundista. Catolicismo y cultura política en la Argentina (1955–1976)*. Buenos Aires: Editorial Biblos, 2021.

Chapter 1

Conflict and ecclesiology: Obedience, institutionality and people of God in the Movement of Priests for the Third World

Pablo Bradbury

In 1968, a network of Argentine Catholic clergymen calling themselves the *Movimiento de Sacerdotes para el Tercer Mundo* (Movement of Priests for the Third World, MSTM) emerged calling for revolutionary social change, inspired by the 'Manifesto of Third World Bishops' disseminated the previous year (16 Bishops of the Third World 1967). Over the following six years, the MSTM became the driving force of liberation Christianity in the country, incorporating perhaps 10 per cent of all Argentine priests, hosting up to 160 participants from across the country at its annual meetings and attracting almost constant media attention. However, they soon faced mounting internal discord over their collective stance on priestly celibacy and their relationship with the country's dominant popular movement, Peronism. By 1973 the organisation could no longer agree on a collective national statement. The fragmentation of the MSTM occurred just as the Peronist administration took power in 1973 in the midst of an intensely turbulent and polarised political atmosphere. As the state sought to demobilise a highly conflictive political arena, largely by ramping up repressive operations (especially following Juan Perón's death in 1974 and the military coup of 1976), the crisis of Argentine liberation Christianity deepened and increasingly drove its adherents towards different paths.[1] To comprehend the distinct forms, political discourses and identities that liberation Christianity assumed in Argentina from the mid-1970s, it is imperative to understand the nature of the MSTM's fragmentation.

Jerónimo Podestá, a former bishop of Avellaneda, identified the dispute over celibacy as a 'practical' question, while the dissension over Peronism has often been discussed in terms of a problem to do with the movement's politicisation (cited in Martín 2013, 29). Nevertheless, this chapter points to a factor that underpinned each issue: the tension between the MSTM as part of a social movement (liberation Christianity) and its relationship with vertically structured institutions (the Church and the Peronist party). At root here was the nature of the Church. Enrique Dussel (1995, 237–8) affirmed that, in the 1960s and 1970s, the Church's 'model' was one of three fundamental challenges for the Latin American Church, as liberationists advanced a paradigm centred on the protagonism of the poor.[2] This chapter explores some of the discussions that took place among the Third World Priests and others in close proximity to the group on the nature of the Church, power and the oppressed, exploring how these debates evolved to engender an internal tension within the movement. It shows that Argentine liberation Christianity, in a period of intense political and religious conflicts and the discursive identification of the Church leadership with privilege and elitism, challenged the institutional and hierarchical nature of the Church. Based on archival research and analysis of key Christian left periodicals, the chapter proposes that an ecclesiology was advanced that emphasised grassroots praxis and challenged both the verticality and institutional nature of the Church. Nevertheless, and especially in the context of the return of Peronism to power in 1973, this ecclesiological issue became internalised within the movement, shaping the disagreements within the MSTM over celibacy, the identification with the institutional Church and the relationship with Peronism.

Studies of liberation theology that take a social movement approach have tended to emphasise its wider, continental existence. For instance, Christian Smith's classic study (1991) analysed the emergence of a network of key liberation theologians by employing a framework rooted in resource mobilisation theory. Meanwhile, Michael Löwy (1996) interpreted liberation theology as the theological expression of a socio-religious movement across the Americas, rooted in a new religious culture and radical praxis. On the other hand, the historiography has also addressed the importance of ecclesiology in liberation theology in a restricted way, frequently without detailed attention to specific contexts and relationships to local conjunctures. Much has been made of the base ecclesial communities (*comunidades eclesiales de base*, CEBs), especially prevalent in Brazil and Central America, identified by Leonardo Boff in *Ecclesiogenesis* (1986) as challenging top-down institutionalism and reinventing the Church. Ecclesiology was also central to other key liberation theologians, such as Juan Luis Segundo, who began his five-volume *A Theology for Artisans of a New Humanity* with a book on the Church (1980). Liberationists' ecclesiology was also a significant target of the institutional counter-offensive against liberation theology in the 1970s and 1980s. This backlash coalesced ten years after the famous Medellín conference in 1979 at the Third Episcopal Conference of Latin America (*Consejo Episcopal Latinoamericano*, CELAM) in Puebla, headed by the conservative traditionalist Alfonso López Trujillo. Pope John Paul II opened Puebla with an address in which he issued an implicit criticism of some elements of liberation theologians' ecclesiology: 'In some cases an attitude of mistrust is produced with regard to the "institutional" or "official" Church, which is considered as alienating, as opposed to another Church of the people, one "springing from the people" and taking concrete form in the poor' (John Paul II 1979).

In the Argentine case, a number of important studies have analysed the history of the Third World Priests, and its relation to both the wider Church and the Argentine political scene.[3] Scholars have insightfully charted the development of liberation Christianity over these years, its links to the insurgent left and its theological production (Campos 2016; Donatello 2010). Moreover, research has pointed to the internal disagreements over the country's dominant popular movement, Peronism, and clerical celibacy that led to the MSTM's dissolution (Magne 2004; Touris 2021). This chapter seeks to build on this pioneering work by situating ecclesiology at the centre of tensions within liberation Christianity and especially within the MSTM. It establishes how the charge of alienation, privilege and elitism aimed at the hierarchy shaped an ecclesiology based on the idea of participatory practice that challenged prevailing forms of institutional hierarchy. This analysis foregrounds the perception of the institutional Church as reproducing, through close relationships with elites and the armed forces, rigidly vertical organisational structures. Liberationists instead sought a more horizontal structure that defied the institutional and disciplinary strictures of the Church. It then shows that the tensions implied by this ecclesiology seemed to become internalised within the MSTM and underpinned its fragmentation over issues of clerical celibacy and political affiliation in 1973–4. In this historically grounded analysis, the chapter helps to explain how the theology of the people, an Argentine variant of socially committed Catholicism, peeled away from other tendencies of liberationist Christianity, despite their shared origins (Remeseira 2022).[4]

Conflict and privilege

In the atmosphere following the CELAM meeting in Medellín in 1968, many Christians across Latin America attempted to rethink the Church's role in society. The Church, it was argued, must recognise its own political function and actively participate in the liberation of the people. In his theological notes at the end of the 1960s, Carlos Mugica, a high-profile figure in the MSTM, affirmed that the Church must be at the heart of the 'fundamental political process of liberation' (Mugica n.d.). However, Mugica contended that this presupposed a particular form of Church: 'We talk of intervention from the Church, but which Church? Without doubt, the People of God' (Mugica n.d.). Exploring the different roles within the Church (bishops, priests, laity), he recognised that his own political commitment to the people as a pastor would inevitably result in confrontation with traditional and hierarchical Catholic sectors (Mugica n.d.). But the notes also point towards explorations of the meanings of the Church as people of God, which had featured prominently in the Second Vatican Council (1962–5). In Argentina, this term unsurprisingly became entwined with political meanings, since *el pueblo* (the people) was one of the principal themes of Peronist discourse (Bonnin 2012). People of God could therefore elicit notions of popular struggle and identity, and, in turn, of popular Christianity.

Implicit in these ideas was a challenge to what he perceived as the traditional parameters of the Church. In this view, the priest's commitment was to the people of God and to a project of liberation from social injustice. Yet institutional Church structures presented an obstacle: 'The priests want to be supported more decidedly in their temporal-political undertaking by the official Church; in general, they are suspected, violently criticised and even slandered. This divides them even more from the visible Church' (Mugica n.d.). Mugica here indicated that legitimate intervention in temporal matters had to be driven by the Church as 'People of God' instigated by the people, rather than as 'institution' initiated by authorities. Despite these notes consisting of occasionally vague ideas and suggestive questions, they provide an insight into his perception of the Church. Above all, they demonstrate Mugica's understanding that the Church as people of God represented a challenge to both the dominant faction of the ecclesial hierarchy and traditionalist Catholicism. This was a sentiment shared more widely among Catholic left circles, and which had evolved and adapted in interaction with the political and religious cleavages in Argentina.

Disputes within the Argentine Catholic Church reached unprecedented levels of drama in the late 1960s and early 1970s. When General

Juan Carlos Onganía took power in 1966, ushering a new cycle of oppressive military rule, the emergence of a movement of revolutionary Christians was accelerated in response. Onganía was keen to use Catholicism to undergird his regime, for example by consecrating the nation to the Immaculate Heart of Mary in 1969. The MSTM, still only a little over one year old, was quick to protest this move to manipulate Christian symbolism to legitimise an authoritarian dictatorship (*La Prensa* 1969). However, the Church itself was widely seen as being a force of legitimisation for Onganía's dictatorship, not least due to the fact that Mons. Antonio Caggiano, then president of the Argentine episcopal conference (*Conferencia Episcopal Argentina*, CEA), regularly appeared in public alongside the general. *Cristianismo y Revolución*, an influential magazine and a formative experience for a range of key liberationist Christians, guerrilla leaders and activists, was created to a large extent as a response to the Onganía regime and perceived it as accelerating revolutionary change by heightening social tensions.[5] The magazine's editor, Juan García Elorrio, used his platform to denounce the institutional complicity between Church and military leaderships: 'the military government errs when it believes that certain presences, support, influences and people are "the whole Church" or simply "the Church". They believed that the verticality of the military commanders equated directly to the verticality of the Hierarchy' (García Elorrio 1966b).

These editorials were not merely a critique of the armed forces' perception of the Church but also a strident reproach of the Church hierarchy itself, perceived to be clinging onto traditional practices at a time of conciliar renewal and social unrest. Faced with an episcopal leadership perceived to be ambivalent at best over implementing Vatican II reforms, García Elorrio rebuked the bishops for focusing on 'the vague generalities of routine and pointing out guidelines for a Christianity that responds neither to the requirements of man nor to the demands of history' (García Elorrio 1966a). He affirmed that the episcopate must shed itself of 'institutional ties with the State' and cease to be a 'Church complicit with the dictatorship' (García Elorrio 1966a). The accusation against the episcopate was not merely one of political complicity; *Cristianismo y Revolución* charged Church leaders with belonging to the ruling class and 'privileged sectors', tying them more organically to reactionary forces: 'A change of system would make them lose that situation of privilege. If they themselves come to condemn the use of force that the dispossessed sectors undertake to modify the situation, it is difficult not to suspect that more than the Christian ideal what they defend is the power of the Church, its privilege' (Mascialino 1968, 15). In contrast, with the emergence of the MSTM, García Elorrio endowed the Third World Priests and sympathetic laity with an authenticity the episcopate lacked, the true embodiment of the people of God through its politicised nature:

> There is a New Church that [the dictatorship] does not know and cannot call upon on the television as an ally of the state of emergency, as an accomplice in the torture, murder, exploitation and poverty of our brothers. From that Church, true Church of the People, true march of the People of God towards liberation, these words are a sign and a testimony: 'The structures of the new order to which many men aspire must form a socialist society' (García Elorrio 1969, 25).

This statement came after the *cordobazo*, an uprising led by militant trade unionists and students in the industrial city of Córdoba in May 1969, in response to which the MSTM affirmed their support for socialism and the abolition of private property.

The dovetailing of political and religious contestation occurred at various local levels, which pointed towards a wider phenomenon of polarisation within the Church. Disputes between priests and their bishops marked many dioceses across the country, especially those headed by traditionalist prelates. It is worth highlighting a couple of these disputes, as they came to assume emblematic cleavages within the Church. In Mendoza, twenty-seven Catholic priests who had previously been at odds with the pro-military auxiliary bishop, José Miguel Medina, over stances on the Second Vatican Council threatened to resign when the latter was promoted to bishop of Jujuy in 1966 and his replacement was imposed without consultation. Archbishop Alfonso María Buteler demanded obedience, publicly accepted their resignations and left the priests marginalised from institutional functions (Concatti 2009, 75–85).

The city of Rosario experienced one of the most dramatic internal Church conflicts. Archbishop Guillermo Bolatti had a tense relationship with the young priests involved in Young Catholic Workers (*Juventud Obrera Cristiana*, JOC) in his diocese from the 1960s, developing a reputation for opposing pastoral reform and continuing the authoritarian style of his predecessor, Antonio Caggiano.[6] When forty priests sent him a private letter in early 1969 suggesting reforms, he responded by claiming the priests had rebelled against episcopal obedience. Bolatti also suspended Néstor García, who had become involved in local union and student movements, suppressed payments for sacramental duties and included dialogue with the congregation during Sunday Mass. When parishioners rebelled, boycotting the prelate's own mass, Bolatti suspended further priests for supporting the indignant faithful, provoking the resignation of some thirty further pastors (*Clarín* 1969). This provoked a firm protest among priests across the country, who noted that the developments presented the image of a 'Church as an institution in which dialogue seems impossible' ('Documento No. 48' 1970, 380). However, in July 1969, the dispute entered a new stage when lay Catholics had occupied the church of one of the rebel priests to prevent a replacement being imposed. In the wake of wider social mobilisations, including the student and trade union uprisings in Córdoba and Rosario in May 1969, armed police officers were called on to remove the parish occupiers, ending in five protesters being shot and wounded and twenty more arrested. Intra-ecclesial conflicts in the second half of the 1960s often originated in disagreements over pastoral reform in the atmosphere of Vatican II. However, they frequently became centred on the issue of apostolic obedience and wider participation in Church practices, and quickly became entangled with political authoritarianism and state repression. Traditionalist bishops, generally dominant in the Argentine Church, were hostile to participatory ecclesial practices that could be engendered by the notion of the people of God and sought to preserve a more hierarchical institutional structure.

Verticality and horizontality

The conflicts of the late 1960s and early 1970s moved many Christians not only to challenge individual conservative bishops but also the episcopal hierarchy as such, signalling the extent to which this was a generalised institutional rift. In Argentina, this must be contextualised with reference to the dramatic conflicts between priests and bishops that tore through Argentine Catholicism. In this atmosphere, many involved in grassroots Catholic mobilisations began to question the very notion of obedience as demanded by traditionalist bishops. Thus, priests from Tucumán, in a letter in March 1969 to then coadjutor archbishop of Buenos Aires Juan Carlos Aramburu, noted CELAM's observation at Medellín of a 'tension between the new demands of the mission and a certain way of exercising authority' (CELAM 1968). Aramburu had previously criticised some of his priests for becoming overtly political (mostly MSTM members), and the *tucumanos* wanted to express their solidarity with their fellow pastors. However, they were quick to point out that they did not reject the bishop's authority: 'the fact that priests or groups of Christians make their voices heard publicly before concrete situations they perceive as anti-Christian does not affect the adequate subordination to the bishop that creates the unity of the people of God' (Enlace 1969a). This cautious appeal should therefore be interpreted as an attempt to prevent a souring of relations and to fashion space in which to manoeuvre.

Nevertheless, the breakdown in relations between the hierarchy and politicised priests and laity over the following months, epitomised by events in Rosario, generated an increasingly anti-authoritarian sentiment. Lucio Gera, a priest and respected theologian in the MSTM, depicted the Christian faith as a critique of power:

> The faith denounces the false abundance of power, of the possession of power, of man only in authority and not in obedience [. . .] This should be the obedience in the Church: a way of living that denounces the false pretension of abundance that expects the possession of power. This should also be the testimony of authority, of power in the Church. Authority, that which is wielded in the Church, must give witness to the fact that power is not the end, taking it as 'service'. (Gera 1969)

Hernán Benítez was forthright in his denunciation of the Church authorities for fostering a climate of bitterness among priests. He excoriated the hierarchy for:

> having worried more for the good of the institution [. . .] [Priests] enter the seminary brought by a vocation for serving their brothers, men. But, once ordained, they find themselves obliged to spend their lives in service, not to men, but to an institution that does not serve or scarcely serves men. They feel, logically, disappointed, deceived and even cheated. (Enlace 1969c)

Imagining he were a bishop, an idea that he confessed descended into the realms of 'absurd fantasies', Benítez suggested an orientation that was suggestive of a liberationist model of intra-ecclesial relations: first, that he 'would try to see in each priest a man rather than a functionary'; and, second, that he would attempt 'to share with all the priests of my diocese the responsibility for it' (Enlace 1969c). This response evoked two of the principal objections that were being aimed at the Church: on the one hand, its institutional nature, which reduced those beneath the bishop into mere subservient administrators; on the other hand, its inflexible verticality, which imposed indisputable authority and obedience on priests and laity.

Benítez's words were indicative not only of a re-evaluation of how bishops should behave, but also a *re-imagining* of how the Church could function and was structured. Susana Bianchi notes that the Catholic Church was organised in a vast centralised hierarchy, descending from the papacy, through the bishops and down to the parishes, which constitute the basic units (Bianchi 2002, 143). Such an analysis interrogates the *spatialisation* of the Church: how relationships between officials and adherents in the ecclesial institution are imagined and understood in their spatial dimensions. This is not to deny the existence of hierarchical practices, but simply to note that the lexicon of verticality is above all a metaphor connected to how people experience the Church. As James Ferguson and Akhil Gupta argue, albeit in relation to states rather than churches, spatialisation is constructed through quotidian experiences of regulation and bureaucratic practices.[7] Of course, bishops do not literally exist *above* priests, monks, nuns and the laity, but experiences of how the Church functioned produced an imagined understanding of ecclesial structures as rigidly scalar and hierarchical. Thus, the authoritarian practices of bishops such as Guillermo Bolatti reinforced vertical understandings of the Church.

The traditionalist conception of the Church, which saw the hierarchical institution as the perfect society, conformed to this verticality, thus reinforcing many bishops' handling of their priests. At the heart of the dispute was the notion of apostolic obedience, which in Catholic ecclesiology forms an essential part of communion between members of the Church, and was outlined in one of the Second Vatican Council's documents, *Presbyterorum Ordinis* (Paul VI 1965). The document affirmed that bishops should 'regard priests as their brothers and friends' and 'consult them and engage in dialogue with them in those matters which concern the necessities of pastoral work and welfare of the diocese' (Paul VI 1965). On the other hand, priests were expected to recognise 'the fullness of the priesthood which the bishops enjoy' and 'respect in them the authority of Christ, the Supreme Shepherd. They must therefore stand by their bishops in sincere charity and obedience' (Paul VI 1965). In the context of intra-ecclesial conflicts, bishops could appeal to this formulation of apostolic obedience, emphasising reverence to Christ's authority in the episcopate.

Liberationist Christians, on the other hand, adopted the notion of the Church as people of God in a context in which the term *people* had profound political connotations that contrasted with the notion of the oligarchy. When conflicts with the bishops escalated, the priests and laity involved did not necessarily experience an alienation from Church structures in general (as they often remained active in parishes and base communities). In a meeting of MSTM regional organisers during the movement's Second National Encounter, priests emphasised that they should take 'all possible measures to avoid being excluded from the structural Church' (MSTM 1994d, 74). Moreover, they insisted that any division or opposition should not be 'between Movement and Hierarchy but between one part of the Hierarchy [. . .] which is part of the people and another that is in fact against the people' (MSTM 1994d, 74). Nevertheless, the distancing from the hierarchical elements reinforced their identity as the Church of the people, in contradistinction to, as one editorial in the MSTM's bulletin put it, a Church institution characterised by an 'oligarchic' constitution of power (Enlace 1969b). This text argued that an outdated traditionalism understood authority to emanate from God through those in positions of power, but that a new conception of authority had emerged: 'Authority comes from God directly, but not immediately. Between God and the hierarchical structure there is a Medium: the People, the Community' (Enlace 1969b). As such, 'the true and fundamental "institution" of Christ would not be a "hierarchy" but a Community based in love: the People of God' (Enlace 1969b). Power and authority had thus been inverted in their spatial dimensions. This was not an outright rejection of episcopal authority but an affirmation that the authority of God passed through the people rather than the bishops. Although authority retained its vertical aspect with relation to God, the immediate medium was the people, while the episcopate was expected to reflect 'the new consciousness' and 'convert itself into authentic servants of man' (Enlace 1969b). This clearly encountered a tension with the notion of apostolic obedience to which the bishops appealed, that placed liberationist priests in an unclear position with respect to hierarchical structures. Thus, the tension between verticality and horizontality was closely interlinked with an ambiguity over identification with the ecclesial institution, an ambiguity in which many priests, members of religious orders and Catholic laity all became involved.

Containment and transgression

In October 1970, a group of lay militants in Buenos Aires called for the formation of a 'Lay Movement of the Third World', in parallel to the Movement of Priests for the Third World ('Para un movimiento de laicos del tercer mundo' 1970). This was a direct response to the robust censure that the CEA published, in which the Church hierarchy demonstrated itself to identify 'with the capitalist regime' by rejecting the socialisation of the means of production ('Para un movimiento de laicos del tercer mundo' 1970).[8] In this strong denunciation of the hierarchy, the group called for all Argentine Christians sympathetic to the cause to prepare for a 'National Assembly of the Third World Church' ('Para un movimiento de laicos del tercer mundo' 1970). The wording of this last statement is perhaps slightly ambiguous: was this a call for the formation of a new Church? Were they calling for a schism? No evidence supports the notion that this was indeed a rallying cry for a breakaway Church. Nevertheless, this document demonstrates the heightened tensions between a sector of Christians in Argentina and the official Church structure.

The identification of a tension between containment and transgression is a concept borrowed from Charles Tilly and Sydney Tarrow's social movement analysis. They argue that social movements are in a process of tension between contained and transgressive contention: 'Contained contention takes place within a regime, using its established institutional routines, while transgressive contention challenges these routines and those it protects' (Tilly and Tarrow 2015, 62). In their analysis, social movements often occupy an ambiguous political space that can hover between conforming to the legitimate practices or channels of a state and defying those channels, seeking to construct new structures. While Tilly and Tarrow use this to refer to social movement contention within the political and legal system, this frame can also help to explain liberationist Christian contention in Argentina in this period. Priests and lay Catholics were increasingly defying the established routines of the Catholic institution, challenging the authority of the bishop and denouncing the financial and political practices that tied the Church to the ruling elites. These internal tensions occurred throughout all sectors of the Catholic Church, with many politicised priests, nuns, monks and even a bishop (Jerónimo Podestá) abandoning their institutional functions. It should come as little surprise that those alienated from ecclesial structures in bitter disputes with episcopal authorities were often those most prepared to condemn the institution. For example, Raúl Marturet, excommunicated by archbishop of Corrientes Francisco Vicentín, made plain his feelings about the election of Adolfo Tortolo to replace Caggiano as president of the CEA: 'The election of monsignor Tortolo means that the church in Argentina begins its suicide [. . .]. This ultra-right, which found its way onto the managerial posts of all the commissions and of the presidency through a very intelligent and shrewd man, as is monsignor Tortolo, is proof of the hierarchical orientation of the Argentine church' (Marturet cited in *Cristianismo y Revolución* 1970, 19).[9] Many lay militants underwent a similar distancing from the Church, as the phenomenon of generalised social protest among students and workers entered into ecclesial spheres.

Politicised Christians, who understood their faith as demanding a commitment to the poor rather than to an institution bound up in spheres of power, often expressed their uneasy relation with the traditional Church. In the short-lived magazine *Tierra Nueva*, which assumed the humanist language redolent of the new left and hoped to offer a critical voice within Catholicism at a time of modernisation, the young priest Alejandro Mayol wondered whether the Church had become a 'corset for the New Man' (Mayol 1966, 9). Mayol questioned whether the Church, with its 'feudal structure' and 'monolithic concept of obedience', was for 'the modern believer [. . .] another alienation, alongside many others that imprison the human being today' (Mayol 1966, 9). Indeed, the Church appeared to many people as 'governed by the dead, by the past' (Mayol 1966, 10). And one of the key poles of conflict was 'the problem of frontiers': 'the believer before was only comfortable conversing with another believer. It is typical of a ghetto. Today we witness a new phenomenon. In a great number of cases there is much more profound dialogue with non-believers than with Christians' (Mayol 1966, 10). This view of the institutional Church as restricting would reappear frequently among those in or close to the MSTM, especially as the disputes with members of the hierarchy multiplied.

The fractious relationship with the Church institution was a long-running issue for the MSTM, but tended in official proclamations to reassert affiliation with the institution, albeit insisting on the need for reform and popular empowerment within ecclesial structures. For example, the group's Third National Encounter affirmed 'an unbreakable will of belonging to the Catholic Church', but demanded that the ecclesial hierarchy implement what was elaborated in Medellín and in San Miguel (MSTM 1994a, 100).[10] The following year, a public rebuke by the CEA, now led by Mons. Tortolo, criticised the movement's stated commitment to the socialisation of the means of production and reminded them of their obligations of communion with the hierarchy, demanding submission and deference: 'Let us ask for this grace. For us to know the truth well and to say it with clarity and charity; and for you to understand it, accept it and undertake it' (CEA 1970). The MSTM felt compelled to respond at length, defending their political positions as well as affirming, among other things, the necessity of the ecclesial institution, but insisted that it must be 'at the service of faith' (MSTM 1994c, 121). They emphasised that the notion of the Church as people of God did not imply the exclusion of hierarchical structures (MSTM 1994c, 160).

Nevertheless, the MSTM affirmed in 1972 that they understood their priestly commitment not as service to the bishop or the institution but 'as service to the people of God' (MSTM 1972, 201). Consequential here was the notion that the commitment to the *pueblo* – the oppressed and marginalised – could be framed increasingly in conflict with the traditional form of the Church.[11] For some, such a dilemma would bring them to a critical tension, even a breaking point, with the Church. One MSTM member, Rubén Dri, reflecting on his trajectory in the movement and his eventual resignation from his ministry in 1974, was clear about his sense of incompatibility of institutional ecclesial structures:

I felt within the Church. But the thing is, for me the Church is not an institution. I believe in the *ekklesia*, really, that is the assembly Church. I feel inside the Church to the extent that I work collectively, to the extent that I meet up with my companions. That we believe in determinate fundamental values for which we fight [...] I maintain those fundamental values, that fundamental faith, but I do not at all believe in the ecclesial institution. I am outside.[12]

This may have been among the more radical of the liberationist positions, especially among the Catholic clergy, but it was logically and analytically coherent and certainly not a unique outlook.

The rejection of the Church institution can be seen within the context of a conceptual distinction of the people of God from the hierarchical ecclesial structures. There is some parallel here with the separation of planes and the ecclesiology of New Christendom that emphasises the Church as the *corpus mysticum*, the mystical body of Christ: in this, the juridical Church is separated from the mystical Church.[13] As such, according to William Cavanaugh, liberal elements in the Church 'used the mystical body emphasis on the invisible church to distance themselves from institutional, especially Vatican, control' (Cavanaugh 1998, 210). This distinction was a development that built upon the theology which had propagated the notion of the Church as people of God in the conciliar constitution *Lumen Gentium* (Paul VI 1964). For the liberationist Christians, however, the separation is between the Church as a people, functioning as a social movement, and the Church as a politico-juridical institution tied up in the oppressive social structures of capitalist society. This notion of the Church was seen by many as a rediscovery of an authentic Christianity. Writing in 1969 in the MSTM's bulletin, *Enlace*, Jerónimo Podestá affirmed that the Church understood as people of God, 'as a community of believers', enabled a distinction between two aspects of the Church's temporal activity: 'the active presence of the Christians – laity or priests – in temporal or political issues' and the 'explicit or implicit pronouncement of the Hierarchy, in other words, the Official Church' (Podestá 1969).

According to Podestá, the 'primordial Church' of the community of believers found itself in struggle with an institutional model characterised by rigid authoritarianism and associated with the wider interest of the prevailing social order:

> There are those who want to accentuate [the hierarchical function] to such a degree that the Church would give a monolithic Image, of absolute verticality. These confuse the Church, People of God, with the Church Institution, not seeing anything but this last aspect [...]

Generally those who encourage the Church as Institution stabilising and defending a supposed 'Order' with whose interests it is identified. (Podestá 1969)

These were not merely theological discussions articulated in intellectual forums but serious critiques of the Church's implication in political power that made sense to radical political sectors. Indeed, the Peronist Armed Forces (*Fuerzas Armadas Peronistas*, FAP), closely linked to *Peronismo de Base*, a grassroots militant movement that rejected the Peronist and trade union bureaucracies and emphasised autonomous working class organising, made a similar point, albeit in a more denunciatory key. In an open letter to the MSTM, one of the FAP's affiliated 'detachments' rebuked the Church institution for seeing its function as one of 'organising, talking and dispensing a grace that only it possesses through rites emptied of human reality' (FAP 1970, 18). Although, the letter continued, the institution 'throughout its history has been committed – as a structure – to anti-Christian, anti-human regimes', a more authentic Christian message could be mobilised 'against and rejecting the Church institution':

> It is here that we find the distinction, which theoretically seems inadmissible, in real life: Church-institution and Church people of God [. . .] There are then two Churches. One with all the word, apostolicity and authority, structure and rite. And on the other hand, a Church-people of God full of life, of service, of love, without old rites or signs, that begins to create its own rites and signs born in struggle.
> (FAP 1970, 18–19)

Here, the people of God or the 'assembly Church' appeared to be akin to a social or popular movement whose vitality emerges fundamentally from the struggle of the poor and oppressed, focused on grassroots praxis and in rejection of what were perceived as the institutional confines of a Church tied up with political power. In social movement terms, we might refer to Frances Fox Piven and Richard Cloward, who claimed that movements are at their most radical in the cause of the poor and oppressed when they preserve their 'disruptive capacities', nurture popular rebellion and refuse to institutionalise (Piven and Cloward 1979, 23–7).

Although the MSTM as such never rejected the institutional Church, sharp criticisms of the ecclesial hierarchy, from the priests as well as lay Christians, alongside dramatic intra-ecclesial conflicts were met with accusations of a schismatic orientation. Attacks even came from figures considered broadly sympathetic to the priests and who therefore might have undermined the MSTM's legitimacy among its own supporters, such was the case of Vicente Zazpe, the archbishop of Santa Fe. The document produced in 1971 from the MSTM's fourth annual 'National Encounter', named the 'Carlos Paz Document', had levelled forthright allegations against the episcopate: in the face of the military's encroachment on fundamental human rights, the hierarchy was notable for its 'obsequious silence' and was 'domesticated and servile before the powerful' (MSTM 1994b, 185). Zazpe replied to the MSTM's criticisms by attacking what he described as their 'schismatic ferment' and a 'spirit that was not ecclesial', rebuking the priests for neglecting communion with the episcopate (*El Litoral* 1971). The archbishop's timing could hardly have been worse for the MSTM. It came at a time when four priests in Rosario were detained, another in Resistencia had been abducted by the military and the movement was in the midst of a bitter polemic with Mons. Tortolo, who had downplayed an apostolic blessing from Paul VI by falsely claiming that they had requested it explicitly (Palacios Videla 1971). This came a year after the Tortolo-led CEA's open castigation of the MSTM, discussed earlier. The communion with the hierarchical leadership demanded of the MSTM therefore appeared bound up with a rigid apostolic obedience and a political position in opposition to their revolutionary commitment.

In response to Zazpe, the priests insisted on their loyalty to the Church and noted that 'we have never talked about two Churches; in every case we have referred to diverse positions within the only Church' (quoted in *La Opinión* 1971b). In the midst of feverish media coverage of the fallout, Mugica insisted that the movement was a consequence of, not in tension with, the Church's teachings and rejected the notion of a lack of communion with bishops, pointing to regular meetings between his fellow priests in Buenos Aires and the archbishop, Juan Carlos Aramburu (*La Opinión* 1971c). Nevertheless, the incident contributed to a growing alienation from the hierarchy. For example, hundreds of lay activists in Buenos Aires held a protest and released a document that affirmed that 'the People of God is incarcerated, and their shepherds do not defend them' (*La Opinión* 1971a). Zazpe's attack fed into a sense that the hierarchy had abandoned their own priests when they needed them most, just as state repression against the MSTM was increasing. Moreover, it demonstrated how the two tensions identified here (vertical/horizontal and containment/transgression) were intimately related.

As the MSTM came under sustained attack by the military authorities and ecclesial hierarchy, media coverage of the movement, often little more than conjecture and speculation, wondered whether the priests would break away from the Church. One of the more serious journalists, Tomás Eloy Martínez, writing for *La Opinión*, sparked a minor scandal following the Fifth National Encounter in August 1972 when he claimed that the MSTM had held a secret meeting, attended by married priests, at which they resolved to reject the ecclesial rule of celibacy (Eloy Martínez 1972). A response quickly came from the MSTM, denying that they had even debated celibacy (*La Opinión* 1972). In spite of this clarification, the story generated media speculation, such as in the conservative magazine *Esquiú*, over whether the movement would 'remain within the Church or definitively break from it' (*Esquiú* 1972). Although this question was articulated in rather sensationalist terms, it was not totally immaterial. There was no prospect of the entire movement breaking away from the ecclesial institution; however, what was undoubtedly true was that intra-ecclesial conflicts and the political and theological chasm that existed between different sectors of the clergy meant that many Catholics were increasingly channelling their activities outside of the official institutional structures. In fact, a fundamental challenge existed over the nature of the ecclesial structure and its functioning. The presence of married priests, and priestly celibacy more broadly, was indeed both a source of controversy and symptomatic in this regard, embodying a defiance of institutional rules. This was merely the most acute example of the fact that radicalised Catholic sectors increasingly challenged ecclesial authorities who were perceived to be in league with the rich and powerful and sought to maintain the authority of the institution in society while neglecting the true demands of Christian faith.

Fragmentation

The fact that radical and politicised ecclesiological perspectives drew the ire of even certain sympathetic progressive bishops in Argentina placed significant pressure on the MSTM, especially during a period of heightening political turmoil in the 1970s. After the *cordobazo* in 1969, and other social uprisings, during which workers and students battled a hostile dictatorship, the political scene increasingly became marked by what Sebastián Carassai identifies as a move from social violence to political violence: insurgent guerrilla groups increasingly came into conflict with the state, while armed far-right groups also mobilised (Carassai 2014, 51–101). The political opening in 1973 – in which Peronist candidate Hector Cámpora, friendly with the insurgent left, swept to power – ironically ended in a dilemma for the MSTM. Peronism was now back in power but was unable to contain its own battles. The Peronist left and the revolutionary tendency pointed towards the political and union bureaucracy, seeing it as a solidification of verticalist structures in the Peronist movement and the primary obstacle to Peronism becoming a truly revolutionary force. Cámpora soon resigned to make way for the triumphant return of Juan Perón; but the Ezeiza Massacre, a bloodbath of the left carried out by far-right Peronists during the welcome rally for the arriving leader, augured an intensification of political polarisation.

Although there appeared to be a general tendency among the MSTM to challenge the hierarchical and institutional nature of the Church and advance a grassroots notion of the Church as people of God, in a changing political environment these challenges appeared to become internalised. In the lead up to the Fifth National Encounter in August 1972, clear differences began to emerge. Miguel Ramondetti, the MSTM's general secretary from its beginnings, circulated a letter that summarised the points of difference over five issues: interpretation of the national political reality; understanding of priestly commitment; the form and level of priestly commitment in politics; understanding of the relationship between faith and politics; and understanding of the Church itself (MSTM National Secretary 1994, 245). The priest's movement over the course of 1973 became torn by two apparently intractable disagreements. On the one hand, the question of Peronism became an even more contentious issue than it was before once the Peronist-led coalition took power. The MSTM had initially mobilised in 1968 on the basis of a prophetic denunciation of capitalism and a rather imprecise notion of the need for revolutionary change in the structures of society. Originally inspired by the Message of Third World Bishops, the political model of the MSTM had loosely been some form of socialism: 'true socialism is a full Christian life that involves a just sharing of goods, and fundamental equality' (16 Bishops of the Third World 1967, 144). However, as the priests sought to develop their analysis and commitment, Peronism, the dominant movement among the trade unions and popular classes more broadly, quickly became the immutable point of discussion. Rolando Concatti, a leading MSTM figure in Mendoza, had shaped the terms of debate to some degree, as his assertion that prophetism must lead to more concrete political options was adopted as a core theme in the priests' annual meeting of 1970 (Concatti 1970, 17). Two years later, Concatti and the Mendoza MSTM published an influential pamphlet outlining their 'option for Peronism' – not as a political party, but as the expression of a social force and an oppressed people (Concatti 1972).

With the Peronist party – and Juan Perón himself from September 1973 – in power, however, the distinction between Peronism as an oppressed social force and as an institutional power was less immediate; or, at least, what this meant in practice became less obvious. Figures such as Ramondetti, who maintained a more insistent support for socialism, were clear about their reluctance to support Perón. Even various Third World

Priests who identified personally as Peronists believed a formal identification of the movement with Peronism was an error and that such political allegiances should be personal decisions.[14] Indeed, if it is likely that most MSTM members were Peronist, there remained significant differences between them.

This reflected the deep divisions within Peronism more broadly, a movement that managed to encompass a dizzying array of competing articulations from the far right to the revolutionary left, but also had to do with political verticalism in a similar way to which priests challenged the hierarchical nature of the institutional Church. Buenos Aires MSTM members affirmed loyalty to Perón: the leader, it was asserted, was the highest expression of the Argentine people, so it was necessary to ally themselves with him. From this perspective, the MSTM should be concerned with ensuring that the Church was *'inserted in the People'*, and it was consequently incumbent on them 'to participate in the People and with the People in the National Justicialista Movement' (MSTM Buenos Aires 1973b, 6 and 16). Using *Justicialista* here was a clear allusion to official Peronist party structures, rather than merely the wider identity of Peronism as a social force. In a letter sent to *La Opinión* from Buenos Aires member-priests Alberto Carbone, Jorge Goñi and Rodolfo Ricciardelli just before the election of Perón in September, the priests claimed that 'In Argentina, the work for liberation is hegemonised by Peronism and its leader. Our Movement verifies that fact and as priests we want to illuminate it with the Gospel' (*La Opinión* 1973). The MSTM's role, in this vision, was to ensure the participation of the institutional Church in the official structures of the dominant popular-national movement.

Against this, other MSTM members and branches reaffirmed a more class-based position, often aligned with the Peronist left or the more grassroots current *Peronismo de Base*. Some of these priests, as Concatti had previously advocated, affirmed Peronism to be the identity of an oppressed social force but sought to avoid containment within limits defined by Peronist institutional spaces: 'Revolutionary Peronism is not the only path to Socialism, but it is the *beginning* of Socialism in Argentina, because it is the national movement of the people and of the workers'; the option for Peronism was necessary only insofar as 'in Peronism, the working class has its highest level of organisation and combativeness' (MSTM Mendoza 1973a). However, both the MSTM in Mendoza and Concatti were also embedded in a more plural scene that included a lively ecumenical network that included an important Protestant presence (Concatti 2009). Striking a note comparable to that of Concatti, Rubén Dri articulated a commitment to political praxis from below: the method of the bureaucracy 'goes from top to bottom, imposing a verticalism that intensifies in moments of danger' while that of the grassroots 'goes from bottom to top. Democracy is not a mere theoretical postulate to be applied once one has taken power, but a demand that must be put into practice in the path to taking power' (Dri 1974b, 22). Rather than relying on verticalist political structures, the working classes and the Peronist people, Dri asserted, had to create their own tools and organisational forms, independent of those interests (Dri 1974a, 20–22).

The second intractable disagreement was more directly related to the institutional Church: the problem of celibacy. A number of priests who had been marginalised by the ecclesial hierarchy from their ministries had by 1973 married. This was particularly the case with certain branches in the interior of the country, such as Mendoza and Rosario, where dozens of priests had resigned or been removed from institutional roles in light of conflicts with the conservative bishops in those dioceses. Jerónimo Podestá, former bishop of Avellaneda – as mentioned earlier in this chapter – suggested that this issue was a practical one. However, in elaborating on the disagreement, he pointed towards a deeper tension: priests in the Buenos Aires chapter of the MSTM hoped for the priests to inspire a commitment to the poor among the episcopate, seeing the married priests as an obstacle; meanwhile, many priests in the interior opposed separating classes of priests in canonical terms. In fact, some priests have claimed that, more than ideological or political disputes, disagreements over the question of celibacy initiated the MSTM's fragmentation.[15]

In preparation for a regional coordinators' meeting in May 1973, the Mendoza MSTM elaborated a scathing denunciation of Canon Law on celibacy (MSTM Mendoza 1973b, 1–8). While recognising 'the values and validity of celibacy' for many clergymen, they questioned 'its coercive and imperative character', rejecting its imposition as an 'objective rule of domination and marginalisation' and the most effective way of excluding 'the "rebels" who challenge juridico-Roman totalitarianism' (MSTM Mendoza 1973b, 6). The MSTM, as a result, 'has no other coherent path than that of including our married companions and taking the risk with them and for them' (MSTM Mendoza 1973b, 8). In other words, liberation Christianity as represented by the MSTM transgressed the traditional institutional confines of the Church.

Alberto Carbone recounted how he travelled to Mendoza to explain the position of the Buenos Aires MSTM. The disagreements were so immediate that he found himself taking the 1,000 km bus journey back half an hour after he had arrived.[16] Just as the Buenos Aires chapter affiliated more explicitly with the official Peronist hierarchy, the group also conformed to a more conventional institutionalism over celibacy. Since the Church's Canon legislation rejected the compatibility of the priestly ministry for those who abandon celibacy, 'such people cannot integrate *formally* to the Movement' (Büntig 1994, 312). Carbone ascribed the core difference that divided the MSTM as between those who followed a 'European socialist ideology' and those who adhered 'to a popular Peronism' among 'a majority Catholic people'.[17] This perspective closely followed the analysis of Rafael Tello, a key figure alongside Lucio Gera in a so-called popular pastoral position associated with the Episcopal Commission of Pastoral Ministry (*Comisión Episcopal de Pastoral*, COEPAL), which formed the basis of the so-called theology of the people.[18] In September 1973, Tello claimed that two blocs had emerged in the MSTM: on the one hand was '*enlightened progressivism*', guided by secularising tendencies and foreign Marxism whose logical end point was 'rupture with the institutional Church'; on the other, a '*national and popular*' faction recognised the revolutionary potential and popular essence of the Church (Tello 1994, 324). At stake, for Tello, was the very integrity of the Church, since these elements wanted a rupture with the institution. The Buenos Aires MSTM articulated this analysis publicly, with Carbone telling the liberal daily *La Opinión* that 'some do not want to be in "that Institution" [the Church] as it is now', and a forthright collective statement: 'We understand that [. . .] the rupture of established discipline in [celibacy] produces a rupture with the Church' (quoted in Ruza 1973; MSTM Buenos Aires 1973a, 1).

It may be noted here that the theology of the people pioneered by Rafael Tello and Lucio Gera continued to occupy a relatively significant role in the institutional Church in Argentina, Latin America and, eventually, the Church globally. For instance, Gera had an important role in the drafting of *Iglesia y comunidad nacional*, the Argentine episcopate's attempt in 1981 to appeal to national reconciliation and a potential democratic opening five years into the last dictatorship and following the most intense period of state terrorism (Bonnin 2012). At the continental level, the theology of the people was also influential in the 1979 CELAM conference at Puebla, which reflected the perspective of that tendency by focusing on the evangelisation of culture (de Schrijver 1998). And in more recent years, much has been made of the fact that the theology of the people informed the development of Pope Francis' pastoral thought, with echoes of the tendency marking his papal encyclicals and found in his continuing relationship with some of Argentina's present-day *curas villeros* (Scannone 2016). None of this has been entirely free from contestation within wider liberation theology. Indeed, *Iglesia y comunidad nacional*'s discourse on reconciliation was criticised by the left and parts of liberationist Christianity; many key liberation theologians were excluded from the Puebla conference, in a manoeuvre that attempted to impose institutional discipline from the Vatican; and contemporary *curas villeros* may be seen as divided between two different groupings that somewhat correspond to the MSTM factions that emerged in the 1970s (Bradbury 2023, 228–9). This also raises the question of whether the theology of the people does in fact lie within the liberation theology tradition or, as Claudio Iván Remeseira has recently claimed, should be understood as distinct given its development in opposition to key liberationist positions (Remeseira 2022). In any case, although it is beyond the scope of this chapter to explore later developments fully, the continuing impact shows how the theology of the people was evidently able to consolidate its presence as a major and accepted institutional current.

Conclusion

Over the course of the dictatorship that began with General Juan Carlos Onganía, and continued with Generals Roberto Levingston and Alejandro Lanusse, the MSTM was thrust into political and ecclesial conflicts. These conflicts became central to the construction of the broader movement's identity. Through important publications, such as *Cristianismo y Revolución*, many within the broader movement attempted to construct a popular identity rooted in an interpretation of the notion of the people of God and the people as a historical and political subject. This was constituted in opposition to a political regime, an international system and an ecclesial hierarchy that was deemed to represent an anti-popular alliance that upheld the privileges of the elite and maintained the oppressive conditions of the many. The intra-ecclesial conflicts that were a central fact of the MSTM's existence reinforced this mentality. However, the insurgent identity of the movement encountered a basic problem, related to its relationship with the Church institution. Tensions had arisen, which existed in the liberationist movement more broadly but were especially acute in the MSTM, in two dimensions: whether to remain within the institution or find a path outside of it; and a dispute over verticality and horizontality, that is, the organisational forms that should be developed.

Assessing the fracturing within the MSTM – over obedience to Canon Law on celibacy and between Peronists and revolutionary Peronists – we see how contending conceptualisations and spatialisations of the Church underpinned these divisions. These ruptures emerged in the movement in the context of the growing crises of the 1966–73 military dictatorship. The MSTM thus had to navigate a panorama in which the immediate enemy had suddenly fallen and had to contend with the dilemma of how to relate to a Peronist government. However, this contingent political conjuncture was compounded by the contradictory existence and tensions of the MSTM within the Catholic Church. The Buenos Aires group drew from the nascent theology of the people, rooted in a more traditional nationalist mythology, avowing the inherent Catholicity of the Argentinian people, and associated more closely with hierarchical Church structures. Tello and Gera's popular pastoral line did not demand formal adherence to a political project, and the theology of the people was more heterogeneous than is often allowed (Zanca 2022). However, an affinity emerged between the Buenos Aires MSTM most significantly influenced by Tello and a more orthodox Peronism: the people, to which they promised their loyalty, were both Catholic and Peronist. Thus, the Buenos Aires branch came to represent a position of fidelity to the Church and Perón, submitting to the verticality of the ecclesial institution and that of the *Justicialista* movement.

On the other hand, various other MSTM members challenged such verticalism. This resistance to political institutionalisation was mounted not only by socialists with a more Marxist-Leninist bent but also by revolutionary Peronists. Although individual positions were diverse, a common tendency was the rejection of top-down institutional structures as marginalising those struggling for radical social transformation. Politically, this tended to manifest as a position foregrounding class struggle and autonomous grassroots organisation, as reflected in the support or participation in *Peronismo de Base*; ecclesiologically, we can point to Rubén Dri's (1987) formulation of a Church 'born from the people'. The Church, for Dri, was the assemblies of ordinary people reflecting on their oppressive conditions and political praxis, not the hierarchical institutional arrangement that saw power concentrated in the episcopate.

Studies on liberation theology have previously identified a crossroads in the 1970s and 1980s that presented a choice between democracy and revolution. Nevertheless, the analysis above presents a different dilemma in the case of Argentina, which is also reflected elsewhere, for instance in the writings of Leonardo Boff (1985). This is the paradox of an apparently popular, participatory or grassroots identity existing within an institutional and hierarchical Church. In Argentina, parallel or related issues also characterised the identification with Peronism and the relationship with its institutional organs. How could the Church as people of God, radically participatory and popular, be reconciled with rigid verticalism and institutionalism? This chapter suggests that this issue underpinned the bitter fragmentation of the MSTM, just as it confronts social movements more broadly when they relate to social and political institutions. For some, preserving institutional space in the Church and attempting to engender popular values therein became the priority, especially when the return of

Peronism in power appeared to offer certain opportunities. For others, institutional channels, of the Church but also within Peronism, had come to appear too oppressive and entangled in an unjust social order.

Notes

1. For studies of liberationist Christianity during state terror, see especially Catoggio (2016) and Morello (2015). This chapter builds on research published in my recent book (Bradbury 2023), which analyses the different trajectories of liberation Christianity during the period of state terror.
2. The other two challenges were 'People', as the social bloc and historical subject of the oppressed, and the tension between reform and revolution.
3. The best work on the MSTM remains José Pablo Martín's study (1992), based on hundreds of interviews and textual analysis. However, many other valuable works have been published, including Burdick (1995), Magne (2004) and Touris (2021).
4. For more on theology of the people, see Cuda (2016), Politi (1992) and Scannone (1982).
5. For more on the journal, see Campos (2016) and Morello (2003).
6. Author interview with Oscar Lupori, 9 May 2015.
7. For a discussion of verticality and spatialisation, see for example Ferguson and Gupta (2004).
8. For the hierarchy's document, see CEA (1970). Episcopal declarations are available here: https://episcopado.org/documentos (accessed 19 December 2023).
9. Marturet had defied Vicentín's orders when he performed a public prayer for a student activist killed by police in Corrientes during the May 1969 unrest. The priest became concerned by increased police presence at his own church and by death threats after his homilies, asking the judiciary to investigate. Suspecting Vicentín's collusion with the police, he requested the archbishop appear before the investigating judge to testify. When Vicentín refused, the judge ordered his arrest, and the archbishop responded to the humiliation by issuing Marturet's excommunication (which was quickly confirmed by the Holy See).
10. The San Miguel document was something of an anomaly among Argentine episcopal statements, as it reflected the influence of the minority progressive bishops, offering self-criticism of the Church's historic relationship to elites, renouncing a pursuit for power and foregrounding the need for a Church of the poor. See Bradbury (2023, 86).
11. This theme was explored for instance by Conrado Eggers Lan in 1972 in a chapter entitled 'Pueblo, Iglesia y pueblo de Dios' (2014, 181–97).
12. Author interview with Rubén Dri, 19 February 2015.
13. For a critical perspective on this, see Cavanaugh (1998, 151–252).
14. For example, see Juan Ferrante's and César Raúl Sánchez's testimonies in Diana (2013, 140 and 207).
15. For example, see Juan Ángel Dieuzeide's testimony in Diana (2013, 117).
16. Alberto Carbone's testimony in Diana (2013, 117).
17. Carbone's testimony in Diana (2013, 117).
18. Set up in 1965, COEPAL was tasked with elaborating a national pastoral plan, but was dissolved in 1973.

References

16 Bishops of the Third World. 'Gospel and Revolution', *New Blackfriars* 49, no. 571 (1967): 140–48.

Bianchi, Susana. 'La conformación de la Iglesia Católica como actor politico-social. Los laicos en la institución eclesiastica: las organizaciones de elite (1930–1950)', *Anuario del IEHS* 17 (2002): 143–61.

Boff, Leonardo. *Church, Charism and Power: Liberation Theology and the Institutional Church*. New York: Crossroad, 1985.

Boff, Leonardo. *Ecclesiogenesis: The Base Communities Reinvent the Church*. Maryknoll: Orbis Books, 1986.

Bonnin, Juan Eduardo. *Génesis política del discurso religioso. 'Iglesia y communidad nacional' (1981) entre la dictadura y la democracia en Argentina*. Buenos Aires: Eudeba, 2012.

Bradbury, Pablo. *Liberationist Christianity in Argentina, 1930–1983: Faith and Revolution*. Woodbridge: Támesis, 2023.

Büntig, Aldo. '"Informe-síntesis" sobre la reunion de Coordinadores y Responsables Zonales del Movimiento'. In *Documentos para la memoria histórica*, edited by Domingo Bresci, 311–15. Buenos Aires: Centro Salesiano de Estudios, 1994.

Burdick, Michael. *For God and the Fatherland: Religion and Politics in Argentina*. New York: State University of New York Press, 1995.

Campos, Esteban. *Cristianismo y Revolución. El origen de Montoneros. Violencia, política y religion en los 60*. Buenos Aires: Edhasa, 2016.

Carassai, Sebastián. *The Argentine Silent Majority: Middle Classes, Politics, Violence, and Memory in the Seventies*. Durham: Duke University Press, 2014.

Catoggio, María Soledad. *Los desaparecidos de la iglesia. El clero contestatario frente a la dictadura*. Buenos Aires: Siglo Veintiuno Editores, 2016.

Cavanaugh, William. *Torture and Eucharist: Theology, Politics, and the Body of Christ*. Malden: Blackwells, 1998.

CEA. *Declaración de la Comisión Permanente del Episcopado Argentina a nuestros colaboradores: Sacerdotes diocesanos y religiosos y a todo el pueblo de Dios*, 12 August 1970.

CELAM. 'Second General Conference of Latin American Bishops'. In *Documentos finales de Medellín*. 1968.

Clarín. 'Exhortación del arzobispado de Rosario a los 29 sacerdotes que han renunciado', 18 March 1969.

Concatti, Rolando. 'Profetismo y política', *Enlace*, July 1970.

Concatti, Rolando. *Nuestra opción por el peronismo*. Buenos Aires: Movimiento Sacerdotes para el Tercer Mundo de Mendoza, 1972.

Concatti, Rolando. *Testimonio cristiano y resistencia en las dictaduras argentinas. El movimiento ecuménico en Mendoza, 1963–1983*. Buenos Aires: Centro Nueva Tierra, 2009.
Cristianismo y Revolución. 'Raúl Marturet: "Un problema para el Obispo"', June 1970.
Cuda, Emilce. *Para leer a Francisco. Teología, ética y política*. Buenos Aires: Manantial, 2016.
de Schrijver, George, ed. *Liberation Theologies on Shifting Grounds: A Clash of Socio-Economic and Cultural Paradigms*. Leuven: Leuven University Press, 1998.
Diana, Marta, ed. *Buscando el Reino. La opción por los pobres de los argentinos que siguieron al Concilio Vaticano II*. Buenos Aires: Planeta, 2013.
'Documento No. 48: Solidaridad de sacerdotes de todo el país con los renunciantes de Rosario'. In *Los católicos posconciliares*, edited by Alejandro Mayol, Norberto Habegger and Arturo Armada, 380–82. Buenos Aires: Galerna, 1970.
Donatello, Luis Miguel. *Catolicismo y Montoneros. Religión, política y desencanto*. Buenos Aires: Manantial, 2010.
Dri, Rubén. 'La alternativa y la lucha de clases', *Militancia*, 31 January 1974a.
Dri, Rubén. 'Los aspectos de la alternativa', *Militancia*, 24 January 1974b.
Dri, Rubén. *La Iglesia que nace del pueblo*. Bogotá: Editorial Nuestra América, 1987.
Dussel, Enrique. 'La Iglesia ante la renovación del Concilio y de Medellín (1959–1972)'. In *Resistencia y esperanza. Historia del pueblo Cristiano de América Latina y el Caribe*, edited by Enrique Dussel, 237–8. San José de Costa Rica: Editorial Departamento Ecuménico de Investigaciones, 1995.
Eggers Lan, Conrado. *Peronismo y liberación nacional*. Buenos Aires: Editorial Maipue, 2014.
El Litoral. 'Posición arzobispal ante el Tercer Mundo', 21 August 1971.
Eloy Martínez, Tomás. 'Honda fisura entre la Iglesia y los curas del Tercer Mundo', *La Opinión*, 6 September 1972.
Enlace. 'Carta de sacerdotes tucumanos remitieron a Mons. Aramburu', March 1969a.
Enlace. 'La política: Estado e Iglesia, Gobierno y Jerarquía', May 1969b.
Enlace. Interview with Hernán Benítez, March 1969c.
Esquiú. '¿Seguirán fieles a la Iglesia?', 17 September 1972.
FAP. 'Carta de las FAP a los Sacerdotes para el Tercer Mundo', *Cristianismo y Revolución*, November–December 1970.
Ferguson, James, and Akhil Gupta. 'Spatializing States: Towards an Ethnography of Neoliberal Governmentality', *American Ethnologist* 29, no. 4 (2004): 981–1002.

García Elorrio, Juan. 'Carta abierta al Episcopado argentino', *Cristianismo y Revolución*, October–November 1966a.
García Elorrio, Juan. 'El signo revolucionario', *Cristianismo y Revolución*, September 1966b.
García Elorrio, Juan. '"Tiempo social" con "estado de sitio"', *Cristianismo y Revolución*, July 1969.
Gera, Lucio. '¿La Iglesia debe comprometerse en lo político?', *Enlace*, October 1969.
John Paul II. *Address of His Holiness John Paul II*. Puebla, Mexico, 28 January 1979. https://www.vatican.va/content/john-paul-ii/en/speeches/1979/january/documents/hf_jp-ii_spe_19790128_messico-puebla-episc-latam.html. Accessed 22/11/2024.
La Opinión. 'Las Comunidades Cristianas critican a la jerarquía', 28 August 1971a.
La Opinión. 'Polémica de monseñor Zazpe y sacerdotes tercermundistas', 27 August 1971b.
La Opinión. 'Sobre la polémica de Santa Fe. El Padre Mujica dice que se quiere dividir a la Iglesia', 29 August 1971c.
La Opinión. 'Aclaración de los curas del Tercer Mundo', 8 September 1972.
La Opinión. 'Exponen sacerdotes tercermundistas las bases de su acción política', 14 September 1973.
La Prensa. 'Documento de los Sacerdotes para el Tercer Mundo', 27 November 1969.
Löwy, Michael. *War of Gods: Religion and Politics in Latin America*. London: Verso, 1996.
Magne, Marcelo Gabriel. *Dios está con los pobres. Los sacerdotes del tercer mundo*. Buenos Aires: Imago Mundi, 2004.
Martín, José Pablo. *El Movimiento de Sacerdotes para el Tercer Mundo. Un debate argentino*. Buenos Aires: Editorial Guadalupe, 1992.
Martín, José Pablo. *Ruptura ideológica del catolicismo argentine. 36 entrevistas entre 1988 y 1992*. Los Polvorines: Universidad Nacional de General Sarmiento, 2013.
Mascialino, Miguel. 'Apuntes de Migue Mascialino', *Cristianismo y Revolución*, July 1968.
Mayol, Alejandro. 'La Iglesia: ¿Corset del Hombre Nuevo?', *Tierra Nueva*, October–November 1966.
Morello, Gustavo. *Cristianismo y Revolución. Los origines intelectuales de la guerrilla argentina*. Córdoba: Universidad Católica de Córdoba, 2003.
Morello, Gustavo. *The Catholic Church and Argentina's Dirty War*. New York: Oxford University Press, 2015.

MSTM. *Sacerdotes para el Tercer Mundo. Documentos, reflexión*. Buenos Aires: Publicaciones del movimiento, 1972.

MSTM. 'Comunicado del Tercer Encuentro Nacional'. In *Documentos para la memoria histórica*, edited by Domingo Bresci, 99–101. Buenos Aires: Centro Salesiano de Estudios, 1994a.

MSTM. 'Documento del Cuarto Encuentro Nacional'. In *Documentos para la memoria histórica*, edited by Domingo Bresci, 179–86. Buenos Aires: Centro Salesiano de Estudios, 1994b.

MSTM. 'Documento "Nuestra reflexión" enviado a los obispos en respuesta a la declaración de la Comisión Permanente del Episcopado referida al Movimiento'. In *Documentos para la memoria histórica*, edited by Domingo Bresci, 111–62. Buenos Aires: Centro Salesiano de Estudios, 1994c.

MSTM. 'Síntesis de las conclusiones de los equipos regionales'. In *Documentos para la memoria histórica*, edited by Domingo Bresci, 73–5. Buenos Aires: Centro Salesiano de Estudios, 1994d.

MSTM Buenos Aires. 'La pastoral de la Iglesia en la historia'. August 1973a. Archivo MSTM, Caja 8, Buenos Aires, Argentina.

MSTM Buenos Aires. 'Reflexiones de Mayo de 1973: Iglesia y política'. August 1973b. Archivo MSTM, Caja 8, Buenos Aires, Argentina.

MSTM Mendoza. 'Peronismo y Socialismo'. 30 July 1973a. Archivo MSTM, Caja 8, Buenos Aires, Argentina.

MSTM Mendoza. 'Sobre el celibato', *Enlace*, January–February 1973b.

MSTM National Secretary. '"Análisis situacional del movimiento" en preparación al Quinto Encuentro Nacional'. In *Documentos para la memoria histórica*, edited by Domingo Bresci, 243–51. Buenos Aires: Centro Salesiano de Estudios, 1994.

Mugica, Carlos. 'Para reflexionar sobre "política y pastoral"'. n.d. Archivo Carlos Mugica, Caja 3, Buenos Aires, Argentina.

Palacios Videla, Ignacio. 'Bendición controvertida y texto que no aparece', *La Opinión*, 26 August 1971.

'Para un movimiento de laicos del tercer mundo'. October 1970. Archivo MSTM, Caja 4, Buenos Aires, Argentina.

Paul VI. *Lumen Gentium*. 21 November 1964. http://www.vatican.va/archive/hist_councils/ii_vatican_council/documents/vat-ii_const_19641121_lumen-gentium_en.html. Accessed 22/11/2024.

Paul VI. *Presbyterorum Ordinis*. 7 December 1965. http://www.vatican.va/archive/hist_councils/ii_vatican_council/documents/vat-ii_decree_19651207_presbyterorum-ordinis_en.html. Accessed 22/11/2024.

Piven, Frances Fox, and Richard Cloward. *Poor People's Politics: Why They Succeed, How They Fail*. New York: Vintage, 1979.

Podestá, Jerónimo. 'Contestando tres preguntas', *Enlace*, October 1969.

Politi, Sebastián. *Teología del pueblo: Una propuesta argentina a la teología latinoamericana, 1967–1975*. Buenos Aires: Editorial Guadalupe, 1992.

Remeseira, Claudio Iván. 'Analytical and Native Concepts in Argentina's Post-Conciliar Catholicism: The Case of "Liberationism", "Popular Pastoral Theology", and "Theology of the People"', *Religions* 13 (2022).

Ruza, Rodrigo. 'Elecciones plantean disidencias entre los sacerdotes tercermundistas', *La Opinión*, 5 September 1973.

Scannone, Juan Carlos. 'La Teología de la Liberación. Caracterización, corrientes, etapas', *Stromata* 38, no. 1–2 (1982): 3–40.

Scannone, Juan Carlos. 'Pope Francis and the Theology of the People', *Theological Studies* 77, no. 1 (2016): 118–35.

Segundo, Juan Luis. *A Theology for Artisans of a New Humanity. Volume I: The Community Called Church*. Maryknoll: Orbis Books, 1980.

Smith, Christian. *The Emergence of Liberation Theology: Radical Religion and Social Movement Theory*. Chicago: University of Chicago Press, 1991.

Tello, Rafael. '"Aporte" para el Sexto Encuentro Nacional'. In *Documentos para la memoria histórica*, edited by Domingo Bresci, 322–30. Buenos Aires: Centro Salesiano de Estudios, 1994.

Tilly, Charles, and Sydney Tarrow. *Contentious Politics*. New York: Oxford University Press, 2015.

Touris, Claudia. *La constelación tercermundista. Catolicismo y cultura política en la Argentina (1955–1976)*. Buenos Aires: Editorial Biblos, 2021.

Zanca, José. 'Discovering the People: Theology, Culture and Politics in the Argentine Catholicism of the Seventies', *International Journal of Latin American Religions* 6 (2022): 73–97.

Chapter 2

Legacies of the 'bridge man': Catholic accompaniment, inter-class relations and the classification of surplus in Montevideo

Patrick O'Hare

Those who come bearing gifts

It was early January 2014 and I had only been at my fieldsite in Montevideo, Uruguay, for a few weeks. The families of the *Cooperativa de Vivienda de Familias Unidas* (COVIFU) housing cooperative where I lived were gathered around the red-brick *Cañales* after-school club, chatting excitedly on a day Latin American children await more excitedly than Christmas: the Epiphany, or *Reyes Magos*. On this hot summer's afternoon, I stood around with the others on the expansive sports fields waiting for the nativity to get under way. Teachers, children and benefactors had been preparing for the event over the past week, fitting costumes out of long pieces of shiny synthetic material, crowns out of crepe paper, and a nativity of palm leaves sunk with concrete into used car tyres. Some little girls appeared as angels with wings, other personifications were unclear, but all the child actors gathered in a procession behind Mary and Joseph, who were mounted with a plastic doll on my neighbour's mare, proudly lent for the occasion.

The director of the centre, a softly spoken teacher trained in the Salesian tradition, offered a few words about the importance of the day for those of Christian faith. Representatives of the audience (a pupil, an educator, a nun and benefactor) were then asked to come forward with pieces of coloured card onto which they had fixed photographs of important figures to be remembered that day. Those profiled made for rather strange companions: a mixture of persons of local, national and international stature, from Sister Raquel, who had spent many years volunteering at the centre, to the recently deceased Nelson Mandela. Those who came forward read out a sentence on why each figure was inspirational for them. 'Ruso' Pérez, benefactor of the *Cañales* and one of the upper-class Catholic Montevideans who 'accompanied' the families through their resettlement from a shantytown to COVIFU, moved to the front holding up a picture of Padre Cacho.

Ruso, dressed in trousers and checked shirt, with a simple wooden cross around his neck, which mirrored that worn by the figure who appeared in the photo, told those present that the Uruguayan priest had been an inspiration for his social commitment and *acompañamiento* (accompaniment) of the poor since Ruso had lived with him in a shantytown as a young man. The crowd nodded in recognition. It was the first time I had met Ruso, and I was intrigued but not surprised to find the presence of Padre Cacho, known for his association with the poor and informal sector recyclers (known as *clasificadores* or classifiers, in Uruguay). A majority of COVIFU residents were *clasificadores* after all, and the peak of the municipal landfill rising above the flat Montevidean landscape formed a backdrop to the ceremonies.

The event ended with the families being presented with large hampers with which they posed for photographs, smiling. I made my way back across the fields to COVIFU *rural* with my neighbours, who had hoisted the colourful boxes onto their shoulders. Back at home, they tore them open to find a selection of crisps, fizzy drinks, games, footballs and *pan dulce*. The children kept hold of their toys while the foodstuffs were collected by the adults for a celebration later on that night. Those who had contributed the gifts on the occasion of the Epiphany were not kings or even necessarily wise men, but the *Cañales*' benefactors – principally upper-class Montevidean Catholics – some of whom had known the families for at least a decade.

What brought people like Ruso Pérez and Monja Raquel to the neighbourhood and of what did their 'accompaniment' of the poor consist? Why did upper-class Montevideans cross the geographically short but symbolically enormous gulf which separates their affluent Carrasco neighbourhood (poverty levels 1 per cent), to establish relations with residents of *Cruz de Carrasco* and *Flor de Maroñas* (poverty levels of 15 per cent and 24 per cent respectively) (INE 2009)? By exploring the dynamics of religious social work conducted with the poor at the COVIFU housing cooperative, this paper seeks to understand *why* the upper class and religious engage with the poor at my fieldsite; it asks *what* is the nature of that engagement; and explores *how* such relations are sustained. I argue that upper-class Catholic engagement with the poor must be understood in relation to the genealogy of the Catholic 'preferential option for the poor' and the particular manifestation that it took in Uruguay in the work of Uruguayan priest Padre Cacho, as well as to post-dictatorship mechanisms for managing social polarisation. I outline how the nature of the engagement with the poor in my fieldsite is characterised by the concept of *acompañamiento* (accompaniment) and reciprocity which, I argue, sit tensely with both the Catholic prerogative to engage in unconditional charity and the continued existence of hierarchy and what liberation theologians denounced as 'structural sin' (Aguilar 2008, 124). Finally, I argue that engagement with the poor is sustained through the appropriation and rechanneling of surplus, not as waste but as donation. Following the model established by Padre Cacho, Ruso and others act as bridges between rich and poor, but materials themselves can also be understood as constituting non-human bridges which connect different social strata.

Much has been written in Southern Cone anthropology about the effects of neoliberalism and casino capitalism, social exclusion, poverty and the growing gap between rich and poor (e.g., Abelin 2012; Álvarez-Rivadulla 2007; Grimson 2008; Saravi and Makowski 2011; Svampa 2008 [2001]). Less has been written about initiatives that seek in various ways to connect the rich and poor, and the texture of inter-class relations. Uruguay, the least unequal country in Latin America (CEPAL 2014), is an appropriate ground for such an endeavour. Known not only for its relative equality but also for its secularism, the influence of Catholicism there has been historically downplayed (Caetano 2013). In recent years, as elsewhere in Latin America, Catholics in Uruguay have also struggled to compete with the increasing appeal of Pentecostal and Evangelical Christianity, especially among the popular classes. The magnetic appeal of Pentecostalism and neo-Pentecostalism has also driven the social science research agenda (Lehmann 2016). Yet Catholicism has remained strong among the influential and affluent Uruguayan upper and middle classes and, as I go on to describe, plays a key role in shaping the praxis of social and charity work with the poor.

In exploring the nature of the church-mediated relation between rich and poor at my fieldsite, I set out to make a contribution to lacunae in several areas. First, I attempt to complement ethnographic writing on social exclusion with a focus on attempts to build bridges between different social classes. Second, I examine class not by focusing on a *particular* class, as is the norm even for those who espouse a class perspective (as in many contributions in Kalb and Carrier 2015), but by focusing on the relation *between* classes. Third, my interest lies in Catholic theology and praxis, the study of which has been marginalised in the growing literature on the anthropology of Christianity.

Roots of Catholic confluence in the Cruz

I visited and volunteered at the *Cañales* throughout my fieldwork year, and the nativity was about as religious an activity as I encountered. The centre was explicitly secular, featuring barely a cross or representation of Jesus Christ, and religious observance was required neither of its teaching staff, nor of the children who attended. The grounds included only a simple clearing with a statue of the Virgin of Guadeloupe where those who wished could engage in contemplative prayer. Such subtle signs of religion suited the parents of COVIFU rather well, for although most residents were baptised as Catholics, few if any were practising, and many were hostile to religion altogether. It also fitted well into Uruguay's secular climate.

Yet as I came to realise, Catholic faith and organisation played a key role in framing the social and charitable work conducted with COVIFU residents and, in particular, in shaping the nature of the relation between my low-income neighbours and the upper-class Catholics who visited them regularly at the *Cañales* and their homes. The socio-religious fabric which facilitated the creation of COVIFU (and subsequently *Los Cañales*) was stitched of threads of Franciscan, Salesian and Ignatian charisms and owed a debt to the lingering influence of liberation theology and the mythical figure of Padre Cacho. Before moving on to the discussion of these religious roots, it is important to briefly survey the Catholic presence at my fieldsite.

The religious figure I had known longest was David, nicknamed 'the monk', a self-styled 'lay missionary' who had come back to Uruguay in the early 2000s after a long *misión* in El Salvador, where he was strongly influenced by the teachings of slain Salvadoran Archbishop Óscar Romero. David relocated to the Cruz de Carrasco, staying in a house belonging to a small order of nuns. The nuns had a base nearby where the relatives of many of my neighbours and informants lived and the sisters often welcomed us round for a cup of coffee or a hot meal, amidst catechism and a flurry of visits from neighbourhood children. These women were the first to 'insert' themselves into the neighbourhood in the 1980s under the influence of radical Catholic social thought, including liberation theology but also adjacent political and pedagogical concepts like

Paulo Freire's pedagogy of the oppressed. The current congregation stalwart, María Inés, explained in our interview that 'insertion' into the community and living closely with the poor stemmed from the model of ecclesial base communities, which were popularised throughout Latin America from the 1980s.

As a nun with the congregation in the 1970s and 1980s, the COVIFU social worker founded the house where the sisters would live for the following decades, while the nuns also supported the first cooperative housing project in the neighbourhood, COVICRUZ. One of the houses in the cooperative was granted to the nuns, but since the congregation already had a base, a priest from the nearby Catholic private school was invited to take up residence. The 'brother' thus also opted to insert himself into a poor and humble neighbourhood, thereby initiating a long-lasting association between underprivileged neighbourhood residents and the privileged pupils of the school. It was in this house that David now lived, its walls decorated with images of Archbishop Romero, Jesus Christ, Ernesto 'Che' Guevara and Camilo Torres. David had been granted a house in COVIFU but was reluctant to leave his home in the Cruz, and so had agreed to let me stay there while conducting my fieldwork.

David 'discovered' the *Villa del Cerdo* (pig town) – so-called because of the pigs raised there atop an old, contaminated landfill – soon after he arrived in the neighbourhood in 2004. He collaborated with another social worker, applying for funds for a relocation project on a cooperative housing model, and he also brought together several social actors in the neighbourhood to create a working group focused on improving the quality of lives of *Villa* residents and securing relocation. These included the nuns and alumni of the private school, like Ruso Pérez. The relocation was achieved over the course of several years with *Villa del Cerdo* residents building their cooperative homes on land acquired nearby, a section of which was donated by Opus Dei in Uruguay through its Asociación Técnica y Cultural. This donation was secured by the Catholic connections of the alumni. The bulk of the funding for the construction of the houses, some US$600,000, came from the United States government's independent overseas aid programme, administered by a local NGO run by affluent Catholic mothers of Carrasco. Other supporters included the Ministry of Social Development (*Ministerio de Desarrollo Social*, MIDES), the embassies of Ireland and Japan, and organisations that brought together the alumni of the Christian Brothers school.

Thus, *Villa del Cerdo* became COVIFU and the Catholic *acompañantes* whom I encountered in the neighbourhood were the legacy of this relocation project, consisting principally of upper-class alumni of Stella Maris, the Franciscan nuns, David, social worker and former nun Sara, the staff of the *Cañales*, and local Cruz de Carrasco priest Pablo Bonavía. The *Cañales* had been partly financed by the upper-class *acompañantes* in the years after the completion of the homes in order to maintain a connection with parents and children who would attend the centre. To the different charisms and theological approaches present was added that of the Salesians, to which the centre's director and many of its teaching staff belonged. Social and charity work was monopolised by these Catholic actors, with other faith or state actors largely absent.

The arrival in the neighbourhood of Catholic activists and social workers cannot be understood without reference to the changes which took place in the Catholic Church in the second half of the twentieth century. The Second Vatican Council (1962–5) ended with a call to take the Church out of the institutions and into the world, while a group of bishops signed the 'Catacombs Pact', which committed them to living in poverty, rejecting symbols of power and privilege, and placing the poor at the centre of the Church. Three years later, in 1968, the Latin American episcopal conference (*Consejo Episcopal Latinoamericano y Caribeño*, CELAM) held in Medellín was pivotal in shaping the orientation that many radical and progressive Latin American Catholics would take towards 'the poor'. Specifically, it marked the beginning of Marxist-influenced 'liberation theology' and a 'preferential option for the poor'. Liberation theologians drew extensively on the words and acts of Jesus in the Bible to justify their focus on the poor, using Bible citations such as 'Blessed are you who are poor, for yours is the kingdom of God' (Luke 6: 20).[1] The 1979 Puebla CELAM conference then resulted in the publication of the so-called 'Puebla Document' ('Evangelisation in the Latin American present and future') that, although considered a compromise between traditional Catholicism and liberation theology, nevertheless condemned repressive governments and international capitalism while asserting the importance of ecclesial base communities and a preferential option for the poor.

For liberation theologians, the poor were seen as the chosen people of God, whose 'crying out' caused the intervention of God in the Bible and might well also provide the key for the return of Jesus Christ. The foremost passage of the Old Testament referred to in order to support this claim was from Exodus, where the 'Israelites groaned in their slavery and cried out, and their cry [*clamor*] for help because of their slavery went up to God. God heard them in their groaning and he remembered his covenant with Abraham, with Isaac and with Jacob' (Ex 2: 23–24). In the words of Jon Sobrino (1992), 'to experience God's revelation it is necessary to experience the reality of the poor' (Sobrino 1992, 55), while José Porfirio Miranda argues that 'God . . . presents himself as knowable exclusively in the cries of the poor and weak who demand justice' (Miranda 1975, 115).

Theologians like Ricardo Antoncich have argued that different times and places require different biblical exegesis and hermeneutics. The 1970s conditions of dictatorship, repression, savage inequality and extreme poverty called for a specific 'Latin American reading of Catholic social teaching' (1987 [1980]). The anchor for this reading, he writes, was 'the perspective of the cause of the poor' (83) and he notes that the bishops at Puebla had urged not only clergy but all 'without distinction of classes, to accept and make their own the cause of the poor as if they were accepting and making their own the cause of Christ himself' (in Antoncich 1987, 82). Poor-centred Latin American Catholic theological praxis was not, Antoncich asserts, simply one acceptable variant of Catholic social work among many but a return to the 'original intention of the church's social teaching' (83) as evidenced in the example of Christ. That is to say, for Antoncich, liberation theology was the particular Latin American expression of Catholic social teaching, responding to the urgent contemporary demands of poverty, exclusion and repression. In so doing, the bishops at Medellín also coined the concept of 'structural sin' to argue that 'within the salvific and theological context of Latin America, there were social structures that were sinful because they discriminated among God's children' (Aguilar 2008, 124).

Catholics influenced by liberation theology were also inspired by the attention Jesus paid to the poor, marginalised and excluded. Such was the case for Cruz de Carrasco priest Pablo Bonavía, who writes that Jesus got close to 'the poor, the blind, lepers, sinners, widows, prostitutes ... the New Testament singles out the "poor" and "sinners" as privileged recipients of Jesus' work' (1994, 18). Bonavía's view is that the latter were not 'vague categories' but 'perfectly identifiable groups who shared an implacable marginalisation as well as being systematically and explicitly blamed and disdained' (1994, 18). Not only was the group's status identified in the Bible, argues Bonavía, but the book also demonstrated the praxis to be adopted towards them. 'More than charitable "help" which did nothing more than deepen their dependency and victimisation', he writes, 'these people needed to recover consciousness of their dignity, worth and personhood' (1994, 18). Liberation theology, alongside the pedagogy of Brazilian educator Paolo Freire, played an important role in directing development trends in the continent away from supposedly disempowering charity (*asistencialismo*) towards reciprocal aid (*promoción social*). It contributed to 'shifting the idea of charity – with its connotations of short-term alleviation – toward structural change as a more enduring way of caring for one's neighbor' (Lehmann 2016, 747).

The religious figure most recognised in Uruguay for living out a 'preferential option for the poor' is the one whose image Ruso Pérez had glued on to a piece of coloured card that day in the *Cañales*: Padre Cacho. In the years of 1970s and 1980s dictatorship, Cacho breathed the Uruguayan airs of subtle Catholic radicalism under the protection of Montevideo's Archbishop, the quiet but virtuous Carlos Partelli (Clara 2012). Cacho lived in a poor community in provincial Salto before returning to Montevideo in 1978 where he established himself first in the shantytown of Placido Ellauri, then in neighbouring Aparicio Saravia. He lived in shacks (*ranchos*) 'no different from the rest . . . a little house of wood and metal, a bed, a table, 3 plates, glasses, a pot and some clothes' (2012, 35). He wanted to move to the shantytowns, he told a fellow priest, because 'that is where God is, and I want to find him' (2012, 29).

Cacho did not only privilege the poor, but he also prioritised a subsection within them: the informal sector waste pickers who were his neighbours. He became known as the *cura de los carritos* ('the priest of the little carts') for his close association with them and helped change their popular nomenclature from the semi-disdainful *hurgador* (rummager) to the more dignified *clasificador* (classifier). Waste pickers represented a population of special interest for the priest not only because many of his neighbours engaged in the activity but also because they appeared as particularly marginalised and scapegoated. Cacho recognised the important environmental role played by these 'ecological agents', arguing that 'the injured dignity [of the *clasificador*] calls out for us to recognise him as a worker, prophet and citizen' (Alonso 1992).

In many ways, Cacho's way of relating not only to the poor but also to the rich set the tone for a certain form of Catholic social work which would resonate in Uruguay in the following decades and play a direct role in the creation of COVIFU. While he challenged the dictatorship, even finding himself briefly placed under arrest when he went to a police station to lobby for the release of a neighbour, ultimately, he focused on living humbly and 'accompanying' the poor. Moreover, although influenced by the preferential option for the poor and liberation theology, Cacho was no Marxist. Rather, he was what his biographer Mercedes Clara (2012) has called a 'bridge man' (*hombre puente*), forming a bridge between rich and poor. When I interviewed the then head of *políticas sociales* at Montevideo's municipal council (*Intendencia*), a former Catholic youth activist, she told me that Cacho 'brought together a part of the population with whom he felt a Christian sensitivity . . . with intellectually and economically powerful sectors of society . . . with people who were able to help them'. Through his 'triangulation', she continued, the 'distributive role which should be the responsibility of the state also starts to emerge from civil society'.

In particular, Cacho helped to link professionals and upper-class Catholics in the Carrasco neighbourhood with Aparicio Saravia through the organisation *Juntos Podemos* (Together We Can). The Carrasco parishioners donated food and began fundraising for the neighbourhood, getting enough money together to pay for the breeze blocks needed for the construction of houses (2012, 70). For Mary Larrosa, who arrived in the neighbourhood via Cacho and helped in the collation of neighbourhood histories and publications, Cacho 'made it possible to get close to the poor, because sometimes it's not so easy . . . you want to but don't know how' (2012, 72). One of those who arrived in the neighbourhood as an eager *Carrascito* (posh Carrasco kid) was Ruso Pérez. Born into a family with a history of charitable Catholic work, Ruso told me that from an early age he was taken along to *asentamientos* and shown different realities, while at home the family opened their doors to poor children who came to beg.

Ruso's family provided examples of traditional but also radical ways of engaging with the poor. It was his cousin Pablo Bonavía who had sent him to stay with Cacho after Ruso had expressed an interest in travelling to India to work with the poor. 'You're crazy, there's as much poverty here as in India!', Bonavía had told him. His aunt Ana was a nun in the 1970s and 1980s whose congregation became influenced by the winds of change in the Latin American Church. In our interview in Ruso's living room, she told me that she had been teaching in the upper-class Sacred Heart girls' school in Carrasco but from there had decided to go and live in a poor community in the Uruguayan provincial town of Durazno. She 'took off the habit', and visited neighbours at home, finding that 'this is where people [were] hungry for the gospel!' The nuns faced suspicion and hostility from religious conservatives and former pupils, who accused them of being communists.

Ana and her colleagues were inspired not by Moscow, however, but by Latin American colleagues, explaining that 'we started to study popular education and Paulo Freire, to establish popular education networks all over Latin America, to communicate our experiences, to exchange'. María Inés, Sara and other Franciscan nuns also spent extensive periods with congregations in Brazil, where they learned of popular education methods, participative democracy and community organisation. The model of the church was one, explained María Inés, which 'mixed the ecclesial with popular struggle'. The poor served by the missionaries in the Cruz de Carrasco were essentially those residents who came in two 'immigration waves' in the 1980s and 1990s from the Uruguayan countryside and the slums of Montevideo. These immigrants formed settlements or *asentamientos* in the land between the church and the landfill, quarries and marshes, which constitute the *Cruz*'s boundary.

Not all the backgrounds of those undertaking religious social work with the *Villa* and COVIFU can be placed within a framework of liberation theology, progressive Catholicism or opposition to dictatorship. Pedro Silva was, alongside Ruso Pérez, one of the first and most consistent Stella Maris alumni to engage with families in the neighbourhood, having been involved in three housing cooperative projects and the establishment of the *Cañales*. A land surveyor by profession, Silva attended the state *Universidad de la República* during the dictatorship, a time when, he argued, it was 'very fashionable' to be left wing in student circles. Silva, on the other hand, was, in his own words, a 'posh kid, from a posh neighbourhood, right-wing, fascist'. Pedro justified his position by telling his student antagonists that he was going to take advantage of his position in life, and 'from there, help the other [*el otro*]'.

At the Stella Maris school, Ruso did not remember Irish Catholic priests advocating social work with the poor, while Pedro recalled pupils being told to 'take up, not abandon their [social] position, and from there help the poor'. Pedro's wife, Carmen, also from an affluent family background, acted as the *pro bono* notary for COVIFU, the *Cañales* and several other neighbourhood social projects. Her trajectory in *acompañamiento* of the poor was different still, as she formed part of the post-dictatorship policy-makers who aimed, in her words, to 'look for mechanisms so that one sector of society was not so opposed (*enfrentado*) to the other, and that this wouldn't lead to civil war again'.[2] One way of avoiding this 'conflict' resurfacing, she maintained, was to 'ensure that one sector of society took responsibility for the other'. Ruso also held his class partly responsible for increasing social polarisation and insecurity, arguing that 'we've somehow gone very wrong, not just the government but society as a whole . . . we're responsible for not thinking about other people'.

In looking at the roots of various Catholic actors' engagement with the poor in my fieldsite, we find a confluence of diverse Catholic activists motivated by different strands of Catholic social teaching and/or radical theological developments, who nonetheless became bedfellows in the post-dictatorship period to constitute what I would call, following Antoncich, a politically ambiguous, and particularly Uruguayan, expression of Catholic social teaching. Undoubtedly, the Second Vatican Council, the Medellín conference in 1968 and the 'preferential option for the poor' were important regional and global events in the genealogy of their praxis. So, too, however, were events at a national level, such as the role of the Catholic Church as a tolerated space for activism during the dictatorship. Clearly, a radical Catholic orientation toward the poor inspired by liberation theology continued to consciously influence some neighbourhood Catholic activists such as David, the Franciscan nuns and Fr. Pablo Bonavía. These collaborated closely, however, with others like Pedro and Carmen from the opposite side of the political spectrum, who sought through their work to avoid the repeat of what they understood as a 'civil war' sparked by social polarisation. The work of Padre Cacho in synthesising a preference for accompanying the poor – *clasificadores* in particular – with the creation of bridges between upper and underprivileged classes shaped the Catholic social praxis that I explore in the following sections, directly influencing figures such as Ruso Pérez and Pablo Bonavía who had worked alongside him.

Aside from family, religious and class ties, what brought diverse Catholic actors together in the neighbourhood was a commitment to what they all termed *acompañamiento* (accompaniment) of the poor. In the following section I seek to trace the contours of this concept for upper-class Catholics, arguing that its enactment involves balancing, on the one hand, unconditional charity with reciprocal relations, and, on the other, 'residues' of radical Catholicism with enduring 'structural sin'.

Acompañamiento amid structural sin: between reciprocity and unconditional charity

'These guys give their lives to the poor' was the glowing endorsement by which 'Rama' López introduced my partner and me to friends at a dinner he had invited us to at his plush home in Carrasco. The successful owner of a large hardware wholesaler, López had for a year been 'accompanying' several of my COVIFU neighbours in a pig-rearing venture for which he provided financial, advisory and veterinary support. Embarrassed by the praise, we quickly tried to explain that I was living in COVIFU principally for research purposes, not as a charity worker or volunteer, religious or otherwise. Yet our objections were to no avail – we were sometimes referred to as 'missionaries' during the course of our stay and praised by upper-class *acompañantes* for our commitment to living among the poor. We were seen as following the example of Padre Cacho by enduring the hardships of the neighbourhood and enacting the aspired-to moral value of 'accompanying the poor'.

Rama was a cousin of Ruso Pérez and it was through him that he found his way to the neighbourhood. Both were jovial, outgoing and charismatic men, just as likely to be found talking respectfully with neighbourhood women as joking with men or engaging in horseplay with some of the adolescent boys. It was Ruso who drew a connection between our presence and Cacho's praxis, which he described as 'putting oneself in the skin of the other' and 'feeling like them':

> Because when you think like the other, you . . . fight for a different reality, for a change. If you don't think like the other, it's very difficult. When we have meetings, I always say, 'imagine that you lived here'. And not 'I'm going home in my car to my warm house', which is very different. You live here and you know what the cold is like . . . the swearing matches, the stress, and so you have to feel like the other, put yourself in their skin, as Cacho used to say, to be able to understand and act. And that's what one tries to do, no?

As an adolescent, Ruso had spent several days a week living with poor young men in the house that Cacho shared with them in the shantytown, even covering for the priest when he was away. As he became older and married his wife Laura, Cacho told him to keep a distance from the increasingly dangerous *barrio* and concentrate on raising his family. Yet Ruso maintained a close friendship with a godson whom he invited, with his fiancé, to marriage preparations that Ruso and Laura were undertaking with other upper-class fiancés in Carrasco. They thus learned of the worries facing a couple from another social class, something which Ruso described as an 'enriching experience'. 'When you feel like the other', he reiterated, 'the worries of the other will be your worries . . . if you don't put yourself in the other's skin, the other's worries are ridiculous'. Cacho and Bonavía officiated at both weddings, that of Ruso and his godson.

While *acompañamiento* in Ruso's account came close to *being* the other, others emphasised the importance of *being with* the other but maintaining boundaries. Pedro and Carmen both spoke of the importance of long-term accompaniment, which they compared to accompanying a son or daughter: 'if we are chasing after our children for 30 years, then how can we leave these others alone? They need double the amount of *acompañamiento*'. Carmen in particular stressed that the poor 'couldn't be left alone', that they might need more or less *acompañamiento* in different areas but that they needed a 'permanent model/example [*referente*]'. Given Carmen's understanding of the Uruguayan 'civil war', this 'permanent accompaniment' might be understood critically as a form of surveillance which kept the behaviour of the poor in check. Rather than political activists, however, Pedro told me that he was more interested in keeping away the *malandraje* (rogues/criminal elements) from the housing cooperative. Others were more nuanced in their approach, with Sister Macarena pondering the diminished organisation of another neighbourhood housing cooperative when left without the *acompañamiento* of the nuns. It was Ruso who spoke most of *acompañamiento*, however, which for him meant 'being with, listening to, sharing with, and understanding the other'.

Ruso speaks of a 'before and after' of work with Cacho, where his attitude changed from 'doing social work' and 'giving a hand to poor folk' to seeing the poor like equals and realising that the relationship with them was reciprocal. Ruso received as much as he gave in encounters with the poor, he told me, and without them his life felt incomplete. It could be argued that Ruso thus embodied a shift in Uruguayan Catholic social praxis, from traditional Carrasco Catholic charitable *asistencialismo* towards something more horizontal and reciprocal in line with Latin American Catholic thought in the late twentieth century. Yet moves towards reciprocity were not bereft of tension. How to reconcile the establishment of reciprocal, personalistic relationships with the Catholic imperative to conduct unconditional charity with the poor? How to deal with the 'radical residues' of Latin American Catholicism – its egalitarian and even revolutionary ethos – when structural class positions ('structural sin') endured in twenty-first-century Uruguay?

As noted by Laidlaw (2000), Graeber (2012, 109) and others, major religions, including Christianity, have placed an important emphasis on an unconditional and anonymous giving which does *not* spark reciprocal relations. Within Catholicism, this unconditional charity is linked closely with the unconditional love which Jesus felt towards humanity and which his followers should seek to emulate (Jackson 2003). For those inspired by liberation theology, much of this charity and focus should be conducted with 'the poor' as a theologically broad category that has been translated into a particular poor at different times and places. I argue that upper-class Catholic informants at my fieldsite thus experienced a tension in their praxis of *acompañamiento* between conducting unconditional charity with 'the poor' and establishing reciprocal bonds with particular poor residents of COVIFU.

For example, Ruso and Laura Pérez established a close friendship with the Rosas, the family who had initially taken me in to stay when I first arrived in the neighbourhood. The Rosas' daughter had often been around to their house when she was small, and Ruso and Laura enjoyed passing by Juan Rosas' home to drink *mate* tea together. The Pérez did of course spend time with other families, with Ruso supporting the pig-rearing enterprise and Laura a soap project with other women. Yet the affective bonds established between the Pérez and the Rosas meant that when the former had donations to distribute (the mechanics of which I explore later), they often found their way to the house of the latter.

On several occasions, the Pérez would pass on donations to my partner and me, hoping that they would reach beyond it. The affective relations between the two families aroused jealousy among other neighbours, who appealed to the Catholic imperative to help the poor indiscriminately. 'It seems that the more you have, the more you get around here', complained one neighbour, making reference to the Rosas' relatively well-off status, indicated by their ownership of a car and pick-up truck, while other families did not even possess a motorbike. 'They [*acompañantes*] should be helping everyone around here', said another, 'but there are some families who just grab everything'.

The tendency of upper-class families to establish personalistic relations with particular families is, I would argue, to a large extent due to attempts to introduce reciprocity into relationships, establishing a flow of affects, materials and obligations. At events such as the Epiphany celebration with which I started this paper, they were caught between attempting the perhaps unrealisable ideal of the 'free gift' and the Maussian gift which 'makes friends', entails reciprocity, and establishes and maintains social relations (Benedict XVI 2005, no. 31; Laidlaw 2000; Mauss 1990 [1925]; Sahlins 1972). As Laidlaw notes, 'religious charity and philanthropy in all the great religions have repeatedly rediscovered the supreme value of the anonymous donation, only to find that time and time again donors have been more attracted to the benefits of the socially entangling Maussian gift, which does make friends' (2000, 632). The relation of reciprocity was specifically sought by Catholic actors, with priest Pablo Bonavía arguing in our interview that the 'heart of the social and anthropological problem is that of moving from relations of dependence to relations of reciprocity'.

Upper-class informants did not demand any direct spiritual return for their charity: no receiver was obliged to go to church or profess a belief in Christ or a Catholic God. Nor was there a vote-winning or political dimension or a direct obligation to labour involved which would link this relationship with anthropological literature on patronage and clientelism. If Padre Bonavía and Ruso aimed for reciprocity, of what, then, did this consist? When upper-class Catholics gave their time, money, gifts and contacts to COVIFU residents, what did they expect or receive in return? This is as much an ethnographic as an analytical question, as my poor neighbours often expressed suspicion about what rich volunteers were getting out of a connection with them:

> It's hard to understand, isn't it? A bit untrustworthy. You don't know if it's done in good faith or for their own benefit. Like with Rama López. There's a lot of stuff like, if you set up an NGO then the government

excuses you from taxes and things like that. I'm not sure exactly how it works though. They discount some of your taxes if you're good to the plebs [*pichaje*], I think that's what they do.

To recap, *acompañantes* pass on gifts to the poor as part of their *acompañamiento*, but the counter-gifts in kind, characteristic of gift exchange economies, are neither expected nor possible because of structural and class differences. Reciprocity is nevertheless sought out and thus returns on gifts cannot be in kind but must vary. It is at this point that I turn to the writings of David Graeber (2001; 2010; 2012) on the different moral logics that underlie gifts, modifying somewhat his schema. In the first instance, Graeber argues for the existence of 'closed' and 'open' reciprocity, where closed reciprocity is closer to market exchange and open reciprocity is more balanced (2001). Elsewhere, Graeber has sketched out communism, exchange and hierarchy as different moral logics underlying forms of gifting (2010; 2012).

For Graeber, 'baseline' or 'everyday' communism can be found in instances where the principle of 'to each according to his need, from each according their ability' are in operation and where people are in 'permanent mutual debt' with one another (2010, 9). Ironically, this description fits rather nicely with my upper-class informants' conceptualisation of long-term, permanent accompaniment. Within this relationship, the upper class provide what they believe is within the scope of their abilities – money, materials, contacts, encouragement – and expect in return from the poor only what was within their sphere of capability. The description of such a relation as a form of communism is ironic, of course, because it entails a long-term relationship of mutual commitment which does not approximate equality or the end of class society but rather thrives on it.

With regard to what the poor might give back, *acompañantes* expected neighbours to demonstrate a 'willingness to labour' in cooperative ventures like the pig-rearing enterprise or the housing project that preceded it. In a particularly Uruguayan variation of the development adage taken up by James Ferguson (2015), Pedro Rodríguez said that the poor should be taught to fish alone, but be accompanied and served *mate* as they did so. A scenario to be avoided, however, was the *acompañante* fishing *for* the poor, while the latter sat drinking *mate*. Padre Bonavía had indeed witnessed something akin to this scenario when a group of Swiss volunteers had visited the COVIFU construction site for several weeks. 'I visited the site and the Swiss were working while the neighbours sat drinking *mate*. What was *promocional* (empowering) about that?!'

In some instances, the poor were meant to deliver a clear output in exchange for accompaniment. 'There are conditions (*contraprestaciones*) [for our help]', Carmen clarified: 'the kids who go to the *Cañales* have to go to school and everything'. During the COVIFU building project, one donor, a philanthropist founder of a local charity, wanted stringent conditions in exchange for his donation of land. The sugar magnate demanded that parents report directly to him every year with paperwork demonstrating that they had given their children vaccinations and sent them to school. This conditionality was too personal even for the other *acompañantes*, and he was pressured to back down.

What happened when the poor did not meet their side of the bargain? This is perhaps where Graeber's logic of exchange enters the fray. 'Exchange', as Graeber argues, 'allows us to cancel our debts' (2010, 9). He makes this assertion with reference to a framework of equivalence: if one gift is equivalent to another, it can cancel it out and therefore stop the flow of social relations in its tracks. Yet as we know, gift and *contraprestación* might continually be renewed even as they neutralise each other, as long demonstrated by the literature on the gift in anthropology. In the case of the pig-rearing cooperative, if my poor neighbours carried out a week's labour, they would not expect the flow of financial and other support to be extinguished but rather renewed. In order to break off relations with my neighbours, then, upper-class Catholics instead had to find an instance of lack of equivalence, where the poor failed to reciprocate with an expected *contraprestación*.

Given their emphasis on and commitment to long-term relations of *acompañamiento*, it is not surprising that Pedro, Ruso and others did not often seek to break off relations with my neighbours. Rama, on the other hand, did not have experience in working with the poor and soon found himself frustrated with the discord and lack of progress and indeed cooperation in the pig-rearing cooperative. After coming back from a trip to Europe to find a dead pig, which had apparently been floating in a pool of water for days without anyone seeking to remove it, he decided to cut his losses. The lack of commitment to the project, hard work and care for the animals with which the cooperativists should have reciprocated his time, money and energy was cited as cause for disengagement. Expectations of reciprocity can thus be mobilised as a way of introducing conditionalities into supposedly unconditional Catholic charitable engagement.

When questioned about the affective relations and friendships established between the poor and *acompañantes* like cousin Ruso, Pablo Bonavía emphasised the structural opposition between classes: 'the interests and the causes of the world of the poor, whatever the good relations that might exist . . . are opposed to the interests and causes of the world of richest sectors'. In such circumstances, he warned, relations of reciprocity might slip into those of dependence. Indeed, Graeber (2010) has argued that hierarchy might be considered the opposite of reciprocity, involving mostly uni-directional flows of materials such as tribute sustained by custom and habit. How, then, did upper-class *acompañantes* reconcile pronounced social hierarchies – what liberation theologians considered 'structural sin' – with an attempt to maintain reciprocal relations partly inspired by residues of radical Catholicism? I would argue that in their relations to the poor, the upper class sought to resolve this tension by engaging in strategies to underplay hierarchies and temporarily reverse them.

First, Ruso and others sought out common ground with the poor. A passion for animal husbandry and country pursuits constituted a shared interest between conservative landowners such as Rama, and neighbours of the poor urban-rural periphery. Javi, who used his horse and cart to transport recyclables from the dump, often enquired after Paco's polo performances at weekends, while Juan and Rama compared notes on how to castrate piglets. Some upper-class *acompañantes* clearly drew inspiration from (imagined) class relations in the countryside, with Carmen arguing that 'in the *interior*, people with land or interests always "collaborated"' and Ruso telling me that in the countryside people felt more equal given their vulnerability to the elements. Paco, whose family held the monopoly on the import of certain car brands in Uruguay, also gave mechanics classes to parents in the *Cañales*, trying to find mutuality in a passion for cars, motors and how they worked, quite aside from the purchasing power of each in relation to car ownership.

Acompañantes also attempted to instil a separation between the economic sphere and that in which they conducted their work with the poor. Different rules applied in each area, with professionals such as Pedro and Carmen charging for their services in their working lives, but offering them *pro bono* when engaged in social work with the residents of COVIFU. Rama, meanwhile, reacted strongly when Javi's wife denounced him as the 'boss' of the pig-rearing cooperative, making it clear that, while he was in charge at his company, these rules did not apply in his social work, where the men or families of the pig-rearing cooperative were the 'owners'. As might be expected, *acompañantes* modestly attempted to downplay wealth which they possessed, such as the large expanse of land and woods which Rama had recently acquired and which he would ultimately leave the pig enterprise to spend more time on.

Hierarchies were not always ignored, however – sometimes they were also temporarily reversed. Precedent for this is clearly found in the Catholic ideal of 'serving the poor' generally and specifically in the approach advocated by Padre Cacho. When challenged about being 'used' by the poor, Cacho countered that 'they have been used and manipulated their whole life by those who have power, so it's alright that sometimes things are the other way round' (Clara 2012, 107). In my fieldwork site, Catholic social workers were worried about the poor becoming dependent upon them at the same time as they professed a model of 'continuous accompaniment'. Yet instead of the poor seeking a relationship of dependency with the rich, what occurred in the Cruz de Carrasco was the reverse: the rich unexpectedly turned up at the door of the poor, asking if they might serve *them*. This was a theological praxis integral to liberation theology, where missionaries of various stripes would appear in poor neighbourhoods and attempt to ascertain, through popular education workshops, how they might best serve communities. 'There's something wrong with you', *asentamiento* neighbours told Sara when she first appeared with other nuns in the neighbourhood, 'we want to get out of here while you want to come and live here!'

Catholic service among the upper classes (but not the Franciscan nuns) also suggests a time-limited role reversal analogous with the carnevalesque (Bakhtin 1941; DaMatta 1997). During the week, upper-class Catholics are bosses and professional workers in positions of authority who have subordinates labouring for them – and this is also the future which awaits many young Catholic private school students. On Saturday mornings and special occasions, however, Ruso would bring groups of teenagers to carry out menial work and take orders from the poor, either at the pig-rearing enterprise, at another cooperative housing construction site, or at the *Cañales*. There they would bow to the knowledge of the poor over matters related to building and animal husbandry, or simply serve food and drinks in the *Cañales*. One particular occasion of the latter was the fifth anniversary of the *Cañales*, when the neighbours dressed up in their best and were served sumptuous mixed cold meats and cheese platters by Ruso and other *acompañantes* dressed as waiters.

Such moments of the carnevalesque allow the popular classes to enjoy a temporary status reversal but also maintain inequalities and hierarchies, as normal service is resumed after the time for licence has expired. Roberto DaMatta's (1997) analysis of carnivals in Rio de Janeiro and New Orleans stresses the temporary transgression of societal values (egalitarianism in the United States, hierarchy in Brazil). If this is an inversion of James Ferguson's (2015, 142) example of the Black poor in South Africa clamouring to serve and establish relations of dependency with a bemused rich American, it is hardly incidental. In this case, we might make the claim that upper-class Catholics attempting to live a moral, spiritual and 'full' life *depend* on the temporary role reversal involved in serving the poor as opposed to being served by them. While one should perhaps not exaggerate the importance of such rituals in maintaining structural inequalities, they were certainly not transformational, limited as they were to particular times and places. If a COVIFU resident appeared in the office of Rama's wholesale hardware company and started giving him orders, she would soon find out that she was not in a position to dictate the terms of the latter's service.

Since the 'structural sin' of class society endures in time, upper-class Catholics, influenced by a legacy of progressive Catholicism and its penchant for reciprocity, attempt to create spaces in which inequality and hierarchy are either temporarily downplayed or reversed. Such spaces are far removed from the revolutionary and subversive potential of liberation theology when it first emerged, but their importance in tackling social exclusion and material poverty should not be underestimated. Indeed, such direct, affective relations between rich and poor families and communities does not appear to be common in other parts of the continent, and may be a direct legacy of Padre Cacho, the 'bridge man'. In the following section, I turn to the question of how charity with the poor was enabled through the establishment of a series of 'bridges' and the channelling of surplus. Prioritising and establishing certain reciprocal relations with the poor might have been desired, but it appears that such links can only materialise with the help of non-human actants (Latour 2004) diverted from the waste stream.

Bridges, networks and the (in)dignity of waste

'Padre Cacho brought together two sectors', said the former municipal director of environmental development Martín Ponce de León at a special parliamentary session to remember the priest in 2002: 'He was a man who integrated neighbourhoods and the most diverse social sectors.' The other side of the *acompañantes*' attempts to find commonalities between rich and poor was an acceptance that the poor lived in a different world, with different codes and temporalities. Crossing from one side to the other necessitated the construction of bridges, and the building of relationships depended on the flow of materials across them.

Ruso and Laura Pérez became such bridges for many of their friends in Carrasco. Due to their reputation for 'social engagement', neighbours would drop old and unwanted things off at their house, establishing the couple as a conduit to the poor. 'It's like a chain, people call up, sometimes my house resembles *Emaús*, full of clothes, blankets, beds, televisions that people leave you, this and that – it starts filling up, you see? Because they know that it [sic] will have a good destination.' This happened when flooding occurred in the nearby shantytown of Paso

Carrasco – Ruso posted a note on Facebook calling for donations that soon streamed in from neighbours, friends and contacts. Most of these donations came from Carrasco, Ruso explained, 'because that's where the money is'.

Conversely, Ruso and Laura also acted as a bridge via which the poor could reach the rich. Although the pig-rearing cooperative was meant to represent a process of formalisation, the bulk of the pigs were in fact sold to friends, neighbours and relatives of the *acompañantes*, filling up their freezers and leading their families to complain about feeling sick from eating pork most nights of the week. In the circles of the rich, the butchered pigs could be sold for prices comparable with those of the up-market *Grands Magasins* supermarket rather than the poor neighbourhood *almacén*. At the other end of the gender (and olfactory) spectrum was Laura's involvement in a micro-enterprise with some women from COVIFU *urbano* who put floral, decorative and festive transfers onto bars of soap. These were then sold on at a much higher price within Carrasco ladies' circles.

Through the *acompañantes*, donations flowed from rich to poor, and commodities from the poor to rich. *Acompañantes* constituted 'bridges' in the social network theory definition of connectors between nodes within networks which would otherwise be separate and not in contact with each other (Wasserman and Faust 1994, 114). The connections to the upper class which allowed my neighbours to intercept the surplus material I go on to describe were, in the language of development and political science, 'cross-cutting ties' (Narayan-Parker 1999, 14) or 'bridging social capital' (Putnam 2000). The rich and poor are not always situated in discrete networks, but the existence of parallel networks of commodity circulation is clear in the case of pig rearing. Through contact with Rama, the cooperativists bought a prize hog at the exclusive Prado country fair, instead of sourcing one through contacts in informal neighbourhood networks. They initially managed to sell the pork at a high price in elite circles (Carrasco families or, in one case, a Spanish cruise ship) facilitated by their *acompañantes*. But when the cooperative folded, the residents had to revert to selling it to friends, family and contacts at a lower cost. Materials for the construction of pig shelters were either donated by the *acompañantes* at discounted rates or sourced by *clasificadores* from the landfill.

It was not only the poor who accessed waste materials, however; many donations were also forms of surplus which were 'reconfigured' as donations by passing through the hands of *acompañantes* or being intercepted before they entered the urban waste stream. In enumerating examples of this practice, I wish to make two points. The first is that although both rich and poor can access waste and surplus, the rich intercept them earlier in the chain which links production and disposal, when they have greater value and can be classified as 'donations' partly because they have not been mixed with other wastes. The second is that while those like Ruso and Rama can be seen as bridges between rich and poor, non-human material such as waste can also form bridges between people from these different classes.

Let us take the case of a 'donation' of seed, to be used as pig feed, organised by Ruso. Upper-class networks played an important role, since he secured the pick-up after mentioning the COVIFU project to a friend who happened to be one of the largest importers and distributors of seed in the country. This donation consisted of sweepings from the factory floor which would otherwise have to be disposed of as waste at a cost to the importer or dumped illegally. Instead, Ruso paid for the collection of the seeds which were re-routed to the cooperative and used both to feed pigs and grow eclectic mixed lawns of soy, wheat and ryegrass. Another donation secured by Laura was of surplus bread, biscuits and sandwich cuttings from Aperitivo, the catering company that supplied sandwiches to the *Grands Magasins* supermarket chain. On alternate days, Laura and the nuns from the Cruz would pick these up and distribute them among neighbours in COVIFU and the Cruz de Carrasco respectively. The interception of *Grands Magasins* food waste soon after its production (before it even reaches the supermarket) can be compared to the *Grands Magasins* waste received at Juan Rosas' wife's family recycling yard. The best of this waste had already been siphoned off by the family that collected it from the supermarket, leaving the *clasificador* family to cobble together sandwiches out of stale bread and the off-cuts from the supermarket delicatessen counter.

As for Rama, he arranged for the cooperative to collect surplus from a catering factory, Fresh Fare, managed by his brother. If the condition for the collection of the bakery goods was that they be converted into a donation to be consumed by the poor, it was something precisely forbidden in this case, as the factory wastes fell within the municipal waste management regulatory framework. Food waste had long fed Montevideo's pigs in informal arrangements which the *Intendencia* was trying to discourage and regulate (Santandreu, Castro and Ronca 2002). Only a registered 'waste transporter' could collect the waste, and proof had to be shown that the plastics and cardboard with which the food waste was mixed were properly separated and disposed of, preferably in Felipe Cardoso. The arrangement would probably not have been possible without another contact of Rama's at the *Intendencia*'s department of rural affairs, to whom he sent pictures of neatly classified bales of cardboard and separated food waste while the scheme lasted.

In all of these cases of *acompañante*-mediated transactions, waste is effectively intercepted at the source of its creation, before it has entered the waste stream. They provide examples of how the rich can access surplus of a quality and scale which is very difficult for the poor to acquire directly. In his book on household food waste, David Evans (2014) argues that food passes through the stages of 'surplus' then 'excess' before being placed in a bin and finally becoming 'waste'. The only way COVIFU *clasificadores* could otherwise have intercepted the surplus secured by the *acompañantes* would have been at the landfill, after it had been mixed in with heterogeneous municipal solid waste. There, they would have had to struggle with other *clasificadores* for a share and been pushed quickly to extract as much as possible before machines sped past to spread and flatten. Quality, composition and freedom from contamination could not have been assured, and removal from the *cantera* might have been difficult. In Evans' model, my informants' connections with the upper classes – their 'bridging social capital' – facilitated the interception of surplus *before* it became waste. If figures like Padre Cacho and Ruso made it 'easier to get close to the poor', then material surplus also helped to grease the wheels of inter-class contact. The sticky, odorous materiality of the mixed waste bags, the expectations of *acompañantes* and the regulatory waste framework combined in a hybrid agency. Sometimes, a diverse array of discards fell into the hands of human actors, their materialities acting on humans and bringing about new tensions, altering relations and establishing new connections.

In studies of international charity and development work, examples of asymmetrical relationships sustained by the circulation of discards abound. In one case, Britt Halvorson (2012) looked at how American Lutherans maintained contact with a former mission site in Madagascar through the donation of medical supplies. She argues that the affirmation of moral relations through the donation of objects deemed obsolete and useless in an American hospital setting is a paradox resolved by 'concealing the institutional life of the medical technologies' (2012, 209) transformed into charitable donations. Echoing Thompson's (1979) classic thesis, materials are 'devalued' to be subsequently 'revalued' or reclassified. There are clear parallels between Halvorson's case study and the 'surplus transactions' made at my fieldsite. Like the American hospitals that decrease the costs of classification and disposal by passing these on to the NGOs to whom they donate materials (2012, 217), factories in my fieldsite saved money by 'donating' waste materials to my informants. Yet if Halvorson's focus is the 'redemptive economy' of international Protestantism, to close this paper I return to the particularities of

Uruguayan Catholicism, in particular the perceived relationship between (in)dignity and waste (work).

To some degree, the fact that *acompañantes* used surplus materials as ways of establishing relations with the poor was uncomfortable, if not paradoxical. As in Halvorson's case, the nature of discards was thus sometimes disguised in different ways. Some materials, such as those left at Ruso's house by his neighbours, avoided categorisation as waste altogether. In the case of the seed factory's sweepings, these were never formally classified as waste or donation, but were referred to as the latter by informants and they escaped the costs associated with the former. Bread and cakes from *Aperativo* were intercepted as surplus and reconfigured as donations before they became waste, while the material from Fresh Fare was formally positioned within the framework of municipal waste management and can only secondarily be considered a donation. The stage at which surplus material was intercepted had implications with regard to perceptions of the dignity of consumption. For the *acompañantes*, it was clearly more dignified for *acompañados* to receive a donation before material had officially entered the waste stream and where they had been, we might say, 'blessed' by their intermediation.

Yet there is an obvious irony nonetheless. *Clasificadores* are identified by some Catholics as worthy of theological attention partly because of their appearance, if not actual embodiment, as the poorest of the poor, whose condition in living from society's discards is seen as undignified. Padre Cacho is not the only religious figure to accord waste pickers such importance as the kind of marginalised group favoured by Christ. Pope Francis, formerly Archbishop Bergoglio of Buenos Aires, used to conduct mass in the city for prostitutes and *cartoneros*.[3] He maintained a connection with waste picker organisations on assuming the papacy and invited *cartonero* leader Sergio Sánchez to his inauguration in Rome. In one Buenos Aires mass, Bergoglio drew a direct link between 'throwaway society' and those who are the 'leftovers of society', speaking of 'the existential skips full of disdained men and women' and how those who represented society's leftovers were 'denied work, bread and dignity' (*Clarín* 2009).

The indignity of waste work was echoed by several religious informants. Former nun and social worker Sara found a polluting influence in any work with society's leftovers. 'Whatever name you stick on it, rubbish is rubbish. It's what others throw away, what others don't want . . . and working with waste leaves a mark on the person throughout their life.' For Sara, rubbish indelibly marks those who work with it, and such an essentialist position with regard to waste ('rubbish is rubbish') might even amount to a critique of the surplus offered by some *acompañantes* as donations. A more common position was that although the work was ecologically important, *conditions* should be dignified. Thus, Ruso argued that 'a *clasificador* is as dignified as a nuclear engineer' and it was the conditions – such as a man pushing a cart twenty kilometres a day – which were undignified. In order to dignify such work, *acompañamiento* was necessary: 'through organizing and with *acompañamiento*, [classification] could become a very dignified job'. My accompaniment of neighbours to the landfill and consumption of food recovered there were, for Ruso, a bridge too far.

All this points to the difficulties of enacting the biblical prerogative to help the poor, without interpreting that poverty through a value system maintained by some Catholics which presupposes that the poor must recover a dignity which they have presumably lost and which can only be recovered if they are gently taken by the hand and *accompanied* out of the trash. It is the relation with discards that partly justifies the theological importance paid to *clasificadores* and other waste workers, but upper class Catholics themselves mobilise the materiality of surplus in order to establish reciprocal relationships with them. While it is, at times, useful to distinguish between surplus, excess and waste, I suggest that we might do the opposite here, by looking to the Uruguayan word which stretches to cover recoverable waste, rubbish, surplus and perhaps even donation: *requeche*.

Requeche is a slang word for 'leftover' applied particularly to food, such as the leftovers from a Sunday lunch which one might use for the next week's sandwiches. Amongst *clasificadores*, the word can refer to anything recovered from the trash, but is also customarily used for food. '*Requeche* is what rich people don't eat but instead throw away', explained Pato from the *clasificador* trade union UCRUS (*Unión de Clasificadores de Residuos Urbanos Sólidos*), 'it's what we eat'.[4] Unlike *hurgador* (rummager), *requechero* (the word for those who live from leftovers) was not a term considered undignified or insulting by Pato or the UCRUS. 'What bothers me is when they call us *hurgadores* because it's pigs that rummage', she explained in one interview, 'but we are *requecheros* . . .'.[5] *Requeche* (leftover); *requechar* ('to gather leftovers'; 'to create something new from leftovers'; 'to consume other people's leftovers'); *requecheros* ('one who consumes or lives from the consumption of leftovers'): definitions of the word only make it into online regional slang dictionaries, if at all. Yet the term can perhaps be added to the waste scholar's theoretical toolkit in order to bring together domestic and industrial surplus materials which might have similar physical characteristics but have been placed in different legal or moral classificatory regimes. Recognising the validity and dignity of the *requechero* performs the dual move of freeing *clasificador* dignity from a dependence on the intermediation of Catholic *acompañantes* and recognising that which all 'leftovers' – whether classified as surplus, donation or waste – share in common.

This discussion helps to emphasise the important role played by surplus and waste in bridging social relations between rich and poor in my fieldsite, in line with a move from recent waste scholars to reconsider the agency of their subject matter and recognise the ways in which waste is constitutive, and not a residue, of the social. Thus Gille (2010) argues that complementing the circulation of value, 'we also find in any economy a circulation of waste' in which 'one form of waste metamorphoses into another' (2010, 1060). In a critique of an economics that focuses exclusively on value production and ignores waste, Gille argues that 'as long as the point of departure remains the assumption of value production and realisation, waste will always be a *theoretical* by-product, residual, epiphenomenal, and inconsequential for the understanding of the social' (2010, 1054). My description of the movement of surplus materials – both by-products and the results of overproduction – renders these visible and central in enabling particular social relations. Rather than intra-waste metamorphosis, however, my research describes waste being transformed into donation, or being intercepted as surplus before it even becomes waste. These materials are channelled through but also help enable and modify the dynamics of a socio-religious matrix of *acompañantes* and *acompañados*.

Conclusion

The landfill has long been heralded a somewhat sacred site for the conversion or renewed faith of key religious figures, from Archbishop Romero in El Salvador to Mother Teresa (Aguilar 2008, 17). In this paper I have sought to explore what brought upper-class Catholics close to the Montevidean landfill of my fieldsite, delving into the origin and dynamics of Uruguayan religious social work and inter-class collaboration. Liberation theology's 'preferential option for the poor' found its way to the Uruguayan Church and upper class via Brazil and through figures like Padre Cacho. It came together with post-dictatorship governmental attempts to encourage the upper class to 'take responsibility' for the poor as a mechanism for avoiding social polarisation, creating the particular configuration of the 'Catholic social' found in my fieldsite.

Inherent to these inter-class, church-mediated relations are a series of theological tensions which I have explored in the second part of this paper. One such tension is the attempt to reconcile Catholic doctrine that advocates the conduction of charity with a universal poor and Padre Cacho's example of establishing relations of friendship and reciprocity with a particular poor. From the seeking out of a connection, upper-class *acompañantes* received a series of returns, from affects to tax rebates. Although they looked to the example of St Francis and to the Franciscan nuns in the Cruz de Carrasco, affluent *acompañantes* maintained their class positions as 'structures of sin' endured. This tension was assuaged by several strategies, from the attempted separation of the economic and social realms, to spaces of carnivalesque role reversal.

The points of contact between rich and poor in my Montevideo fieldsite are rare bridges in a continent where gated communities, *favelas* and social polarisation are more common topics of research. While connections with the upper classes might be considered as the poor's 'bridging social capital', it is the networks of the rich which allow materials to be intercepted as 'surplus' before they enter the waste stream. While the intermediation of *acompañantes* channels this material to the *acompañados* in the form of 'donations', surplus material can also be seen as agentive in constituting a bridge through which the rich can establish and maintain relations with the poor. To a certain extent, Catholic engagement with the poor in my fieldsite was about accompanying them to recover their dignity, and certainly led to a greater standard and quality of life in the COVIFU housing cooperative. At the same time, dignity was also used as a relational concept, whereby consumption of surplus materials blessed by the early interception and intermediation of the *acompañantes* was regarded as more dignified than its posterior recovery from the waste stream. Even if, beyond classificatory regimes, it was all a matter of *requeche*.

Notes

1. Uruguay was home to one of the most influential liberation theologians, the Jesuit Juan Luis Segundo, who stayed in the country during the dictatorship, writing articles calling for the release of political prisoners and the restitution of democracy (Aguilar 2008, 59).

2. She described the Uruguayan dictatorship as a 'civil war', a position adopted by the right and related to post-dictatorship President Sanguinetti's 'theory of two demons' (a thesis rejected by the left and human rights activists).

3. The Argentine equivalent of *clasificadores*.

4. Romero, Federica (Dir). 2010. *Requeche*, Montevideo: Calma Cine.

5. Gatti, Daniel. 2013. La Vida en un Carrito. *Brecha*. 13 October. https://brecha.com.uy/la-vida-en-un-carrito/.

References

Abelin, Mireille. '"Entrenched in the BMW": Argentine Elites and the Terror of Fiscal Obligation', *Public Culture* 24, no. 2(67) (2012): 329–56.

Aguilar, Mario. *The History and Politics of Latin American Theology. Volume 3*. London: SCM Press, 2008.

Alonso, Isidro. 'Profeta de la Ciudad', *Novamerica* no. 53 (1992): 22–3.

Álvarez-Rivadulla, María José. 'Golden Ghettos: Gated Communities and Class Residential Segregation in Montevideo, Uruguay', *Environment and Planning A* 39 (2007): 47–63.

Antoncich, Ricardo. *Christians in the Face of Injustice: A Latin American Reading of Catholic Social Teaching*. Maryknoll: Orbis Books, 1987 [1980].

Bakhtin, Mikhail. *Rabelais and His World*. Bloomington: Indiana University Press, 1941.

Benedict XVI. 'Encyclical Letter Deus Caritas est. Of the Supreme Pontiff Benedict XVI to the Bishops, Priests and Deacons, Men and Women Religious and all the Lay Faithful of Christian Love', 2005. https://www.vatican.va/content/benedict-xvi/en/encyclicals/documents/hf_ben-xvi_enc_20051225_deus-caritas-est.html. Accessed 22/11/2024.

Bonavía, Pablo, and Javier Galdona. *Neoliberalismo y fe cristiana*. Montevideo: Obsur, 1994.

Caetano, Gerardo. 'Laicidad, ciudadanía y política en el Uruguay contemporáneo: Matrices y revisions de una cultura laicista', *Cultura y Religión* 7, no. 1 (2013): 116–39.

CEPAL. *Social Panorama of Latin America*. Santiago: ECLAC, 2014.

Clara, Mercedes. *Padre Cacho: Cuando el otro quema adentro*. Montevideo: Trilce/OBSUR, 2012.

Clarín. 'Rodeado de cartoneros y prostitutas, Bergoglio condenó la "esclavitud"', 5 September 2009. https://www.clarin.com/ediciones-anteriores/rodeado-cartoneros-prostitutas-bergoglio-condeno-esclavitud_0_BkbZPR_CaKx.html. Accessed 22/11/2024.

DaMatta, Roberto. *Carnavais, malandros e heróis: Para uma sociologia do dilema brasilero*. Rio de Janeiro: Editora Rocco, 1997.

Evans, David. *Food Waste: Home Consumption, Material Culture and Everyday Life*. London: Bloomsbury Academic, 2014.

Ferguson, James. *Give a Man a Fish: Reflections on the New Politics of Distribution*. London and Durham: Duke University Press, 2015.

Gille, Zsuzsa. *From the Cult of Waste to the Trash Heap of History: The Politics of Waste in Socialist and Postsocialist Hungary*. Bloomington: Indiana University Press, 2010.

Graeber, David. *Beyond the False Coin of our Dreams: Towards an Anthropological Theory of Value*. London: Palgrave MacMillan, 2001.

Graeber, David. 'On the Moral Grounds of Economic Relations: a Maussian Approach', *OAC Press Working Papers Series* no. 6 (2010): 1–17.

Graeber, David. *Debt: The First 5,000 Years*. London: Melville House, 2012.

Grimson, Alejandro. 'The Making of New Urban Borders: Neoliberalism and Protest in Buenos Aires', *Antipode* 40, no. 4 (2008): 504–12.

Halvorson, Britt. '"No Junk for Jesus": Redemptive Economies and Value Conversions in Lutheran Medical Aid'. In *Economies of Recycling: The Global Transformation of Materials, Values and Social Relations*, edited by Catherine Alexander and Joshua Reno, 207–33. London: Zed Books, 2012.

Instituto Nacional de Estatística. *Encuesta Continua de Hogares*, 2009. https://www4.ine.gub.uy/Anda5/index.php/catalog/51. Accessed 22/11/2024.

Kalb, Don, and James Carrier, eds. *Anthropologies of Class: Power, Practice and Inequality*. Cambridge: University of Cambridge Press, 2015.

Jackson, Timothy. *The Priority of Love: Christian Charity and Social Justice*. Princeton: Princeton University Press, 2003.

Laidlaw, James. 'A Free Gift Makes No Friends', *Journal of the Royal Anthropological Institute* 6 (2000): 617–34.

Latour, Bruno. *Politics of Nature: How to Bring the Sciences into Democracy*. Cambridge, MA: Harvard University Press, 2004.

Lehmann, David. 'The Religious Field in Latin America: Autonomy and Fragmentation'. In *The Cambridge History of Religions in Latin America*, edited by Virginia Garrard-Burnett, Paul Freston and Stephen C. Dove, 739–63. Cambridge: Cambridge University Press, 2016.

Mauss, Marcel. *The Gift*. London: Routledge, 1990 [1925].

Miranda, J. P. *Marx y la Biblia*. Salamanca: Sígueme, 1975.

Narayan-Parker, Deepa. 'Bonds and Bridges, Social Capital and Poverty', *World Bank Policy Research Working Paper*, 1999.

Putnam, Robert. *Bowling Alone: The Collapse and Revival of American Community*. New York: Simon & Schuster, 2000.

Sahlins, Marshall. *Stone Age Economics*. Chicago: University Press, 1972.

Santandreu, Alain, Gustavo Castro and Fernando Ronca. *La cría de cerdos en asentamientos irregulares: Desafíos legales, sanitarios, sociales y ambientales de una práctica extendida de agricultura urbana*. Montevideo: Unidad de Montevideo Rural, Intendencia Municipal de Montevideo, 2002.

Saravi, Gonzalo A., and Sara Makowski. 'Social Exclusion and Subjectivity: Youth Expressions in Latin America', *The Journal of Latin American and Caribbean Anthropology* 16, no. 2 (2011): 315–34.

Sobrino, Jon. *El principio-misericordia*. Santander: Salterae, 1992.

Svampa, Maristella. *Los que ganaron: La vida en los countries y barrios privados*. Buenos Aires: Editorial Biblos, 2008 [2001].

Thompson, Michael. *Rubbish Theory: The Creation and Destruction of Value*. Oxford: Oxford University Press, 1979.

Wasserman, Stanley, and Katherine Faust. *Social Network Analysis: Methods and Applications*. Cambridge: Cambridge University Press, 1994.

Chapter 3

Orlando Fals Borda's participatory action research: At and beyond the crossroads of Camilo Torres's neo-socialism and liberation theology

Juan Mario Díaz-Arévalo

Orlando Fals Borda's (1925–2008) pioneering contribution to the inception and development of participatory action research (PAR) made him one of the most influential Latin American intellectuals of the second half of the past century. The centrality of ethical principles, informed by his upbringing and education in the Presbyterian tradition, is a recurring reference in the literature on Fals Borda. Similarly, it has been generally acknowledged that his friendship with the Catholic priest Camilo Torres strongly influenced his radical thinking. Paradoxically, the analysis of the religious element in his career has been one of the most neglected aspects of the intellectual history of Fals Borda. With a few exceptions (Díaz-Arévalo 2017; 2018; 2022a; Moreno 2017; Poggi 2015; Rappaport 2020; Restrepo, G. 2016), religion has been described as a sort of passive influence rather than a field of active and creative engagement in his career. This chapter examines the cross-fertilisation of ideas and methods between sociologists and theologians concerned with human emancipation and liberation that underpins Fals Borda's praxis as engaged social researcher. To do so, it examines the intellectual journey that goes from his analysis of political violence in Colombia, to his ideas of moral subversion, to his engagement with the peasant movement's struggle for land, which resulted in his *sociología del compromiso* (engaged sociology) in 1970, and *investigación activa militante* (militant action research) in 1977. This chapter argues that this trajectory, which ultimately led to the inception of PAR, sprang not only out of his rupture with the functional positivist framework of sociological analysis but also out of two intertwined aspects: first, personal and professional convictions rooted in an ethically and theologically informed vision of social justice that he actively rendered into his *praxis* as an action-oriented researcher; second, his determination to contest a system of political exclusion and extreme social inequality without abandoning his role as a social researcher.

As Fals Borda himself recalls, 'PAR had a demonic midwife: ancestral political violence that climaxed in the *bogotazo* of 1948 and [still] continues' (2013, 162), a reference to the assassination of the Liberal leader Jorge Eliécer Gaitán, which resulted in the destruction of the centre of Bogotá and marked the beginning of a decade of civil strife. He also reminds us that at the inception of his method of PAR there were two tendencies among intellectuals: 'the belligerent one represented by Camilo Torres, one of our founding fathers, who saw the only possible way forward in weapons and historical guerrilla wars'; and the other path of 'civic resistance that was taken by autonomous institutions' (2013, 162–3) such as the Rosca Foundation, a grassroots organisation that Fals Borda himself founded to support the peasant struggle for land in the early 1970s (Rappaport 2017). This provides us with a lens to examine the origins of PAR in a different light.

For the benefit of conceptual clarification, this study differentiates Fals Borda's early formulations of militant action research (1979), which paved the way for the inception of PAR, from the most mature systematisation of PAR developed in the early 1980s (Díaz-Arévalo 2022; Fals Borda 1988; 1991; Hall 2005). This is not to suggest that the seeds of PAR were not already there in his radical activism. It simply means that his praxis as an intellectual of the peasant movement, which allowed him to transform traditional and innovative methods of research into participatory experiences, was also marked by a series of epistemological and methodological deficiencies, as will be discussed later. Fals Borda (1979) himself acknowledged that his early action research was conceptually and methodologically ambiguous. However, these deficiencies, which belong to a stage of intense searching and experimentation, are often uncritically transferred to the more mature elaborations of PAR. This is the case of Boaventura de Sousa Santos's (2018) celebratory version of Fals Borda's PAR, which lacks an empirically grounded account of how PAR was practised in Colombia and other places, contributing to not only a general amnesia about the origins of PAR but also underestimating the role that it still plays in the emergence and expansion of artisanal knowledges.[1]

In a previous article (Díaz-Arévalo 2022a), I looked at the relations and experiences within the Protestant tradition that overlapped with Fals Borda's ideas about social change, and how this appears in his academic works. This chapter focuses instead on Fals Borda's relations and experiences within the Catholic field; chiefly, his encounter with the priest Camilo Torres and subsequently with the theology of liberation, elaborated by Catholic and Protestant theologians alike, which enabled him to incorporate elements of Catholic humanism into his radical thinking. As the Presbyterian theologian Richard Shaull observed, what captured the imagination of the young generation committed to the struggle of the masses, of which Fals Borda was a part, was the humanism embodied in local ideologies: ideologies such as the Indigenous Marxism of the Peruvian José Carlos Mariátegui and Jorge Eliécer Gaitán's autochthonous socialism that Shaull saw as being rooted in 'the traditional humanism of the Iberian soul' (1962, 14).

Drawing upon archival research, this chapter is divided into five parts. The first part looks at the process that goes from Fals Borda's analysis of the period known in Colombia as *la Violencia* (the Violence) to his ideas of *moral subversion*, a framework to examine social change. The second part examines Fals Borda's interpretation of the historical and political significance of Catholic priest Camilo Torres's revolutionary decision. The third part focuses on the question of social ethics, a point of contention between conservative Christianity and engaged sociologists and theologians. The fourth part looks at the two-way methodological interaction between action-research-engaged theologians in the early 1970s. The chapter closes by highlighting both epistemological differences between liberation theology and PAR and common challenges ahead.

From critique of violence to rebellious social science

The role of violence in the break with traditionalism

In 1959, with the decisive collaboration of Camilo Torres, Fals Borda founded the School of Sociology at the National University of Colombia, the first of its type in Latin America. Like most programmes of sociology created across Latin America during the early 1960s, this became integral to the implementation of the US developmental policy for Latin America. Although Colombia became the showcase for the Alliance for Progress, Fals Borda considered that an adequate response to war-torn Colombia not only required economic development and agrarian modernisation but also necessitated overcoming the legacy of the country's most recent past: a decade of political violence known as *la Violencia*, from 1948 to 1958, which began with the assassination of the Liberal leader Jorge Eliécer Gaitán and spiralled into all-out conflict between the Conservative government, which deployed a political police force and paramilitary squads, and improvised self-defence Liberal guerrillas. This turbulent period, with a death toll amounting to 200,000 civilians, had given way to the establishment of the National Front, a power-sharing agreement that provided for alternating Conservative and Liberal presidencies and an equal representation in all executive and legislative bodies which endured from 1958 to 1974 (Gutiérrez and Guataquí 2009). In contrast to the attempts of this bi-partisan coalition to consign *la Violencia* to oblivion, Fals Borda thought that facing it was a vital step towards overcoming it (in Guzmán, Fals Borda and Umaña 2005 [1962], 11–18).

Moreover, as vice-minister of agriculture, 1959–60, he grew concerned with the socio-political disadvantages of top-down reconciliation which did not permeate or benefit the social bases that had been devastated during the 1950s. As a rural sociologist, he was also dissatisfied with official narratives that depicted *la Violencia* as the result of the peasantry's natural aggressiveness and moral disorder.[2] There was still a more personal reason to break the curtain of silence drawn over the country's immediate past: a sense of moral responsibility as a member of a new generation, a generation that, he thought, had the responsibility to 'foster change for the better of the country' (ACH-UN, FOFB. Instituto Antropología Social, 2).

The combination of all these aspects impelled Fals Borda along with a group of researchers from the newly founded Faculty of Sociology to write the first sociological analysis of *la Violencia*. To produce this book, the authors drew on the personal archive of Monsignor Germán Guzmán, one of the eight members of the National Commission to Inquire into the Causes and Present Situation of *la Violencia* in the National Territory (a body created by the interim government in 1958) and the only one that had kept the records of thousands of interviews with individuals and groups involved in the conflict across the country (Jaramillo Marín 2012). The resulting text was the first volume of *La Violencia en Colombia: Estudio de un proceso social* (LVC) (Guzmán, Fals Borda and Umaña 2005 [1962]).[3]

Although the compendium of atrocities and despicable crimes became the most conspicuous face of *la Violencia*, Fals Borda's analysis did not dwell on these horrors. His analysis instead focuses on two crucial aspects of the conflict: first, what he calls 'structural cleavage', that is, the loss of the monopoly of legitimate violence when the coercive institutions of society (such as the political police and the army) turned into predatory forces, and the law courts began to grant impunity to cover up political crimes (1964, 28); second, the transfer of power from the centre to the periphery, which led, he argues, to the break with traditionalism. For Fals Borda, such a complex and accelerated process of social disintegration and integration at various levels of power, top-down and bottom-up, gave rise to a radical transformation of collective values or a 'moral crisis'; a state that he defined as 'anomical' rather than anarchic and that went hand in hand with the abolition of core features of the legality and the legitimacy of state institutions.[4]

Distressing as it was to read, LVC was highly praised by politicians and even high-ranking military officials who agreed that, first, such a thoroughly documented account sadly bore faithful witness to the most recent history of the country (*El Espectador* 12 July 1962) and, second, that any attempt at reconstruction of the war-torn social fabric should acknowledge that the main causes of *la Violencia* were social inequality, fanaticism and a political system which deterred social change by democratic means.

Despite its initial positive reception, the book soon became the target of virulent attacks after Liberals and Conservatives used it as a tool of mutual recrimination at congressional debates. While avoiding comments on any topic in the volume, the Conservative press went from criticism of the 'sectarian' and 'poisonous' book to personally attacking its authors – a 'renegade priest and friend of criminals', 'a Protestant sociologist' and 'a freethinking lawyer' – arguing that their personal backgrounds made them incompetent to analyse Colombian reality (*El Siglo* 15, 20, 25, 28 September, 1, 4 October 1962). After four months of acrid debate in the national press, the leadership of both parties claimed the National Front was established in order *not* to speak of *la Violencia* anymore (Fals Borda 1963, 49), and that any attempt to analyse its origins or who bore responsibility for the conflict might destabilise the Grand Coalition (*El Tiempo* 24 December 1962).

The decision of the establishment to consign *la Violencia* to silence deepened Fals Borda's distrust of the National Front's ability to understand the extent and depth of the damage caused by *la Violencia* and to act accordingly. Intellectually, the writing of LVC marked Fals Borda's move away from functionalism as a framework of analysis, as its focus on social structure, institutions and social functions was found to be of limited use in understanding the dynamics of conflict in Colombia (Cendales et al. 2005). Moreover, the reaction to LVC confirmed his fears that the establishment was reluctant to ground policy on scientific research. Thus, LVC marked the beginning of a shift that can be described as moving from attempting to inform policy to directly supporting the oppressed in their struggle for liberation (Feagin, Vera and Ducey 2014, 165–94).

Subversion as a framework of socio-historical analysis

After the second presidential period of the National Front from 1962 to 1966, which became a symbol of 'elitism, authoritarianism, aloofness and corruption [. . .] often under the control of personal fiefdoms' (Gutiérrez and Guataquí 2009), Fals Borda and many representative members of this generation found their politics to be increasingly revolutionary. Thus, the pertinent question became *how* to be a revolutionary. According to Fals Borda (1970/71), the deaths of both the Catholic priest Camilo Torres (who was killed during his first combat as a guerrilla fighter in February 1966) and Ernesto 'Che' Guevara (who was killed in Bolivia in November 1967) marked the climax of a type of revolutionary endeavour in Latin America. 'Now', he argues, 'follows the anti-climax . . . the examination and careful reorganisation . . . New utopias, new directives toward dissent will very likely appear because the basic problems of Latin American society persist and invite rebellious thought and action' (1970/71, 77).

Subversion and Social Change in Colombia (1967; 1968; 1969; henceforth *Subversion*) was Fals Borda's first attempt to examine the revolutionary potential of Torres's message, while exploring new models of socio-political contestation. While other commentators at the time portrayed Torres as an 'immature' and 'defrocked priest' trapped in Marxist dialectics (see, for example, *El Tiempo* 17 February 1966; *La República* 18 February 1966; Andrade 1966, 177–81), in this book, Fals Borda did not seek to challenge this portrayal, entrusting this task, instead, to Torres's biographers (Broderick 1975; Caycedo 1972; Guzmán 1967; 1967a; Habegger 1967. See also Villanueva Martínez 1995; Lüning 2016 [1969]). Nor did Fals Borda attempt to provide historical background to those narratives that depicted Torres as a 'martyr' of a popular cause. Instead, by approaching Torres in a manner reminiscent of that of Benjamin's 'dialectical image' (Benjamin 2006), Fals Borda sought to recover his political significance; that is, to retrieve his moral subversion as a positive category for social transformation able to lead a new cycle of civil resistance (Fals Borda 1969, xiii).[5]

To accomplish this task, *Subversion*, a book written during the academic year of 1966 when Fals Borda was visiting professor at the University of Wisconsin, broke out of the chronological straitjacket into which partisan historians had constricted national historiography. Calling into question the truth of the past embedded in such exclusionary narratives, it aimed to take a snapshot of four social orders in the history of Colombia, while highlighting the factors that influenced the transitional process of radical social change in Colombia.[6] With 'moral subversion' as a framework, the book sought to actualise a not-yet-encountered but already-imagined order defined by the ideals of a more just and equitable society. *Subversion*'s aim, as will be explained in the next section, was to connect the struggles of the socialist movement since its origins in Colombia in the 1920s with Camilo Torres's neo-socialist attempt to subvert the liberal-bourgeois social order established by the National Front (Fals Borda 1969, xii).[7]

Sociologist José A. Silva Michelena, to whom Fals Borda had shown the first draft of *Subversion* (1967), asked him why he had not simply used the term 'revolution' instead of subversion (ACH-UN, FOFB. Subversión, 52). For Fals Borda, 'subversion' was a notion loaded with historical meaning, whereas 'revolution' was a household word devalued by historical events as much as by timid institutional attempts at social reform in Colombia, such as Liberal President Alfonso Lopez Pumarejo's Revolution on the March of 1934–8 and 1942–5.[8] Moreover, the nature of power in the late 1960s – based on the advanced technologies of war and repression, sophisticated social control and the increasingly complex social organisation of urban-industrial communities – had rendered obsolete the classical model of revolution originating in eighteenth-century Europe. Hence, Fals Borda's main concern was how to contest what Latin Americanist William McGreevey (1970) described as 'the porosity of Colombia's elite' and its ability to co-opt dissident movements without causing social change.

The first edition of *Subversion* (1967) was encouraged by signs of ideological and political renewal that had arisen from within the Liberal Party in the mid-1960s, which Fals Borda rushed to interpret as the emergence of a real opposition to the National Front (1968, xiv).[9] The lack of real opposition to bi-partisan coalition created a 'revolutionary social vacuum', which led Fals Borda to see the creation of a movement that could lead the country towards a new social order – the neo-socialist order – as 'the subversive task of the moment' (ACH-UN, FOFB. Europa II, Suiza, 16). Accordingly, the second edition of *Subversion* (1968) was addressed to a new generation of non-conformists, dissidents and political activists beyond the traditional political cadres, and non-sectarian communists and socialists with the aim of contributing to 'doing subversion well' (1968, xvi).

Camilo Torres's pluralism and the liberation social science tradition

In his comments on *Subversion* (1967), Silva Michelena drew Fals Borda's attention to the chronic inability of Colombian subversive groups to become a viable political option – a situation closely related to Colombian social conservatism, which was reinforced not only by the Catholic Church's alliance with the Conservative Party but also through the adoption of traditional values in key social institutions such as the family and schools. Therefore, Silva Michelena wrote, 'this is one of the factors that made Camilo an ideal leader for Colombia but, as you have said, [Camilo] can be revived and it would not be the first time that a dead person makes a revolution' (ACH-UN, FOFB. Subversión, 54).

Although Camilo Torres's vision of a pluralist utopia was distorted by realities almost immediately after he expounded it, Fals Borda agreed with Michelena that there already existed the minimum ideological and organisational elements 'to initiate a new cycle of subversive development in Colombia that will lead to another order, the fifth of the historical series' (1969, 170). If Fals Borda regarded Camilo Torres as the standard-bearer of a new subversion in Colombia, it was not because Torres was a priest who preached the new socialist revolution in religious tones. It was because the moral direction of his pluralist utopia had become the crossroads at which many disenfranchised and even rival leftist factions converged (López-Pacheco 2017, 176; Pereira 2008, 394–5). Moreover, Fals Borda's critical retrieval of Torres's ideological drive was an effort to reclaim the utopian and moral ingredients from those who turned them into a mere justification for armed struggle.

Therefore, Fals Borda's method of 'reviving' Torres consisted in reappropriating through historical inquiry at least three aspects of his pluralism that Fals Borda sought to render into an autochthonous ideological framework for political action: (1) the politics of human dignity, which Torres encapsulated in the concept of 'efficacious love' (Torres 1971, 351; see also Díaz-Arévalo 2022a) – a moral imperative that was at odds with the ritualistic type of religion which has little ethical significance in everyday life. In Colombia, a highly segregated society where most people live in poverty, Torres wrote (*La República* 16 June 1965), effective charity had to point to the practical and social implication of Christian faith; (2) pluralistic dialogue and criticism of false binaries, which aimed at de-spiritualising politics. Torres's dialogue with the Marxists and the communists challenged the ideological Manicheism held by the church–state alliance which had perceived all good to rest on one side, and all evil on the other. Torres's dialectic is no longer between good and evil but between justice and dignity on one hand, and exploitation and oppression on the other. As he put it, when religion makes people take human problems seriously, it is no longer religious alienation. So, in contrast to the dominant groups who blamed the socio-political turmoil on inimical outsiders or foreign conspiracies, mostly communist, Torres declared, 'I am not, nor will I ever become, a Communist. However, I am prepared to fight together with the Communists for our common goals: against the oligarchy and United States domination; for the winning of power by the people';[10] and (3) participatory politics which represented a direct challenge to the National Front's exclusionary politics whose ideology was phrased in terms of internal national security and had allowed the oligarchy to rule uncontested over a society which had been torn asunder.

Fals Borda's actualisation of Camilo Torres as a utopian image for *teletic* – or goal-oriented – politics was by no means uncritical of Torres's final decision. For Fals Borda (1968), the rapid spread of guerrilla warfare throughout Latin American was a 'social fact' that reflected the existence of acute and historical social problems in the region. Therefore, the problem of violence as *ultima ratio* was not so much in its justification as in the conditions and limitations of its use. Justifications had been ongoing for centuries, at least since Thomas Aquinas's classical thesis on just war (Fals Borda 1969, 166). The problem, as Fals Borda noted, was the excessive reliance on military success that led armed groups inspired by the success of the Cuban Revolution to blindly duplicate the Sierra Maestra pattern in the early 1960s (1968, 457). The case of Torres illustrates this point. Torres saw his decision to join the guerrillas as the means to consolidate his previous political work as a leader of the *Frente Unido* (United Front), which had been officially launched just five months before, in May 1965. In his last letter to his brother Fernando, written from his guerrilla campsite in the mountains of Santander, Torres stated that, 'following the work of agitation, this stage is necessary and will consolidate the previous stage. I am prepared for a long struggle but sure of victory ... If I get left behind, because they kill me, I believe that the work already done will prevail' (ACH-UN. Fondo Camilo Torres Restrepo, 81).

For Fals Borda, Torres's self-deluding confidence in the immediate success of armed struggle, as well as that of other popular leaders in the region, was his tactical error. Aware of the need for a long-term and more complex strategy for political action, Fals Borda posited that the alternative was the creation of a popular counter-elite ethically and politically prepared to subvert the unjust social order imposed by the coalition of the National Front. This, however, posed the practical challenge of finding 'strategic groups ... akin to Torres's ideal of service to collaborate with them in the concrete revolutionary task' (ACH-UN, FOFB. RI, Suiza, 18).

One of these groups was Golconda, with which Fals Borda tried to engage. Led by Monsignor Gerardo Valencia Cano, the group was formed by Father René García and a group of priests of the Archdiocese of Bogotá; a group of nuns and teachers of the girls Catholic School Marymount led by sister Leonor Esguerra; and the Marxist mathematician Germán Zabala and a group of his students, with whom he led an educational experience, the Integral Educational Model (*modelo educacional integral*, MEI), at the Central Colombian Institute (Pérez-Prieto 2016, 92). By adopting a 'militant pastoral methodology', which was inspired by the see-judge-act approach of the Young Christian Workers created by the Belgian priest Joseph Cardijn (Cervetto 2017), the articulation of these three groups and their pedagogical practices in the popular districts of Bogotá sought to realise Torres's revolutionary ideal; that is, to create the basis for 'the political, pedagogical and spiritual unity of the popular classes' (Pérez-Prieto 2016, 93).

However, Fals Borda's plan to work with the 'revolution of the cassocks' (Restrepo, J. 1995), as Golconda was known, never came to fruition. On the one hand, Golconda rapidly lost momentum as its members scattered following persecution, the emergence of ideological differences, and the fact that some of its leaders joined the ELN (Ejército de Liberación Nacional) guerrilla group (Zeitlin, in Torres 1972, 45–6).[11] On the other, Fals Borda had decided to create an independent centre for social research in which he sought to employ a group of twelve scholars from the Faculty of Sociology that he had created a decade earlier. This proposal was received with deep reservations with some of Fals Borda's former colleagues deeply concerned about the radicalism of his 'new ideas'.

The ideas that surprised some of Fals Borda's former colleagues were those espoused in his conception of *sociología del compromiso* (engaged sociology) with which he sought to respond to Marx's invitation to change the world instead of just contemplating it (Bonilla et al. 1972, 19–33). Fals Borda's engaged sociology had reached academic prominence at the 9th Latin American Congress of Sociology in Mexico, 1969, where the debate between engaged and objective sociology was at the core of the congress. Arguing that claims to non-involvement, neutrality and objectivity in social inquiry served consciously or unconsciously to preserve social injustice, Fals Borda (1970) spearheaded the arguments in favour of engaged sociology against Aldo Solari's value-free sociology (2011 [1969]). The former's ideas provided the key lines adopted by the conference's final declaration, which defined engaged sociology as a current that sides with the underprivileged, seeking to contribute to empowering key groups for social change while contesting the underlying values of instrumental positivism – chiefly, its self-delusionary notions of 'objectivity' and 'neutrality' and its methodological practice restricted to functionalist research methods (Fals Borda 1970).

Fals Borda's engaged sociology resonated with social researchers, popular educators, Protestant and Catholic theologians and activists, who had all gathered under the emerging ecumenical umbrella of the liberationist paradigm. In fact, Fals Borda's *Ciencia propia y colonialismo intelectual* (1971) – a series of essays in which he further expanded his ideas on engagement, decolonialism and the sociology of liberation – came out at the same time as Peruvian theologian Gustavo Gutiérrez's seminal *Teología de la liberación* (1972 [1971]).

Gutiérrez, a classmate of Camilo Torres at Louvain, had participated in the Second Vatican Council of 1962 to 1965 and was the key ideologue of the Medellín CELAM (Consejo Episcopal Latinoamericano y Caribeño) Conference (Hart 1978, 196). Resident, as he was, of a Lima shantytown, Gutiérrez claimed that neutrality was impossible and that denying the existence of the class struggle was 'to put oneself on the side of the dominant sectors' (1998 [1973], 158). In contrast to dogmatic theology, which prioritises doctrine over mundane realities, Gutiérrez argues that theology, as reflection, is the 'second act' since the first act is 'commitment to the poor' (1973, xxiii). Gutiérrez's experience, like that of many liberation theologians and activists living in marginalised areas across Latin America, fostered the creation of popular biblical circles and ecclesial base communities. The analysis of 'institutionalised violence', similar to what sociologist Johan Galtung would term 'structural violence' a year later (Guardado 2022), led those engaged with the poor to interrogate their own contexts against the teachings of the Gospel (Berryman 1987) and, vice versa, to question, as Fray Antonio de Montesinos did in his sermon on the Sunday before Christmas 1511 in Hispaniola (now Haiti/Dominican Republic), 'For whose benefit?' 'In whose interest is it to make such and such a claim about God?' (in Bradstock and Rowland 2002, 62–3).

Engaged research and the theological question of social ethics

In July 1970, on his return to Colombia after almost three years in Europe, Fals Borda officially resigned from the National University of Colombia in order to dedicate himself to radical activism. One year later, with the aim of advancing social research that supported marginalised groups in their struggles for social justice, Fals Borda established La Rosca de

Investigación y Acción Social (the Circle of Research and Social Action; henceforth La Rosca) along with the theatre director Carlos Duplat and three fellow Presbyterians, namely: Víctor Daniel Bonilla, a journalist and ethnographer, who worked with the newly created Indigenous council of Cauca; Gonzalo Castillo-Cárdenas, a sociologist and pastor; and Augusto Libreros, an economist and Presbyterian pastor.

Elsewhere, I have analysed the impact that the 1966 World Conference of the World Council of Churches had on Fals Borda's critical thinking (Díaz-Arévalo 2022a). For our present purpose, however, it is sufficient to note that this progressive movement led by the theologian Richard Shaull raised concerns regarding the role of traditional theology in times of global challenges such as the nuclear threat, the war in Vietnam and the poverty in which two-thirds of the world population lived, leading to the realisation that renewal of the Church's mission must include concern for the people involved in revolutionary struggles for social justice (ACH-UN, FOFB. Congreso Mundial Iglesias, 65). True to these considerations, La Rosca set its base in the western plains of the Atlantic Coast where the struggle of smallholders and land workers against large landowners was more intense and had a major impact in terms of land distribution (Rappaport 2017; 2020). In 1972, when Fals Borda joined the peasant movement's struggle for land, President Misael Pastrana (1970–74) had begun dismantling the official machinery that had been set up by the former administration to carry out an ambitious agrarian reform (Rivera Cusicanqui 1982; Zamosc 1986). The peasant movement responded to Pastrana's counter-reform with hacienda occupations which were, in turn, violently suppressed. Indeed, along with many others who joined the peasants' action, Fals Borda was jailed for his participation.

La Rosca, however, not only raised concerns within the establishment but also sparked confrontation within the Presbyterian Church over the funding that Fals Borda had secured for La Rosca from the National Committee on the Self-Development of People (NCSDP), an organisation of which Fals Borda was a co-founding member and that works under the auspices of the United Presbyterian Church of the US (Moreno 2017, 141).[12] The Colombian Presbyterian Synod decried the fact that the US Church had funded La Rosca, 'a Communist revolutionary organisation dedicated to promoting class struggle', as they saw it (ACH-UN, FOFB. IAP [Investigación Acción Participativa], 126). Through open letters and leaflets distributed by hand at the NCSDP annual meeting, the National Synod, led by Emery Lorentz, a US missionary based in Colombia, protested against what they saw as NCSDP's interference in national affairs and demanded the US Church revoke its decision. Fals Borda ultimately resigned as a member of the NCSDP and a second instalment of $75,000, due to be paid in early 1974, was suspended. In addition, the conflict with the Synod escalated to the point that Fals Borda was excommunicated because of his alleged communism. Nonetheless, Fals Borda found a generous source of financial support for La Rosca in the Swedish International Development Agency (SIDA) and, despite his excommunication, also obtained help from the Dutch Churches' Foundation, Cross the Bridge.

The feud with the Presbyterian Synod of Colombia over the NCSDP grant serves as a backdrop for examining the question of social ethics; a crucial point of contention between the liberationist paradigm and what Fals Borda viewed as the churches' old paradigm. While the former was aligned with the principles of engagement with the poor previously mentioned, the latter was crudely described by Fals Borda as characteristic of 'institutions loaded with the most conservative views, far from the genuine interests of the people in need [and] adept at giving moral support to an unjust system' (ACH-UN, FOFB. Alterantiva, 50).

The discussion of the relationship between religion and social action had been addressed by Fals Borda and theologians such as W. César and Richard Shaull in the book *Protestantismo e imperialismo* (César et al. 1968). However, the specific question of social ethics became an issue of analysis for La Rosca after some leaders of the peasant movement expressed their concern about the influence of fast-growing evangelical groups which were indifferent or even opposed to the peasants' struggle for land in the region (CDRBr//M, fol. 0731, 4081). La Rosca therefore launched a research project on the experience of participation in the Pentecostal community in Córdoba, on the Atlantic Coast, an area under the influence of the peasant movement.

The research project, coordinated by María Cristina Salazar, Fals Borda's wife, explored the socio-historical and theoretical basis for the traditional conservatism of the Protestant churches in Latin America, given that their members seemed uninterested in the socio-political destiny of their countries (CDRBr//M, fol. 0731, 4099). Through a comparative analysis of the development of Protestantism in Colombia, Chile and Brazil, and the adoption of the critical views of theologians such as Rubem Alvez (1970), César Waldo (1968) and Lalive d'Epiney (1967), Salazar argues that the lack of a clear social ethics in Protestant churches relates to the fact that their message appeals to the individual, requiring him or her to make a decision of a religious nature, yet leaving them to their own devices in the political and social spheres (Tilich 1962, in Salazar CDRBr//M, fol. 0731, 4082). Moreover, as Libreros (1969) argues, the relationship between the individual and the social is presented as a duality, not a dialectic. While the latter suggests a tension that demands the active engagement of the individual to transform society, the former suggests an irreconcilable either/or type of relation.

For d'Epiney the reactionary role of Protestantism in Latin America (a sort of 'Latin American McCarthyism' or passive socio-political strike) resulted from the attempt to shift the Protestant groups too quickly towards structures and conventions that had dominated the older churches in Latin America. As d'Epiney had concluded at the Conference of Church and Society held in Uruguay in 1967, these older churches were founded on the same principles as the traditional hacienda in Latin America: 'they offer men a possible escape from their historic situation, from their responsibility as men, from their solidarity with other men' (ACH-UN, FOFB. Congreso Mundial Iglesias, 384).

For Rubem Alvez, head of the Union Theological Seminary and new director of studies of the Latin American Committee of Church and Society, the roots of the problem of the churches' conservatism were not only socio-cultural. He argued that they were also part of the spiritual inheritance of Latin American Protestantism, which is encapsulated in the motto 'convert the individual then society will be transformed' (1970, 10). Social ethics based on this principle can hardly produce categories for understanding problems of a structural nature. According to Alvez (1970, 11), the mutation of the political character of Calvinism (transformation of the world for the glory of God) into individualistic ethics, based on the consciousness of being morally different or superior, had stripped Calvinism in Latin America of its social ethics. Hence, for the Latin American Protestant, man does not change his world, he rejects it: 'Criticism of the structures is avoided, and criticism of the individual takes its place. It is the same ideology which in the US ascribes the plight of the poor to the fact that "they do not try hard enough"' (1970, 11–12).

Salazar concludes by arguing that by replacing the critique of the structural with the critique of the individual, Protestant ethics manage to create an illusory happiness that is stronger than in traditional peasant Catholicism due to its emphasis on emotions and very intense sentimental experiences (CDRBr//M, fol. 0731, 4112). Therefore, under the current social structures of the country, the lack of social concerns in Pentecostalist groups appears to be detrimental to the historical tasks of the Colombian peasantry for its own liberation (CDRBr//M, fol. 0731, 4113).

In search of a methodological approach to Praxis

Fals Borda and his associates were aware that an ethical framework for social action also required methodological strategies able to connect theory and practice. Therefore, they also found the attitude of left-wing groups towards the fast-growing influence of evangelical groups in the region extremely concerning. As Fals Borda wrote, 'there is no known concrete plan of action to counteract this counter-revolutionary influence, except to bemoan it or ignore it; that is, to underestimate it' (CDRBr//M, fol. 0731, fol. 4162).

Seeking to render their action-oriented research agenda into methodological approaches to work with the marginalised became one of the major epistemological questions with which La Rosca was confronted. The various labels created to name their work as engaged social researchers, such as engaged sociology, committed sociology and the sociology of liberation, among others, are indicative of their efforts to connect Freire's ongoing spiral of praxis with scholarly inquiry and theorising, as well as with their pastoral work.

The same was true for most theologians and social researchers seeking authentic engagement with the poor. The creation of ecclesial base communities and cadres demanded novel methods and strategies of participation, which resulted in an intense period of experimentation in action-oriented research and reflection undertaken with the bases. With their multiple variations, approaches such as the action-research cycle (inquiry-reflection-action) and the militant pastoral methodology (see-judge-act), then widely adopted by liberation theology (Girardi 2012, 5), developed in parallel within the framework of praxis defined by Paulo Freire. This demanded that the oppressed engaged in reflection on their own reality: 'reflection – true reflection – leads to action', wrote Freire. As he continues, 'when the situation calls for action, that action will constitute an authentic praxis only if its consequences become the object of critical reflection . . . Otherwise, action is pure activism' (2005 [1970], 66).

According to Fals Borda, the link that allowed engaged groups to combine thought and action in the praxis research process was the adaptation of Marxism to local conditions (1974, 61). Following Mariátegui's refusal to abide by dogmatic or mechanical Marxism while seeking to adapt Marx to Peruvian reality (Munck 2022), La Rosca, as its funding act indicates, sought to adopt the technical-practical aspects of Marxism as a working method, not as ideology and even less as dogma, with the aim of adapting it to Colombian rural reality (ACH-UN, FOFB. IAP, Rosca, 202). Something similar applied to most liberation theologians, who did not adopt Marx's ideas wholesale but, always within the *modus cogitans* of religious epistemology (Lamola 2018), borrowed concepts and methodological pointers which they found helpful.

This section focuses on three techniques developed by La Rosca which are illustrative of at least two aspects: first, an intense period of methodological exploration of theologians and sociologists united by their commitment to the struggle of the marginalised; and second, efforts to integrate practical aspects of Marxism into a methodology that, at the same time, responded to a theologically informed framework of social ethics.

Participation-insertion

Participation-insertion rather than a technique of research was a *sine qua non* condition for genuine engagement. According to La Rosca associates, only those embedded in popular struggles are able to discover what their skills are and how these can be most useful to the cause of the poor (Bonilla et al. 1972, 37). The practice of 'insertion' (*inserción*) sought to curb the facile enthusiasm which had led many to interpret the connections between *liberation, commitment* and *social science* superficially and hence identified the task simply as a form of *intervention* and *agitation* of the masses (Fals Borda 1974, 63–4). It also aimed to respond to the failure of traditional techniques such as observation by participation and observation by experimentation (intervention) effectively to connect scientific research and political action, let alone to advance the fight for liberation. The notion of 'insertion' also emerged from activist theologians and pastors – within their revolutionary or pre-revolutionary commitment – providing a clearer methodological framework, something like a 'breakthrough' (1974, 62). Echoing Gustavo Gutiérrez, for whom insertion was the first and most basic stage of praxis as a method, Fals Borda stated: '[insertion] implies that the scientist *is involved as an agent within the process he is studying*, because [he learns] not only from his observation but also from the work he carries out with the persons with whom he identifies' (Fals Borda 1973, 27; italics in original).

The practice of insertion was guided by three basic principles: (1) it is inextricably linked to the social groups with which the researcher works; (2) it varies, evolves and is modified according to local political conditions or the correlation of social forces in conflict; (3) it depends, to a large extent, on the overall social change strategy adopted in the short or medium term. In practical terms, it was considered a gradual process of preliminary analysis that did not necessarily include the participation of community members. Some of the aspects of this non-linear approach included: getting familiar with the local group and its history and conditions, establishing contact with key internal and external actors, identifying potential strategic sub-groups, documenting conflicts and tensions, and conducting socio-demographic analysis (Bonilla et al. 1972,

39–43). Again, more than a new approach, this technique summarises aspects that Fals Borda had put into practice during his previous research experience with rural communities in the 1950s.

Knowledge through action

The aim of militant research was not only to collect, systematise and accumulate scientific knowledge on and for the masses. More importantly, Fals Borda (1974, 65) argued, the purpose of action-oriented research was to strengthen the opportunities of the marginalised to act upon their reality in ways that would accelerate social change (ACH-UN, FOFB. IAP, Rosca, 241). Seeking to engage local people, La Rosca trained cadres of militant researchers, which included teaching them how to read and write, training them in the use of ethnographic techniques of self-investigation and the analysis of class struggle, and forming circles for critical thinking and collective analysis (Fals Borda 1974a; 1979, 48–50). This not only implied replacing academic audiences with local groups but also adjusting the process of knowledge production and dissemination. Inspired by Mao Tse-tung's 'militant observers', through which he sought to advance his motto 'to the masses – from the masses – to the masses' (Bonilla et al. 1972, 35), La Rosca prioritised the needs and issues identified by the peasants they worked with, facilitated research on the historical roots of the conflicts identified, and developed different levels of scientific language to communicate effectively with intellectuals, activists and the masses (Fals Borda 1974, 4). The most significant of these was a technique called systematic devolution (*devolución sistemática*), which consisted of 'returning the results of the research to these key sectors or groups with a view to achieving greater clarity and effectiveness in their action' (Bonilla et al. 1972, 45). As Rappaport (2020, 93) has pointed out, rather than 'returning' finished outputs to a passive audience, systematic devolution facilitated 'the creation of educational vehicles geared to their audiences' capabilities and needs' (2020, 133), including graphic stories, pamphlets and puppet shows.

From a pastoral perspective, engaged praxis departed from the traditional approach, which focused on the cult, indoctrination or charitable work. This engaged approach included the creation of ecclesial base communities and biblical circles where people read and interpreted the Bible or formed communal organisations that also helped the participants understand the conditions under which they lived. For Fals Borda, however, it was crucial that social research did not become subordinate to pastoral ends. On the role of the churches in setting out the early stages of the research agenda, Fals Borda wrote that 'the blessing of the church opens doors and destroys cultural resistances. Pastors, priests and missionaries have frequently cooperated in this field, but it is important to remember that the aim is the stimulation of self-development and the people's own sense of responsibility' (1974, 66).

Encouraging liberation through the critical recovery of history

Commitment to the struggle of oppressed groups and identification of potential avenues for action also required various techniques to encourage people to pursue desired goals. Chief among the 'techniques of incentivisation' (*incentivación*) was the critical recovery of history (Bonilla et al. 1972, 50–51). By increasing historical awareness and mobilising wider support for the peasants' struggle for land, critical recovery of history was seen as the means to bridge the gap between research and action. This technique brought together researchers and cadres to carry out historical analysis, giving attention to life stories, communal enterprises, structures or institutions of self-governance or resistance in the past, which could be reactivated in class struggles of the present (Fals Borda 1974, 66). The medium to disseminate this new knowledge also differed from traditional outputs. Fals Borda and his associates produced, for example, a series of graphic stories seeking to activate the collective memory of a community. In this way, critical recovery was intended to help increase the agency of the community while allowing the researcher to 'begin his work at the real level of the political awareness of the people, and not at his own' (1974, 66).

The technique of the critical recovery of history allowed La Rosca to retrieve narratives that belonged to the Christian history of salvation, that is, those of the Old and New Testaments as seen from the perspective of liberation. In stark contrast to the Christ of colonial times, liberation theology rediscovered the praxis of Jesus and the prophets whose words and deeds no longer served or justified the vested interests of the groups in power (Berryman 1987, 28; Gutiérrez 1998 [1973], 12). One of La Rosca's graphic brochures, *Escucha Cristiano*, merits particular attention in this regard. Derived from La Rosca's research project into the political conservatism of Protestantism in Latin America led by Salazar and discussed previously, it displays theological-political content with a view to promoting ecumenical liberating praxis among traditionally conservative evangelical groups. Contrasting images of opulent lifestyles with the plight of the poor, *Escucha Cristiano* uses biblical quotations to criticise believers' disregard for social injustice and inequality. These pamphlets, as Rappaport points out (2020, 64), depart from the research report that describes the empirical context and elaborate their graphic narrative based on biblical exegesis, a method commonly used by ecclesial base communities and inspired by liberation theology and by Marxism.[13]

In 1975 La Rosca was legally closed after prolonged conflict with the Maoist left and severe political and ideological divisions within the National Peasant Association (*Asociación Nacional de Usuarios Campesinos*, ANUC). Fals Borda's refusal to establish his own political movement, or to side with either the official line or the radical left of the ANUC, forced him temporarily to abandon his activities in the region (Parra 1983; Zamosc 2009 [1987]), before transforming La Rosca into Fundarco, an organisation primarily concerned with research (Rappaport 2017).

PAR and liberation theology: epistemological differences and common challenges

Thus far, this chapter has examined three stages of Fals Borda's intellectual journey: that of the analyst of political violence in Colombia, of the theorist in search of a *subversive* framework for sociological analysis, and that of the militant researcher who sought to put into practice his own radical sociological ideas.

In the face of the widespread emergence of violent revolutionary movements fighting against exclusion and domination, Goulet defined the late 1960s as the period when many Latin American intellectuals fought their battles around 'conflicting loyalties' (1974). Similarly, he points out, Fals Borda faced three crucial options: 'that of the detached scholar versus the active revolutionary intellectual; that of the institutionally successful professional versus the marginalised outcast; that of the "marker of history" versus the Christian witness to transcendence' (1974, 53). Bringing together three different aspects of Fals Borda's work, this chapter has highlighted that his radical ideas and activism were much less the result of his abandoning the functionalist framework of analysis than a consequence of the vision of social justice that had led him to break the silence surrounding *la Violencia*.

Along the same lines, this chapter has indicated that Fals Borda's engagement with the struggle of the poor designated both a field of action and an epistemological crossroads at which theologians, social scientists, educators and activists converged. Echoing Gutiérrez's (1973, xxiii) theological perspective, according to which commitment to the poor was the 'first act' of the praxis of liberation, the founding act of La Rosca stated that its aim was 'to make of the very politically engaged action with the landless (or militancy) a scientific experience' (ACH-UN, FOFB. IAP, La Rosca, 248).

Looking at the origins of PAR, this chapter has examined a series of overlapping concerns, both conceptual and methodological, between engaged social researchers, activists and theologians. Nonetheless, there are important differences between PAR and liberation theology, as well as common challenges.

As one may imagine, the main difference between social science and theology is of an epistemological nature; that is, the way questions such as what is understood by knowledge, how it is acquired, and how it is justified, are addressed. For all its contributions to validate and legitimise the knowledge-creating capacity of people outside traditional models and institutions (Díaz-Arévalo 2022), PAR, as most approaches within the participatory paradigm, belongs to the sphere of the scientific paradigm, in which knowledge is gained through the process of data collection, empirical verification and analysis. As indicated earlier, Fals Borda's search for methodological approaches to transform reality were meant to validate action as a *locus* of scientific knowledge production, and not only as the means to support a political struggle.

The *modus cogitans* of liberation theology is instead grounded upon religious epistemology and, hence, mediated through religious notions of social practice. By looking through the epistemological lens of the poor, liberation theology departed from the classical models of theological production, helping to create an alternative way of doing theology within the Christian tradition (Boff 1989). Lamola, however, contests the assumption that this represented a materialist-transformative epistemological break, and goes even further by questioning the possibility of liberation theology becoming a theoretical tool for socio-political transformation (2018). Given its commitments to metaphysics, ecclesiastical orthodoxy and fidelity to biblical reflection, liberation theology's concept of orthopraxis, Lamola argues, results in a mystification of historical reality (2018, 2). For others, liberation theology's concern with human suffering and social injustice represents a novel framework for theological analysis. However, as Alberto Parra has pointed out, Gutiérrez's liberation theology's singular merit is not the inclusion of 'new topics' for theological reflection but 'a new way of doing theology whose principle, means and end is the praxis of liberation' (2021, 58 and 228). Such an innovation spread beyond Latin America and Roman Catholicism, giving way, for instance, to Black theologies of liberation and Islamic liberation theology, or influencing the emergence of other critical theologies such as feminist and eco-theology (Guardado 2022).

The widespread legacies of both militant action research and liberation theology suggest that a good way to conclude this chapter is by pointing to a challenge that both PAR and liberation theology, each within their own epistemological spheres, have faced since their origins: the participation of the marginalised.

Looking at the links between liberation theology and PAR, Girardi recalls that liberation theology's option for the poor was to be only an initial stage, whereby the Christian community should commit to a moral and intellectual conversion; that is, to promote the full realisation of the people as the subject of theology (2012). 'Ultimately, we will only have an authentic Liberation', Girardi states, 'when [the oppressed themselves] become the protagonists of theological reflection and research' (2012, 5) and the role of specialists be that of stimulating and promoting their initiatives.

The challenge to liberation theology was not simply to create more inclusive hermeneutical communities but to contribute to the genuine participation of those traditionally marginalised and excluded from theological elaboration. This meant nothing less than critically analysing and transforming the *docente-discente* divide on which the churches had established their prerogative to teach, preach and indoctrinate. For Presbyterian theologian Richard Shaull, recognising the hermeneutical privilege of the poor is the task of a new generation of liberation theologians (Barreto 2004). They do not want simply 'to be with the poor and do theology for them', Shaull argues: 'instead, they wanted theology to rise from the poor themselves' (cited in Barreto 2004, 169). In order to take up this task, one would have to take into account the socio-historical analysis of the development of liberation theology and its influence on contemporary critical thinking within and beyond the theological realm.

The history of PAR has been beset by similar concerns. As argued in the introduction, PAR developed out of Fals Borda's militant research and hence its evolution was conditioned by a conflictive context that demanded radical socio-political action. Retrospectively examining his own engaged (value-oriented) sociology, Fals Borda pointed out that the relation between research and action depended very much on the ability of the conscientious researcher and committed cadres to 'work at the level of political consciousness of the masses to successively bring them to "good sense" and revolutionary class consciousness' (Fals Borda 1979, 46). Alfredo Molano, one of La Rosca's close collaborators, thus stated that militant research was 'a politicized version of participant observation [. . .] a form of "profane evangelisation"' (ACH-UN, FOFB. IAP, Rosca, 208), while others have stressed that the implementation of techniques of militant research, such as the analysis of class struggle and the ideological formation of revolutionary cadres, were not immune to reproducing subject–object asymmetries (Poggi 2015; Rivera Cusicanqui 1987, 51; Sousa Santos 2018, 262). However, 'engagement', which was much more a watchword of the researcher's commitment to the peasant struggle than a methodological guide, served as a first step towards rejecting the traditional distinction between 'observers of the process' and 'people under observation (as in a laboratory)' to start seeing them both as 'thinking and acting subjects within the research task' (Fals Borda 1974, 65).

The popularisation of PAR in the 1980s and 1990s and its use, misuse and abuse by development organisations and donors sparked radical criticism of PAR as instrumental, co-opted and trendy (Cooke and Kothari 2001). However, looking at the guiding principles of Fals Borda's militant research and the techniques tried in the field, it is possible to discern the germ of the three ontological bases that later came to define PAR: a method of social research, an educational act, and a means of taking transformative action (Hall 1975, 1982). Drawing on these pillars, and with an emphasis on participation, Fals Borda redefined the methodological approach of his action research, laying the basis for what became known as PAR: (1) collective and dialogical research through traditional ethnographic techniques as well as art-based approaches including graphic stories, puppet shows and drama; (2) critical recovery of history through exercises of collective memory and analysis of *archivos de baúl* (kitchen archives); (3) valuing and fostering local culture to promote action and participation; (4) co-production and multi-level dissemination of knowledge made accessible through different formats to local communities, organisations and researchers; and (5) systematic devolution that facilitates what Swantz (1975, 45) calls a 'two-way educative communication'. Rather than a fixed set of methodological techniques, these also operate as epistemological principles which aim to challenge the hegemonical distinction between researched and researcher and hence break with the monopoly of knowledge (Díaz-Arévalo and Ruiz-Galvan 2024).

For all the epistemological differences in the ways theological knowledge and social knowledge are produced and validated, the common historical grounds of PAR and liberation theology reminds us that *praxis*, understood as the coherence between knowing, saying and doing (Parra 2021) is the crossroads at which efforts to support people's own struggles through collectively self-deliberated action converge.

Notes

1. Drawing almost exclusively on Fals Borda's *Ciencia propia y colonialismo intelectual* (1970), a book written before his engagement with the peasant movement, Sousa Santos argues that: 'Fals Borda distinguishes between participant-observation, observation-intervention, and observation-insertion, the last one corresponding to PAR' (2018, 331). Sousa Santos's (2018, 247–67) account of Fals

Borda's pioneering work paradoxically presents PAR as synonymous with a technique that Fals Borda himself described as outdated and surpassed by his own experience in the field and theoretical elaborations on more mature ideas on action research (1979).

2. President Alberto Lleras stated in his speech on the day he took office: 'We saw with amazement how there had been a reserve of savagery in our people which defied entire centuries of Christian preaching, of civil order, and of advanced communal existence' (in Fals Borda 1964, 28).

3. The bulk of the first volume of LVC (Guzmán, Fals Borda and Umaña 2005 [1962]) deals with the antecedents, history and geography of *la Violencia* (part 1) and the socio-anthropological characterisation of the groups in conflict (part 2), and was mostly written by Guzmán. With its comprehensive chronology and painstaking descriptions, these two parts made it a 'book-archive' (Sánchez 2007, 21), which remained the main empirical source for academic research on *la Violencia* until the late 1970s. The third part consists of three chapters, the first discussing the social consequences of *la Violencia*. The second, authored by lawyer Eduardo Umaña, examines what Martz (1975, 304) described as 'the total inadequacy of the Colombian judicial system in dealing with [it]', which explains impunity as one of the main causes of the escalation of political violence. The book closes with Fals Borda's sociological analysis of the phenomenon (399–420).

4. For the functionalist framework, the 'anomalous stage' defines a dialectical process according to which the collapse of a system of values does not occur without a corresponding series of values in predicament or transition (Cfr. Fals Borda 1964, 29). In the Colombian case, Fals Borda argues, this transition was accelerated by the drastic changes that conflict imposed in rural areas. Estimates suggest that the number of self-defence guerrilla fighters – men, women and children, mostly former rural workers – was between 40,000 and 55,000 by 1953. The police and paramilitary squads, which also massively recruited among the rural population, according to Ramsey, numbered no more than 25,000 men (Molano 2015, 26; Ramsey 1981, 206).

5. Elsewhere, I have examined the convergence between Fals Borda's historical dialectic between utopia and subversion (1969, xii) and Benjamin's dialectical image insofar as both carry a sense of urgency, as if they were to rescue a memory in danger of sinking into oblivion – something like the 'tiger's leap into the past', as Benjamin wrote in his Thesis XIV, trying to 'seize a momentary flashing image at the moment of its recognisability' (Benjamin 2006, 390–91).

6. The first three social orders are: (1) the rule of the pre-Colombian group, the Chibchas, and its domination by the Spanish conquest; (2) the three-century seigniorial order with its Hispanic peace, and its partial liberal-democratic transition in the mid-nineteenth century; (3) the seigniorial-bourgeois order after the Conservative hegemony, 1885, and the socialist transition, stemming from the ideology that appeared in Colombia after 1925.

7. According to Fals Borda, 'scholars tend to jump from one stage of historical development to another', without giving systematic information about the factors that influenced the transition between social orders (1969, 4). Within the framework of the sociology of conflict, Fals Borda draws on Mannheim's *Ideology and Utopia* (1960) and Ernest Gellner's *Thought and Change* (1965) in search of a 'master theory' to enable analysis of periods of transition leading to or preventing the emergence of new social orders in Colombian history. Following Gellner's socio-historical approach, Fals Borda seeks to understand how hegemonic power is eroded by collective endeavours in Colombia, to which end he considers four components: social values, social norms, social organisation and techniques. The process undermining the old order is 'subversion': a condition reflecting the internal incongruities of the social order recognised during a specified historical period in the light of new, more highly valued goals.

8. Fals Borda traces the origins of the concept *subvertere* as synonymous with violent and destructive actions back to Gaius Sallust's Catilinarian Conspiracy (circa 44–40 BC). Sallust, an aristocrat accused of corruption, described Catiline (who attempted to overthrow the power of the aristocratic Senate) as a deliberate foe of law, order and morality, which allows Fals Borda to argue that this definition, introduced in Western dictionaries, ignores genuine cases of subversion, the promoters of which have over time been recognised as heroes or even saints, especially in Jewish and Christian cultures. As Rev. Castillo-Cárdenas wrote to Fals Borda, the subversion, led by Moses and legitimised by Jehovah himself against the tyranny of the Pharaohs, and the prophetic voices against injustice and oppression in the Old Testament are the backbone of the Judeo-Christian tradition (ACH-UN, FOFB. Subversión, 63). Along these lines, Fals Borda questioned the medieval perception which associated subversion with evil or heresy, as was seen at the trials of advocates of 'social equality and freedom of thought', such as Jan Hus (1415) and Thomas Münzer (1525) (ACH-UN, FOFB. Subversión, 47–51). Ironically, Fals Borda (ACH-UN, FOFB. Subversión, 82) noted, in the Latin American republics, which were established after radical subversions, those who challenge the social order are considered anti-social, no matter how just their causes are.

9. The rebel groups were the *Movimiento Revolucionario Liberal* (MRL), founded by Alfonso Lopez Michelsen, son of President Alfonso Lopez Pumarejo, and himself later president from 1974 to 1978, and *El Grupo de La Ceja*, whom Fals Borda had contacted to offer his intellectual support. Fals Borda's attempts to liaise with a new politically dissident movement within the Liberal Party soon met with disappointment. The La Ceja group disintegrated and the MRL's dissidence was revealed to be a strategic move designed to channel popular frustration, and hence it served to prevent many liberals dissatisfied with the National Front from abandoning the party (*El Espectador* 11 May 1965).

10. Camilo Torres, 'Message to Communists', in Camilo Torres (1971, 371).

11. The group's second meeting in the city-port of Buenaventura was followed by the Golconda Declaration (1968), which reflected on the practical implications for the Colombian Church of the official declaration issued by the Conference of the Latin American Bishops that had been just celebrated in Medellín and inaugurated by Pope Paul VI. Golconda's declaration echoed the Conference's conclusions regarding the need for a Christian theology grounded in critical analysis of the socio-political situation of the region. But the fact that the Colombian hierarchy had delivered their own document rejecting the Conference's final document resulted in the condemnation of Golconda's declaration and, soon after, of the group itself, which was seen as an instrument of Marxist infiltration in the country (Funk 1972, 85).

12. Cintya White, co-founder of the NCSDP, recalled that the concept of self-development entailed that the poor were the real experts of their own reality and knew how to solve their problems: 'They might need financial and expert help but they should remain in control of the solutions' (in Moreno 2017, 144).

13. Rappaport focuses on the experimental nature of the pamphlets and analyses the level of epistemological control taken by the participants over the process of production. *Escucha Cristiano*, she argues, provides us with a good example of early action research methodological experimentation: '[it] is not research in any standard sense of the word, although it constituted research in the [participants'] new understanding of the investigative process' (2020, 64). Poggi, who looks at this graphic story with a focus on the content and use of the material, sees it as a partisan ideological instrument that contributed to reproducing the subject–object asymmetry (2015, 76).

References

Alvez, Rubem. 'Protestantism in Latin America: Its Ideological Function and Utopian Possibilities', *The Ecumenical Review* 22, no. 1 (1970): 1–15.

Andrade, Vicente. 'Quién es responsable de la tragedia de Camilo Torres', *Revista Javeriana* 65 (1966): 177–81.

Archives of the Fondo Orlando Fals Borda. Archivo Central e Histórico de la Universidad Nacional de Colombia, Bogotá (ACH-UN, FOFB).

Barreto, Raimundo. 'Understanding Richard Shaull's Third Conversion: Encountering Pentecostalism among the Poor', *Koinonia* 16 (2004): 161–75.

Benjamin, Walter. 'Theses on the Concept of History'. In *Selected Writings, Volume 4: 1938–1940*, edited by Howard Eiland and Michael W. Jennings, 389–400. Cambridge, MA: Harvard University Press, 2006.

Berryman, Phillip. *Liberation Theology*. Philadelphia: Temple University Press, 1987.

Boff, Leonardo. 'The Originality of the Liberation Theology'. In *The Future of Liberation Theology: Essays in Honour of Gustavo Gutierrez*, edited by Marc H. Ellis and Otto Maduro, 38–48. Maryknoll: Orbis, 1989.

Bonilla, Víctor Daniel, Gonzalo Castillo, Orlando Fals Borda and Augusto Libreros. *Causa popular, ciencia popular*. Bogotá: Publicaciones de La Rosa, 1972.

Bradstock, Andrew, and Christopher Rowland, eds. *Radical Christian Writings*. Oxford: Blackwell Publishers, 2002.

Broderick, Walter. *Camilo Torres: A Biography of the Priest-Guerrillero*. New York: Doubleday & Company, 1975.

Caycedo, Olga de. *El Padre Camilo Torres o la crisis de la madurez de América*. Barcelona: Ediciones Aura, 1972.

Cendales, Lola, Fernando Torres and Alfonso Torres. 'One Sows the Seed, But It Has Its Own Dynamics: An Interview with Orlando Fals Borda', *International Journal of Action Research* 1, no. 1 (2005): 9–42.

Centro de Documentación Regional 'Orlando Fals Borda', Montería, Colombia.

Cervetto, Carina. 'La Juventud Obrera Católica dentro de las instituciones católicas laicas'. *XVI Jornadas Interescuelas/Departamentos de Historia*. Departamento de Historia. Facultad Humanidades. Universidad Nacional de Mar del Plata, Mar del Plata, 2017.

César, Waldo A., Richard Shaull, Orlando Fals Borda and Beatriz de Souza. *Protestantismo e imperialismo na América Latina*. Petrópolis: Vozes, 1968.

Cooke, Bill and Kothari Uma. *Participation: The New Tyranny?* New York: Zed Books, 2001.
Díaz-Arévalo, Juan Mario. 'Orlando Fals Borda or The Ethics of Subversion: Towards a Critique of Ideology of Political Violence in Colombia, 1948–1974'. PhD thesis, University of Roehampton, London, 2017.
Díaz-Arévalo, Juan Mario. 'Orlando Fals Borda, 1948–1958: The Making of an Intellectual', *Revista de Estudios Colombianos* 52 (2018): 1–10.
Díaz-Arévalo, Juan Mario. 'In Search of the Ontology of Participation in Participatory Action Research: Orlando Fals Borda's Participatory Turn, 1977–1980', *Action Research* 20, no. 4 (2022): 343–62. doi:10.1177/14767503221103571.
Díaz-Arévalo, Juan Mario. 'Re-thinking the Role of Religion in Orlando Fals Borda's Ideas of Social Change, 1948–1970', *Latin American Perspectives* 49, no. 4 (2022a): 172–90.
Díaz-Arévalo, Juan Mario and Adriel Ruiz-Galvan. 'Participatory (Action) and Community-based Research'. In *The Routledge Handbook of Conflict and Peace Communication*, edited by Stacey Connaughton and Stefanie Pukallus, 43–53. Abingdon: Routledge, 2024.
Fals Borda, Orlando. 'The Role of Violence in the Break with Traditionalism: The Colombian Case'. In *The Sociologists, the Policy-Makers and the Public: The Sociology of Development. Volume 3*, 21–31. Washington, DC: International Sociological Association, 1964.
Fals Borda, Orlando. *La subversión en Colombia: El cambio social en la historia*. Serie Monografías Sociológicas, no. 24. Bogotá: Departamento de Sociología, Universidad Nacional de Colombia; Tercer Mundo, 1967.
Fals Borda, Orlando. 'The Significance of Guerrilla Movements in Latin America', *Cross Currents* 18, no. 4 (1968): 451–8.
Fals Borda, Orlando. *Subversion and Social Change in Colombia*. Translated by Jacqueline D. Skiles. New York and London: Columbia University Press, 1969.
Fals Borda, Orlando. *Ciencia propia y colonialismo intelectual*. Mexico: Nuestro Tiempo, 1970.
Fals Borda, Orlando. 'Marginality and Revolution in Latin America: 1809–1969', *Studies in Comparative International Development* 6, no. 4 (1970/71): 63–89.
Fals Borda, Orlando. *Ciencia propia y colonialismo intelectual*. Mexico: Nuestro Tiempo & Oveja Negra, 1971.
Fals Borda, Orlando. 'Reflexiones sobre la aplicación del método de Estudio-Acción en Colombia', *Revista Mexicana de Sociología* 35, no. 1 (1973): 49–62.

Fals Borda, Orlando. 'The Social Sciences and the Struggle for Liberation', *The Ecumenical Review* 26, no. 1 (1974): 60–69.

Fals Borda, Orlando, with Augusto Libreros. 'Cuestiones de metodología aplicada a las ciencias sociales'. Draft in ACH-UN, FOFB, 1974a.

Fals Borda, Orlando. 'Investigating Reality in Order to Transform It: The Colombian Experience', *Dialectical Anthropology* 4, no. 1 (1979): 33–55.

Fals Borda, Orlando. *Knowledge and People's Power Lessons with Peasants in Nicaragua, Mexico and Colombia.* New Delhi: Indian Social Institute, 1988.

Fals Borda, Orlando. 'Dogmas, No: An interview with Fals Borda', *Revista Cromos* 3817/18, no. 25 (1991): 12–18.

Fals Borda, Orlando. Speech as the 2007 Martin Diskin Oxfam American Commemorative Conference Speaker of the Latin American Studies Association (LASA), 2013.

Feagin, Joe, Hernán Vera and Kimberly Ducey. *Liberation Sociology.* London and New York: Taylor & Francis Group, 2014.

Freire, Paulo. *Pedagogy of the Oppressed.* New York: Continuum, 2005 [1970].

Funk, Richard Harries. 'Camilo Torres Restrepo and the Christian Left in the Tradition of Colombian Church-State Relations'. PhD thesis, University of Notre Dame, 1972.

Girardi, Giulio. 'Investigación participativa popular y Teología de la Liberación', *Caminos, Revista Cubana de Pensamiento Socioteológico*, 2012.

Goulet, Denis. *A New Moral Order: Studies in Development Ethics and Liberation Theology.* New York: Orbis Books, 1974.

Guardado, Leo. 'After 50 Years, "Liberation Theology" Is Still Reshaping Catholicism and Politics – But What Is It?', *The Conversation*, 2022. https://theconversation.com/after-50-years-liberation-theology-is-still-reshaping-catholicism-and-politics-but-what-is-it-186804#:~:text=Today%2C%20liberation%20theology%27s%20reach%20has,been%20influenced%20by%20liberation%20theology. Accessed 22/11/2024.

Gutiérrez, Francisco, and Juan Carlos Guataquí. 'The Colombian Case: Peace-Making and Power Sharing: The National Front (1958–1974) and New Constitution (1991–2002) experiences'. Conference: Peace and Development Dissemination Conference, Washington, 2009.

Gutiérrez, Gustavo. *Teología de la liberación.* Salamanca: Ediciones Sígueme, 1972 [1971].

Gutiérrez, Gustavo. *A Theology of Liberation: History, Politics, and Salvation*. Rev. ed. Maryknoll, New York: Orbis Books, 1998 [1973].

Guzmán, Germán. *Camilo Torres, el cura guerrillero*. Bogotá: Ediciones Especiales de la Prensa, 1967.

Guzmán, Germán. *Camilo Torres, presencia y destino*. Miami: Book Reprints International, 1967a.

Guzmán, Germán, Orlando Fals Borda and Eduardo Umaña. *La Violencia en Colombia*. Bogotá: Editorial Taurus, 2005 [1962].

Habegger, Norberto. *Camilo Torres, el cura guerrillero*. Argentina: APL Editor, 1967.

Hall, Budd. 'Participatory Research: An Approach for Change', *Convergence* 8, no. 2 (1975): 24–32.

Hall, Budd. 'Breaking the Monopoly of Knowledge: Research Methods, Participation and Development'. In *Creating Knowledge: A Monopoly?*, edited by Budd Hall, Arthur Gillette and Rajesh Tandon, 13–26. New Delhi: ICAE, PRIA, 1982.

Hall, Budd. 'In from the Cold? Reflections on Participatory Research 1970–2005', *Convergence* 38, no. 1 (2005): 5–24.

Hart, John W. 'Topia and Utopia in Colombia and Peru: The Theory and the Practice of Camilo Torres and Gustavo Gutiérrez in their Historical Contexts'. PhD thesis, Union Theological Seminary, New York, 1978.

Jaramillo Marín, Jefferson. 'El libro La Violencia en Colombia (1962–1964). Radiografía emblemática de una época tristemente célebre', *Revista Colombiana de Sociología* 35, no. 2 (2012): 35–64.

Lalive d'Epiney, Christian. 'Pastores Chilenos y apertura hacia el ecumenismo', *Revista Mensaje*, 163 (1967): 478–84.

Lamola, Malesela John. 'Marx, the Praxis of Liberation Theology, and the Bane of Religious Epistemology', *Religions* 9, no. 74 (2018): 1–14. doi:10.3390/rel9030074.

López-Pacheco, Jairo Antonio. 'Orlando Fals Borda: Del cientificismo a la subversión moral', *Ciencia Nueva. Revista de Historia y Política* 1, no. 1 (2017): 170–83.

Lüning, Hildegard. *Sacerdocio y política*. Bogotá: Universidad Nacional de Colombia, 2016 [1969].

Martz, John. *Colombia: A Contemporary Political Survey*. Westport, CT: Greenwood Press, 1975.

McGreevey, William. 'Review of Subversion and Social Change in Colombia, by Fals Borda', *The Hispanic American Historical Review* 50, no. 2 (1970): 392.

Molano, Alfredo. 'Violence and Land Colonization'. In *Violence in Colombia. The Contemporary Crisis in Historical Perspective*, edited by

Charles Bergquist, Ricardo Peñaranda and Gonzalo Sánchez, 195–216. Wilmington, DE: SR Books, 1991.

Molano, Alfredo. 'Fragmentos de la historia del conflicto armado (1920–2010)'. In *Contribución al entendimiento del conflicto armado en Colombia,* edited by Comisión Histórica del Conflicto Armado y sus Víctimas en Colombia. Bogotá: CHCV, 2015.

Moreno, Mónica. 'Orlando Fals Borda: ideas, prácticas y redes, 1950–1972'. PhD thesis, Universidad Nacional de Colombia, Bogotá, 2017.

Munck, Ronaldo. 'José Carlos Mariátegui and Twenty-first-Century Socialism: Recovery and Renewal', *Latin American Perspectives* 49, no. 4 (2022): 13–30.

Parra, Alberto. *'Dicen, pero no hacen': Teología de la acción.* Bogotá: Editorial Pontificia Universidad Javeriana y Univerisdad Loyola, 2021.

Parra, Ernesto. *La investigación-acción en la Costa Atlántica: Evaluación de La Rosca 1972–1974.* Cali: Fundación para la Comunicación Popular, 1983.

Pereira, Alexander. 'Fals Borda: La formación de un intelectual Disórgano', *Anuario Colombiano de Historia Social y de la Cultura* 35 (2008): 375–412.

Pérez-Prieto, Victorino. 'Los orígenes de la Teología de la Liberación en Colombia: Richard Shaull, Camilo Torres, Rafael Ávila, "Golconda", Sacerdotes para América Latina, Cristinos por el Socialismo y Comunidades Eclesiales de Base', *Cuestiones Teológicas* 43, no. 99 (2016): 73–108.

Poggi, Alfredo. 'De lo etnográfico a lo teológico-político: investigación-acción ecuménica de La Rosca en comunidades protestantes de Córdoba, Colombia', *Tabula Rasa* 23 (2015): 59–77.

Ramsey, Russell W. *Guerrilleros y soldados.* Bogotá: Ediciones Tercer Mundo, 1981.

Rappaport, Joanne. 'La Rosca de Investigación y acción social.' In *How the Past Was Used: Historical Cultures, c. 750–2000,* edited by Peter Lambert and Björn Weiler, 231–58. Oxford: Oxford University Press, 2017.

Rappaport, Joanne. *Cowards Don't Make History: Orlando Fals Borda and the Origins of PAR.* Durham, NC: Duke University Press, 2020.

Restrepo, Gabriel. 'Seguir los pasos de Orlando Fals Borda: Religión, música, mundos de la vida y carnaval', *Investigación y Desarrollo* 24, no. 2 (2016): 199–239.

Restrepo, Javier Darío. *La revolución de las sotanas: Golconda 25 años después.* Bogotá: Planeta, 1995.

Rivera Cusicanqui, Silvia. *Política e ideología en el movimiento campesino colombiano: El caso de la ANUC*. Bogotá: CINEP, 1982.

Rivera Cusicanqui, Silvia. 'El potencial epistemológico y teórico de la historia oral: de la lógica instrumental a la descolonización de la historia', *Revista Temas Sociales, IDIS/UMSA* 11 (1987): 49–64.

Sánchez, Gonzalo. 'Los estudios sobre la Violencia: balance y perspectivas'. In *Pasado y presente de la violencia en Colombia*, edited by Gonzalo Sánchez and Ricardo Peñaranda, 17–33. Medellín: La Carreta Editores, IEPRI, 2007.

Santos, Boaventura de Sousa. *The End of the Cognitive Empire: The Coming of Age of Epistemologies of the South*. Durham, NC: Duke University Press, 2018.

Shaull, Richard. *The New Revolutionary Mood in Latin America*. Pennsylvania: Buck Hill Falls, 1962.

Solari, Aldo. 'Algunas reflexiones sobre el problema de los valores, la objetividad y el compromiso en las ciencias sociales', *Revista Colombiana de Sociología* 34, no. 2 (2011): 181–99.

Swantz, Marja Liisa. 'Research as an Educational Tool in Development', *Convergence* 8, no. 2 (1975): 44–52.

Torres, Camilo. *Revolutionary Priest: Complete Writings and Messages*. Edited by John Gerassi. London: Jonathan Cape, 1971.

Torres, Camilo. *Father Camilo Torres Revolutionary Writings*. Edited by Maurice Zeitlin. New York: Harper Colophon Books, 1972.

Villanueva Martínez, Orlando. *Camilo, acción y utopía*. Bogotá: Universidad Nacional de Colombia, 1995.

Zamosc, Leon. *The Agrarian Question and the Peasant Movement in Colombia: Struggles of the National Peasant Association, 1967–1981*. Cambridge: Cambridge University Press, 1986.

Zamosc, León. 'Campesinos y sociólogos: Reflexiones sobre dos experiencias de investigación activa.' In *La investigación-acción participativa. Inicios y desarrollos,* edited by María Cristina Salazar, 85–134. Caracas: Editorial Laboratorio Educativo, 2009 [1987].

Chapter 4

The impact of liberation theology in the Latin American built environment

Fernando Luiz Lara

There is no question that liberation theology has had a huge impact in Latin America. The work of Leonardo Boff, Gustavo Gutiérrez and Juan Luis Segundo, among others, that inspired the 'preferential option for the poor' and the action strategy of the *Comunidades Eclesiais de Base/ Comunidades Eclesiales de Base* (Ecclesial Base Communities) were transformative not only in issues of faith but mostly, and more importantly, in terms of a praxis of empowerment.

One aspect of liberation theology still very much understudied is its influence on architecture and urbanism. For this reason, this chapter looks at a series of initiatives regarding the design and construction of the built environment that were inspired by liberation theology. From the land invasions in Peru in the 1970s to the *Orçamento Participativo* in Brazil in the 1990s, the ideas of liberation theology met those espoused in Paulo Freire's *Pedagogy of the Oppressed* (1968) and changed the way communities organised to improve their dwellings and public spaces. Moreover, I propose that schools of architecture and urbanism such as those found in Valparaíso in Chile and FAU-Santos in Brazil have incorporated the ideas of liberation theology into their design pedagogy. Indeed, dozens of Catholic schools of architecture have student-led design practices that work with impoverished communities as suggested by proponents of liberation theology.

More recently, a wave of design/built collectives (for example, Al Borde in Ecuador, Goma in Brazil, Aqua Alta in Paraguay and Grupo Talca in Chile) have been highly visible throughout Latin America. Although not directly tied to liberation theology, a case can be made that they are following the same concepts that made liberation theology so dangerous to the power structures of the West, including the power structures of architecture.

Participatory processes rising in the 1960s

There is a significant temporal coincidence between liberation theology and participatory design processes around the 1960s. While other chapters of this book elaborate on the roots of liberation theology, as their authors have much deeper knowledge of the movement and the motivations of its proponents within the Catholic Church, I instead focus on what was happening in *architectural* circles.

The idea of participatory design is often associated with self-help and 'architecture without architects' as it reached the public realm in the 1960s in response to the exhaustion of the Modern Movement heterodoxy. In the Global North, those ideas are usually linked to Bernard Rudofsky's MoMA exhibition *Architecture without Architects* of 1964, John F. C. Turner's publications after 1967 and Giancarlo De Carlo's book *An Architecture of Participation* from 1972. Nonetheless, the beginning of the trend can be located in writings by Italian historian Manfredo Tafuri, whose Marxist framework explained architectural design as a peg in the big wheel of capitalism, and, indeed, one which contributed to separating ideas (design) from matter (construction). Later in this chapter, I will discuss this process of abstraction as another stitch binding liberation theology to architecture. However, allow me to point out here that, before elaborating on his Marxist critique of architecture and alienation, Tafuri was a Renaissance scholar who wrote about the roots of the separation between design and construction that facilitates the capitalist sequestering of architecture as a tool for exclusion and territorial control. The architectural establishment on both sides of the Atlantic did not embrace Tafuri's Marxist critique, insisting instead on celebrating form and image as the basis for design, something clearly visible also in Rudofsky's MoMA exhibition. Sociology, economics and politics were pushed aside as variables that should not dictate architectural decisions. This denial – because such factors *do* dictate design decisions whether we like it or not – explains why any attempt to reposition the perceived centrality of the architect in shaping the built environment was resisted and labeled as 'radical'.

Nonetheless, participation would continue influencing many designers, some of whom would in turn become influential in their own right. In the early 1970s Giancarlo De Carlo wrote *An Architecture of Participation*,

Nigel Cross organised a conference on Design Participation and Ralph Erskine completed the Byker Wall complex, all of which strongly promoted participatory design. But, as is well known in architectural circles, this movement was relegated to the periphery of architectural education while the movement for autonomy of form, whose avant-garde was led by then by Peter Eisenman and his journal *Oppositions*, took the day. As De Carlo himself wrote:

> professionals are against participation because it destroys the arcane privileges of specialization, unveils the professional secret, strips bare incompetence, multiplies responsibilities, and converts them from the private into the social. Academic communities are against it because participation nullifies all the schemes on which teaching and research are based. (De Carlo 1980, 79)

Abstraction as a tool for privilege

As a necessary preamble to explain the importance of the present chapter, let us first consider the epistemological underpinnings of architectural design which, of course, emerged simultaneously with architecture as a distinct profession. It is a disciplinary consensus that abstraction is the main component of the modern process of architectural design and students of architecture are taught that the process of design abstraction was developed in the fifteenth and sixteenth centuries. As I will go on to argue, it is no coincidence that the European occupation of the Americas happened at exactly the same time, given that the very process of slicing an object into plan, section and elevation is a process of abstraction, understood here as reduction (Lara 2020; 2021).

To expand on the point: abstraction, as the definition goes, is the quality of dealing with ideas rather than events, or with something that exists only as an idea. The key question here is which facts have been elevated to the realm of ideas and which facts have been discarded in the process? Ultimately, it is my contention that spatial abstraction has been a tool of coloniality and inequality since the world-system took shape in the sixteenth century, and architecture is deeply embedded in this process (Lara 2023). This is to say that modernity was created when we abandoned relational knowledge and adopted a superficial understanding of space (focusing only on the surface) in which the white man is not situated in space but rather has mastery over it, while non-white, non-male and non-human beings are reduced to objects to be plotted and therefore controlled.

Thus, the importance of the task becomes clear. Within architectural pedagogy, we use abstraction to separate our design students from everything they knew before and immerse them in a new set of values, architectural values. Once delinked from any previous spatial relations, our studio pedagogy teaches them to master abstraction, almost always discarding any site context or content in order to manipulate only geometry. Site plans do not register community life. Contours do not tell the history of the land. Plans and sections are arbitrary narratives that force behaviours on people. These are the Janus-faced powers of architecture: it could be used to envision a better world, but 95 percent of the time it is used to reinforce the status quo. If we want to mitigate the erasures embedded in spatial inequality to keep moving toward more inclusive design processes, we need to understand the history of the relationship between design and exclusion. The historical roots of abstraction are intertwined with the historical roots of architectural design, and the Americas played a central role in that development.

Architectural scholarship defines the late fifteenth century as the time in which abstraction took over building practice, defining architecture as a separate discipline altogether. As we are reminded by Dalia Judovitz, 'the scenographic depiction of rationalized space became the impetus for a combined approach to mathematics and philosophy, as figurative science of measure, order, and proportion' (1993, 66). In practical terms, the design techniques of the early Renaissance were optimised to a higher degree of efficiency, giving us the plans, sections and elevations we used until a few decades ago (before the rise of BIM [Building Information Modelling] and fully three-dimensional software capabilities). For most architectural scholars it was Filippo Brunelleschi who achieved this in fifteenth-century Florence, and it was soon to be systematised by Leon Battista Alberti a few decades later. That simplified narrative is once again a Eurocentric construction. Back in the 1970s, Samuel Edgerton showed that Brunelleschi did not invent linear perspective. More accurate would be the understanding that Brunelleschi revisited Ptolemy and 'rediscovered' the technique (see Edgerton 1975). In addition, as discussed by all the latest surveys of architecture (see Ching, Jarzombek and Prakash 2017; James-Chakraborty 2014), the technology of the two-layered dome was used in Islamic mosques centuries before Brunelleschi. The answer to why the Florentine's perspective became so important for Western civilisation was discussed by Edgerton almost fifty years ago: it was developed in parallel to cartographic techniques that allowed Europeans to both cross open oceans and to control territories very far from their homelands. At the heart of those innovations is a new concept of space that is less about Brunelleschi and Alberti and more about the *conquistadores*. Alberti, as explained by Mark Jarzombek, was deeply rooted in medieval thought. His work, so important for us, 'could perhaps be considered a neo-medieval critique of mainstream humanism' (1989, 59). The real change in the concept of space came when the Spanish and Portuguese engaged the Atlantic Ocean and occupied the territories beyond. Patricia Seed reminds us that the Portuguese used points located by observing the skies as both a mapping device and an argument for possession (Seed 1995, 111), while Ricardo Padrón tells us that the new conception of abstract space 'rationalized the known world according to the principles of Euclidean geometry' (Padrón 2004, 32). This process of abstraction allowed the European powers to make the world apprehensible in ways that it had never been before.

As previously discussed, the very process of slicing an object into plan, section and elevation is a process of reduction. By extension, as David Leatherbarrow reminds us, 'abstraction works itself out through a series of filters and distillations – the flat is made flatter, the black blacker. Abstraction tends toward an ideal or an essence' (1987, 9). Ultimately, we discard information in order to be able to manipulate what we consider the essence. But what if the treasure lies in the information discarded? We would never know that we were throwing the baby out with the bath water if we never accepted that there was a baby in the bath. The point here, learned from contemporary scholars who engage Indigenous knowledge in an act of epistemic decolonisation, is that the rise of abstraction in the sixteenth century killed relational processes that we urgently need to bring back to the table.

One of the most cited theories of abstraction in the arts was written by Wilhelm Worringer and uses a scale gradation between abstraction on one end and empathy on the other. According to Anselm Treichler, Worringer's theory of abstraction is:

> a universalist attempt to explain and redefine art history via the opposing poles of the human urge to abstraction and urge to empathy. Empathetic art stands for the happiness that stems from a harmonious relationship with the world, and abstraction stands for mastering *welt angst* or anxiety about the world. Abstraction and empathy form the poles of an all-encompassing spectrum of artistic creation within which forms relate to one another in shifting forms. Therefore, abstraction is not just absolute abstraction; rather it especially reveals itself as a process of abstracting, which in works of art becomes manifest in their charged relationship with nature. (2020, 34)

Following the words of Worringer, then, the important question becomes: are we discarding empathy in the process of distilling the essence or ideal which has been the architectural goal for 500 years?

The geographer Doreen Massey goes some way to answering that question by opening her book *For Space* with a description of the encounter between Moctezuma and Hernán Cortés in Tenochtitlan, some 500 years ago. Massey explains that after the European occupation of the Americas, the idea of space overlaps precisely with the sliding scale hypothesised by Worringer, moving from a deep, relational experience to an abstracted collection of mathematical notations plotted on a flat surface. It is in this context that we should understand Patricia Seed's observation that the Portuguese plotted such a collection of points guided by the sky, not by the territory, and Ricardo Padrón's rediscovery of the notion of the itinerary (in which the narrator is inscribed into the landscape) and its differentiation from modern maps (in which the narrator is removed from the landscape). Read in this way, the geographers Massey, Seed and Padrón join the decolonial theorists Walter Mignolo, Arturo Escobar and Aníbal Quijano in helping us understand that Descartes' *cogito ergo sum* was both a consequence of, and a tool for, the European occupation of the Americas.

For the present discussion, however, the key point is that, in the case of the built and the natural environment, the rise of abstraction as the only possible process of analysis removed any empathy from the design process by removing a relational and situated understanding of space. This dual removal ultimately resulted in a world in which white male *homo sapiens* rule and everything not-white, not-male and, worse, not-*sapiens* should be at their disposal. Nonetheless, while architectural scholarship has scores of books and articles about abstraction, almost all enthusiastically defending it as a core component of design, the vast majority of our scholarship until very recently completely ignored the Atlantic encounter or minimised its role in European developments.[1] This is to say that architectural scholarship has not yet dealt properly with the impact of this encounter.

Participatory processes in Latin American architecture

With a rooted history of exclusion and erasure, Latin American architects have developed in the last fifty years a tradition of participation and activism that, despite some notable successes, has been mostly invisible in the global design scholarship. Despite this omission, the rise of participatory design and construction processes provides a collection of concepts and experiences that could contribute significantly to the crises of ecology and inequality that the world faces today. Regarding the historical development of this trend, however, departing from the Latin American context of the 1960s, I argue that current participatory design processes have their roots in liberation theology and Freire's *Pedagogy of the Oppressed*, but were also influenced by the United Nations Economic Commission for Latin America (*Comisión Económica para América Latina*, CEPAL).[2]

For fourteen years after the end of World War II, Latin American nations were struggling to find a place in the new world order. The proximity to (and the long shadow of) the United States made more difficult any attempt at independent development. The region seemed destined to export raw materials and suffer the political instability of 'banana republics'. In Santiago, Chile, CEPAL has been working since 1948 on analysis and proposals to escape the region's dependency, as theorised two decades later by Enzo Faletto and Fernando Henrique Cardoso (1967). During the same period, in Bogotá, Colombia, the Centro Interamericano de Vivienda y Planeamiento Urbano/Interamerican Center for Housing and Urban Planning (CINVA) was created in 1952 by the Organization of American States with the initiative focused specifically on housing development. Notably, the CINVA was already working with self-help and incremental design as early as 1958. Nonetheless, all of the initiatives above were using developmental tools of the North to 'fix' poverty and underdevelopment in the South. Poverty was perceived as a problem, but the solution proposed would only bring more inequality because development was indeed the cause of such inequality, not a side effect, as Arturo Escobar explained (1995).

The equation experienced further dramatic change on New Year's Day 1959 when dictator Fulgencio Batista fled Havana, accepting the victory of the armed revolutionary Cubans led by Fidel Castro and Ernesto 'Che' Guevara. Unfortunately, the Cuban revolutionary government would soon be pushed into the arms (both the limbs and the war industry) of the Soviet Union, pulling the entire region under the blanket of the Cold War. In response, John F. Kennedy's government proposed the Alliance for Progress and ramped up expenditure in consulting and infrastructure loans to alleviate the urban problems of Latin America (see Gyger 2019; Zoumanas 1986).

In the Anglo-architectural scholarship, British architect John F. C. Turner is credited with elevating self-help and incremental construction to a worthy scholarly topic. Turner arrived in Lima, Peru, in 1957, wrote his first report on housing in 1959, and published his first scholarly article in 1963. In his eight years in Peru, Turner grew from a young architect working for a large international bureaucracy in the developing world to a major reference on self-help and incremental construction processes in the field of architecture and planning. As discussed by Richard Harris, none of those concepts that Turner became famous for were his creations. Some were proposed by Jacob Crane (for example, slums are the solution, not the problem), others by Charles Stokes (for example, slums of hope), and many aspects of his analysis of *barriadas* and *pueblos jóvenes* in Peru were proposed by José Matos Mar and Eduardo Neira (see Gyger 2019). Moreover, all of them were in accordance with Jane Jacobs' classic *Death and Life of Great American Cities* of 1961 in the sense that the modernist *tabula rasa* was creating more despair than improvement. According to Ray Bromley,

> Turner works hit mainstream architecture and anthropology in the United States and other Anglophone countries just as interest in Third World shanty towns was mushrooming. Theirs were not the first studies, or the experiences which formed United Nations, World Bank or Alliance for Progress policy, but they were timely, brief and highly graphic. They supported what seemed a new academic discovery at the time, that the rapidly expanding shanty towns of third world cities were mainly neighborhoods of optimism and progress, rather than festering slums of despair. (2003, 289)

My hypothesis on why Turner became the main reference of self-help for architects is the word 'graphic' as written by Bromley in the previous quote. Turner had the design skills to translate economic and sociological ideas into diagrams and illustrations that resonate with architects, and the connections to publish them in influential journals. An example of that is the fact that architects cite the *Architectural Design* edition of 1963, edited by Turner and entitled 'Dwelling Resources in South America', not the long list of reports and policy papers published by him and so many others. Daniel Kozak adds that John Turner's defence of self-help and incremental construction was instrumental for proponents of postmodernism in the 1970s, such as Charles Jenks, to support the idea that modern architecture was out of sync with contemporary problems (2016).

Less known are the works of Brazilians, Uruguayans and Mexicans in the 1960s and 1970s that were much more participatory in their proposals. In Brazil, Sérgio Ferro, Rodrigo Lefevre and Flávio Império created the group *Arquitetura Nova* in the early 1960s, arguing that architects should be present in the building site, labouring alongside construction workers in order to overcome the alienation brought forward by capitalist specialisation (see Koury 2003). Their work was interrupted by the 1964 military coup in Brazil that sent Lefevre and Ferro into exile, but their influence is still strong in São Paulo, all the way into the twenty-first century. When Ferro theorised their experiences years later, he zeroed in on the relationship between abstraction in the design process and alienation in the Marxist lexicography, two sides of the same process of removing relational knowledge and empathy from the task of building homes (see Ferro 1982). In Mexico, a group of faculty and students launched *Autogobierno* in 1972, proposing to change the way we practice and teach architecture around six points: total knowledge, praxis, architecture to the people, dialogue pedagogy, self-government and self-criticism. For eight years they held studios in which the hierarchy between professor and student and between architect and construction worker was challenged (see Montes 2012). In Uruguay, the housing law of 1968 created a fund to support self-help, sweat-equity initiatives, and in 1972 the Uruguayan Federation of Housing Cooperatives for Mutual Aid (*Federación Uruguaya de Cooperativas de Vivienda por Ayuda Mutua*, FUCVAM) was created to coordinate housing cooperatives around the whole country, building thousands of units for the Uruguayan working class on a highly participatory process of design and construction. All of the above were challenging traditional construction methods but still preserving most design decisions for the trained architect. Nonetheless, any attempt toward a participatory design process, either in the North with De Carlo or Erskine, or in the South with *Arquitetura Nova* or *Autogobierno*, was pushed out of mainstream architectural scholarship and labeled radical for indeed it threatened the fiction of the architect's power to shape the built environment.

More recently, the rise of *colectivos* of architects working with participatory design and participatory construction processes demonstrate how rooted liberation theology and Freire's ideas are in the continent and how they can be instrumental in the twenty-first century.

Liberation theology and Paulo Freire as antidotes to abstraction

Architecture as we know it was born from Leon Battista Alberti's idea of design as something separated from construction. In the Latin languages, the concept of design is expressed by the words *proyecto*, *projeto*, *progetto*, from the Latin *projetare*, meaning to launch forward (in English we were left with projectile, a fancy word for bullet). Before Alberti, architecture was all about how to select the best design based on how we built in the past. After Alberti, architecture became about how we should build in the future. Intellectual concepts now mattered more than construction experience. In a recent publication, I discussed the fact that the rise of architecture as an independent discipline and the European occupation of the Americas are two sides of the same process of modernisation/colonisation of a planet tied together in the sixteenth century as we learn from Walter Mignolo and liberation theology scholar Enrique Dussel (see Lara 2020a). Within this tradition, the *cogito ergo sum* of Descartes has been extensively discussed as the root of both our crisis of inequality (only white men have minds) and ecology (every non-white, non-male is reduced to nature and therefore a resource to be explored), and it, too, is further connected with the epistemology of architectural design.

The act of building used to be a more experiential workshop in which there was, of course, a clear hierarchy, but nonetheless there was plenty of exchange between clients, workers and master builders, soon to be called architects. The growing specialisation of the modernisation processes created a drastic separation among parts of the construction process, reinforcing the narrative that the architect works with his/her mind and everybody else works with their bodies.

Let us depart from the understanding that abstraction, as synthesised by Descartes as the separation between the mind and everything else, lies at the core of the processes of exclusion and erasure that produced the staggering inequalities of the late twentieth century. All non-white, non-male beings were reduced to 'nature' and therefore available for exploitation and abuse. People's lives become data points even under the best intentions of the developmentalist economists of CEPAL and the World Bank (see Escobar 1995). The writings of Enrique Dussel are key here because he is the main link between decolonial theories and liberation theology. In *The Invention of the Americas* (1995), Dussel explained how the world-system as theorised by Aníbal Quijano was a consequence of colonisation, not the other way around. In several books criticising Eurocentrism and the myth of modernity, Dussel elaborated on the modernity/coloniality dichotomy as proposed by himself, Mignolo and Escobar (see Allen and Mendieta 2021). The main point that I take from Dussel, however, is that liberation theology challenged the rule of abstraction by engaging with the concrete, by resorting to empathy. I am no expert in religious studies and have a minimal knowledge of theological theories, but it is clear to me that promising a better life after death is a process of abstraction, while improving your daily life is precisely the opposite. In that sense Paulo Freire did exactly the same with his literacy method: forget the abstract rules of grammar and syntax, and engage the quotidian vocabulary of the hoe and the washbasin. Empathise with your own environment.

Here we have a clear alignment between a participatory architectural practice with liberation theology for both call for a direct engagement with reality, with less mediation from higher authority. I would also like to say that it is difficult to separate the impact of liberation theology from the impact of Paulo Freire's *Pedagogy of the Oppressed* for those very same reasons – in each the relational and contextual realms work as an antidote for abstraction's power system.

Colectivos and the heritage of liberation theology

In the 1970s the Catholic clergy aligned with liberation theology (always a minority within the Church) organised thousands of ecclesial base communities, discussion groups in which passages of the Bible were debated alongside community struggles, politics and the roots of inequality (see Betto 1985). With most of Latin America under dictatorship in the 1970s, the ecclesial base communities used whatever small protection the Church could provide to discuss topics that were brutally repressed in the public realm (see Bustamante 2009).

As noted previously, attempts to develop meaningful participatory design processes, wherever encountered in the world, were deemed to be radical and rejected by the architectural mainstream. Nonetheless, examples of participatory design processes abound throughout the whole South American continent, and very much like their contemporary experiences in the North, they have not been fully researched and brought to light in architectural scholarship yet. However, unlike their Northern relatives, they left a much deeper mark on both the academic and the professional landscape of Latin America.

Examples of participatory design processes abound throughout the whole continent, and very much like their contemporary experiences in the North, they have not been fully researched and brought to light in architectural scholarship yet. Nonetheless, unlike their Northern relatives, they left a much deeper mark on both the academic and the professional landscape of Latin America.

In 1952, fifteen years before liberation theology was properly articulated, the Jesuit priests who run the Universidad Católica de Valparaíso, Chile, decided to add an architecture program to their school and invited architect Alberto Cruz and poet Godofredo Ianni to design a curriculum that became very influential decades later. Their plan for a more meaningful architecture involved the development of poetic sensibilities and an emphasis on the act of building, not on the final result of construction. As analysed briefly by myself and Luis Carranza, and more extensively by Raúl Rispa and colleagues, Doris Reina Bravo, Sony Devabhaktuni and Maxwell Woods, the Valparaíso school focused less on transforming the world at large and more on transforming the world within each designer (see Bravo 2015; Carranza and Lara 2015; Devabhaktuni 2015; González and Nahoum 2011; Rispa, Pérez de Acre and Pérez Oyarzún 2003; Woods 2020). Students built structures at a remote site north of the city called Ritoque, often cannibalising the materials of the previous year's constructions to build their own. The envelope and the final result are less important; what matters is the fact that the students were sawing, hammering, bricklaying and celebrating both their labour and the act of inhabiting it. In several publications from the 1960s and 1970s, issues of Catholic praxis such as 'communion' and 'transcendence' were present (see Woods 2020). The current website of the school has a whole sub-topic of *catolicidad* where those are elaborated.

More research is needed to investigate possible parallels between the Valparaíso pedagogy and liberation theology. Maxwell Woods recently wrote the best analysis of the Valparaíso school pedagogy and has raised more questions than answers regarding their relationship with Catholicism and liberation theology. The use of empathy as an antidote to abstraction is made explicit by Woods in the first paragraph of his book, in his statement that the Valparaíso school 'embrace[d] a poetic foundation for architectural thought and praxis where the poetic is defined as the hospitable discursive space in which to hear the other' (see Woods 2020). It is clear to me that a model of relational engagement as an antidote to abstraction was extremely influential throughout the Americas, from the Rural Studio in Alabama to the Central Valley of Talca, Chile, and dozens of Catholic and Public Universities in between.

Located in the central valley of Chile and catering to the sons and daughters of farm workers, loggers and miners, the Talca school, led by Juan Román Pérez, has one of the most radical pedagogies currently being tested in the world. Inspired by the Valparaíso school experimentations of the 1960s and 1970s where Román himself studied, the Talca school requires that all students build their graduation project in order to claim their diploma (see Uribe Ortiz 2011). You can imagine that they do not design museums or cultural centres; instead, they design and build covered bus stops, platforms for farm-to-market fairs, playgrounds and shaded benches in front of the local health clinic (see Maragaño 2020).

At Talca the students are trained, from the beginning of the studio sequence, to work in groups, cater to the needs of the community and only design what they can actually build. It works with a traditional sequence of four foundation studios in the first two years in which abstraction is certainly the guiding principle. That is balanced in the upper studios with an emphasis on team building and community engagement. In the third year, the students are placed as 'interns' in a team led by someone who is about to graduate. Moving along the vertical sequence in years three, four and five, students are exposed to the whole process: drafting, detailing, specifying, budgeting, revising and fundraising in a sequence of loops that mandates revisions and re-designing. In addition to the holistic processes of design, they also actually saw, sand, nail, weld and assemble the final structure. For five semesters they work for someone else's graduation project. In the tenth studio, they lead the team and have five other students working for them. The result is a school that cares about design, is absolutely rooted in the community, manages to contribute to such a community, and does it all in a very participatory and empowering manner. It may not sound theological, but it is certainly liberating. And, as I have contended throughout this chapter, this focus on relational, situated empathy is one which is shared by liberation theology and participatory architectural design. Indeed, in Latin America, the former unquestionably influenced the latter, albeit in an undercover manner.

Notes

1. New publications dealing with the impact of the American occupation on Renaissance Europe include Kathleen James-Chakraborty (2014), Clare Cardinal-Pett (2015) and Fernando Luiz Lara (2018; 2020; 2020a).

2. In 1984, CEPAL's work expanded to include the countries of the Caribbean, becoming the Economic Commission for Latin America and the Caribbean.

References

Allen, Amy, and Eduardo Mendieta, eds. *Decolonizing Ethics: The Critical Theory of Enrique Dussel*. University Park, PA: Penn State University Press, 2021.

Betto, Frei. 'O que é Comunidade Eclesial de Base' (1985), https://servicioskoinonia.org/biblioteca/pastoral/BettoOQueECEB.pdf. Accessed 12 April 2021.

Bravo, Doris Maria-Reina. 'Adventures on Paper and in Travesía: The School of Valparaíso Visualizes America, 1965–1984'. PhD thesis, University of Texas at Austin, 2015.

Bromley, Ray. 'Peru 1957–1977: How Time and Place Influenced John Turner's Ideas on Housing Policy', *Habitat International* 27, no. 2 (2003): 271–92.

Bustamante, Fabián. 'La participación de las comunidades eclesiales de base (CEBs) en la regeneración del tejido social popular brasileño durante la dictadura militar 1964–1985', *Revista Encrucijada Americana* 3, no. 1 (2009): 177–200.

Cardinal-Pett, Clare. *A History of Architecture and Urbanism in the Americas*. New York: Routledge, 2015.

Carranza, Luis E, and Fernando Luiz Lara, eds. *Modern Architecture in Latin America: Art, Technology, and Utopia*. Austin: University of Texas Press, 2015.

Ching, Francis D. K., Mark Jarzombek and Vikramaditya Prakash. *A Global History of Architecture*, 3rd ed. Hoboken, NJ: Wiley, 2017.

De Carlo, Giancarlo. 'An Architecture of Participation', *Perspecta*, 17 (1980): 74–9.

Devabhaktuni, Sony, Patricia Guaita and Cornelia Tapparelli. *Building Cultures Valparaiso: Pedagogy Practice and Poetry at the Valparaiso School of Architecture and Design*. Lausanne: EPFL Press, 2015.

Dussel, Enrique. *The Invention of the Americas: Eclipse of the Other and the Myth of Modernity*. Translated by Michael D. Barber. New York: Continuum, 1995.

Edgerton, Samuel Y. *The Renaissance Rediscovery of Linear Perspective*. New York: Basic Books, 1975.

Escobar, Arturo. *Encountering Development: The Making and Unmaking of the Third World*. Princeton, NJ: Princeton University Press, 1995.

Ferro, Sérgio. *O Canteiro e o Desenho*. São Paulo: Projetos Editores Associados, 1982.

González, Gustavo, and Benjamín Nahoum. *Escritos sobre los sin tierra urbanos: Causas, propuestas y luchas populares*. Durazno: Edicions Trilce, 2011.

Gyger, Helen. *Improvised Cities: Architecture, Urbanization, and Innovation in Peru*. Pittsburgh: University of Pittsburgh Press, 2019.
James-Chakraborty, Kathleen. *Architecture since 1400*. Minneapolis: University of Minnesota Press, 2014.
Jarzombek, Mark. *On Leon Baptista Alberti: His Literary and Aesthetic Theories*. Cambridge, MA: The MIT Press, 1989.
Judovitz, Dalia. 'Vision, Representation, and Technology in Descartes'. In *Modernity and the Hegemony of Vision*, edited by David Michael Levin, 63–86. Berkeley: University of California Press, 1993.
Koury, Ana Paula. *Grupo Arquitetura Nova. Flávio Império, Rodrigo Lefevre e Sérgio Ferro*. São Paulo: Romano Guerra, 2003.
Kozak, Daniel Matías. 'John FC Turner y el debate sobre la participación popular en la producción de hábitat en América Latina en la cultura arquitectónico-urbanística, 1961–1976', *URBANA: Revista Eletrônica do Centro Interdisciplinar de Estudos sobre a Cidade* 8, no. 3 (2016): 49–68.
Lara, Fernando Luiz. 'Urbis Americana: Thoughts on Our Shared (and Exclusionary) Traditions'. In *Urban Latin America: Images, Words, Flows and the Built Environment*, edited by Bianca Freire-Medeiros and Julia O'Donnel, x–xv. New York: Routledge, 2018.
Lara, Fernando Luiz. 'American Mirror: The Occupation of the "New World" and the Rise of Architecture as We Know It', *The Plan Journal* 5, no. 1 (2020): 71–88.
Lara, Fernando Luiz. 'Towards a Theory of Space for the Americas', *FOLIO – Journal of African Architecture* 2 (2020a): 232–41.
Lara, Fernando Luiz. 'El otro del otro: Cómo las historias canónicas de la arquitectura borraron las Américas', *Anales del Instituto de Arte Americano* 51, no. 1 (2021): 1–14.
Lara, Fernando Luiz. 'Spatial Abstraction as Colonizing Tool'. In *The Routledge Companion to Decolonizing Art History*, edited by Tatiana Flores, Florencia San Martin and Charles Villaseñor Black, 331–41. New York: Routledge, 2023.
Leatherbarrow, David. 'Interpretation and Abstraction in the Architecture of Adolf Loos', *Journal of Architectural Education* 40, no. 4 (1987): 2–9.
Maragaño, Andrés Daniel. 'El arte instalado en la construcción de espacios de aprendizaje. Apuntes sobre proyectos efímeros en la Escuela de Arquitectura de la Universidad de Talca', *Arquitecturas del sur* 38, no. 57 (2020): 38–55.
Montes, J. Víctor Arias. 'Arquitectura autogobierno 40 anos', *Archipiélago* 76 (2012): 58–60.

Padrón, Ricardo. *The Spacious Word: Cartography, Literature, and Empire in Early Modern Spain*. Chicago: University of Chicago Press, 2004.
Rispa, Raúl, Rodrigo Pérez de Arce and Fernando Pérez Oyarzún. *Valparaíso School: Open City Group*. Montreal: McGill-Queen's Press-MQUP, 2003.
Seed, Patricia. *Ceremonies of Possession in Europe's Conquest of the New World, 1492–1640*. Cambridge: Cambridge University Press, 1995.
Treichler, Anselm. 'The Founding of Abstraction, Wilheim Worringer and the Avant-Garde'. In *Iconology of Abstraction*, edited by Krešimir Purgar, 33–47. London: Taylor & Francis, 2020.
Uribe Ortiz, José Luis. 'La Escuela de Arquitectura de la Universidad de Talca: un modelo de educación', *Dearq: Revista de Arquitectura* 9 (2011): 62–73.
Woods, Maxwell. *Politics of the Dunes: Poetry, Architecture, and Coloniality at the Open City*. New York: Berghahn Books, 2020.
Zoumanas, Thomas. 'Containing Castro: Promoting Homeownership in Peru, 1956–61', *Diplomatic History* 10 (1986): 161–81.

Chapter 5

When liberation theology met human rights

Anna Grimaldi

Introduction

Liberationist theologies, philosophies, ethics and practices present a captivating and critical perspective on the Western concept of human rights. This chapter focuses on the encounter between liberation theology and liberal human rights that took place in transnational spheres of opposition to Brazil's military dictatorship of 1964–85. As domestic opposition to authoritarianism brought liberationists into contact with a global network of human rights and solidarity activists, diverse forms of engagement emerged. In dialogue with the work of Mark Engler, I show how political strategies, communication techniques, social networks and group interests came together to shape the ways in which liberation theology interacted with concepts of human rights circulating in Western Europe at the time.

For much of the Western world, the post-war period would have appeared as a time of great hope. The creation of the United Nations (UN) and the Universal Declaration of Human Rights represented the establishment of a common moral commitment to individual freedoms, both political and in terms of enterprise, and grounded the political regime of liberal democracy that united the West against the Soviet Union. Winston Churchill's 1946 'Iron Curtain' speech was followed by the 1947 Truman Doctrine, cementing an alliance between the two world powers. Meanwhile the creation of the CIA, the National Security Council and NATO added US military might to the project.

In theory, the benefits of this new order would also be extended to Latin America. Governments across the region quickly joined the UN, which set up the Economic Commission for Latin America (CEPAL) in 1948 to better understand the specific economic dynamics of the region, while local businessmen and political leaders welcomed the creation of the International Monetary Fund and the World Bank. With promises of import-substituted industrialisation, the diversification of domestic markets, positive relations with the USA and a more prominent position within global trade more broadly, many Latin American nations saw this as a time of continued opportunities to develop and expand state capitalism domestically.

Nevertheless, the freedoms promised by the Western interpretation of democracy and human rights were somewhat conditional. The USA quickly established that Latin America should not continue industrialising but should instead return to the unfavourable position of exporting traditional primary goods. In 1947, the Rio Pact had reasserted the right to interfere militarily in the region, while in 1948 the creation of the Organization of American States (OAS) revealed interest in keeping US–Latin American disputes outside the reach of the UN. Yet through the establishment of new dependences, namely imported technologies and other foreign investments, Latin American countries diversified their economies and exports. By the 1960s, Latin America was seeing significant growth in manufactured exports, as well as good growth in GDP and average income per capita, even if the terms of trade were in decline (Ffrench-Davis, Muñoz and Gabriel Palma 1995, 159–60, 180; see also Furtado 1970).

All the while, Latin American populations were growing at the fastest rate in the world (Merrick 1995, 3). Over the following decades, migration into the region, as well as from rural to urban areas, saw the vast expansion of capital cities and, with it, growing levels of inequality. While between the 1960s and mid-1970s real incomes rose across the board, income concentration grew for top earners, worsening inequality (de Oliveira and Roberts 1995, 294). Cities also saw the growth of shantytowns and proprietary trade and production as a major part of the economy, leaving huge sectors of society to fall to the wayside of any benefits created by economic growth (1995, 277). But the 1960s also brought with it centralised efforts to increase levels of education, public employment and healthcare accessibility, among other things, to meet the demands of the growing concentration of people in cities (1995, 284–5; Merrick 1995, 12, 43). With greater access to schools, hospitals and work, absolute poverty declined, life expectancy rose and birth rates increased. Simultaneously, however, tensions arose between growing numbers of waged labourers and their bosses, with mass strikes becoming more intense and sometimes violent.

In light of the growing conflicts between impoverished masses, waged labourers and the interests of global capitalist trade, the USA feared that wider Latin America might become a breeding ground for 'communism', or another Cuba. Latin America had already been designated a region of priority in the Cold War context in 1954, when a CIA-backed military coup deposed Guatemalan President Jacobo Árbenz. Over the following decades, to varying degrees, this model would be replicated across several other Latin American states. Parallel to these covert interventions, the USA also proposed a number of development aid projects to pacify demands for greater social and economic equality. The famous 1961 Alliance for Progress sought to facilitate greater economic cooperation in the region by setting up infrastructures of technological dependence under the guise of liberal development and democratic values (Taffet 2007). Authoritarianism, local elite interests and liberal development therefore came to depend on one another to sustain capitalist expansion in Latin America.

Proponents of a critical interpretation of the Western model included prominent scholars, intellectuals, politicians and artists, as well as unions, student bodies and various Christian organisations, including more radical activists who took up arms (Marchesi 2018). The potential alliance between liberationist Christians and militants posed a particular threat to Catholic conservatives. From the 1960s, a time when Latin America comprised 35 per cent of the world's Catholic population (Dussel 1995, 549), conservative Catholics feared 'a trend away from church orthodoxy toward a materiality that many felt was inappropriate', and denounced the practice of social critique or Marxist economic analysis by members of the Church hierarchy (Nagle 1999, 466–7; see also Dussel 1995, 552). Such ideas and practices spread to rural, Indigenous and other marginal communities with the growing number of ecclesial base communities (or CEBs, *Comunidade Eclesial de Base* in Portuguese), which by the 1980s had reached around 100,000 in Brazil. CEBs were part of a grassroots movement made up of various 'pastoral agents', who regularly visited mostly vulnerable communities to facilitate collective reflections and discussions and share ways of thinking (Mainwaring 1987). To carry out these social and pedagogical tasks, CEBs drew from liberation theology and critical pedagogies, particularly Paulo Freire's *Pedagogy of the Oppressed* (1967).

In 1968, the Second Latin American Episcopal Conference (*Consejo Episcopal Latinoamericano y Caribeño*, CELAM) in Medellín controversially institutionalised a commitment to the poor and oppressed, a milestone in the broader rupture in the Catholic Church in Latin America. Clergy and Catholic laity across the region, concerned with social justice and equality, interpreted scripture to shed light on the human suffering they witnessed around them, integrating Marxist concepts to critique the 'structures of power and wealth that exploited the oppressed' (Dussel 1995, 551). Liberationists also found an opportunity in recent developments in Rome, where reforms of the Second Vatican Council (1962–5) provided justification for engaging marginalised communities and addressing social injustice.

Brazil's liberation theology and transnational human rights

The fundamental tension between liberation theology and Western human rights emerges from their opposing interpretations of the ongoing marginalisation, poverty and hunger in Latin America during the second half of the twentieth century. A key incompatibility lies in the universalist assumptions encoded in the 1948 Universal Declaration of Human Rights. For liberationists, this particularly hegemonic language of human rights 'is so universal that it masks and justifies the implicit domination and injustice behind it' (Adiprasetya 2013, 167). The prioritisation of individual political and economic freedoms over collective bargaining and public goods was seen as another contradiction. The complicity and impunity of multinational corporations and human rights violations during the Brazilian dictatorship only evidences this further (Filho 2022). When Latin American workers fought back against the bosses of the foreign companies and multinationals for which they worked, or on the rarer occasion that a government might propose reforms in their favour, foreign, often US, officials would decry the violation of individual and property rights to encourage state repression. The dictatorial regimes dealt with this predominantly through infiltrating and replacing union leadership with agents of the regime, arresting, torturing or disappearing union activists and generally repressing strike action with violence (Moreira Alves 1985, 46–7, 127–8). This was incompatible with what liberationists understood to be the problem of Latin America: inequality. If individual rights are universal, in other words, if they are to be distributed evenly, the structures that underpin inequality will remain undisturbed. The liberationist 'preference for the poor' instead begins on the premise that inequality can only be addressed through solidarity, which requires some to renounce or forfeit their own rights and privileges for the benefit of those who need them more.

Drawing from key publications of the period, Mark Engler's 'Toward the "Rights of the Poor"' (2000) provides an excellent analysis of liberationists' evolving relationship with Western human rights. Engler conceptualises the fundamental contention between Latin American liberationists and Western human rights through 'four dangers'. First, 'human rights language does not provide the conceptual tools with which one could even understand oppression in institutional, rather than individual terms' (2000, 346). Second, therefore, human rights language condones oppression by acclaiming the capitalist world as a model for global order. Third, human rights can provide the bases (in some cases, legally) for condemning genuine attempts to fight back against oppression – here we can refer back to the de-legitimisation of collective bargaining and public protest, which under the authoritarian regimes of the era were met with heavy repression, often under the pretext of defending property and other rights. The fourth and final danger is the fact that, being rooted in the historical trajectories and moral and philosophical reference points of the Global North, human rights as devised by the UN cannot include the voices of the globally marginalised, rather, it denies agency and frames the oppressed as beneficiaries.

Liberationists saw oppression as the fundamental violation of human dignity. Influenced by Marxism, liberationists interpreted the 'structural sin' of injustice through broader economic structures of exploitation that marginalised large sectors and generated poverty and hardship. Political repression, in this context, served only as a supplementary mechanism that enabled structural violence, exploitation and oppression to be maintained. Examples of political violence such as illegal imprisonment, torture and disappearances were therefore interpreted as further symptoms of the prevailing inhuman structural conditions in Latin America. Western human rights, on the other hand, placed individual political and civil rights at the core of their analysis. One of the most impressive organisations of the period was the human rights advocacy group Amnesty International, which brought about such levels of international public awareness and engagement that they succeeded on multiple occasions to secure the release of specific political prisoners. At the same time, and like many others, Amnesty International took the position not to approach the topic of broader oppressive social and economic structures that might also explain the violation of political rights (Grimaldi 2023), demonstrating the dominance of liberal frameworks.

The problem with Western human rights is also illustrated by contrasting the liberationist remedies to conditions of oppression, which were very different to those promoted by mainstream humanitarian and human rights organisations at the time. Whereas liberationists sought to address poverty and inequality by fostering social awakening and structural change from within, the Western world offered charity, development aid and financial investments or loans. In other words, solutions to oppression were imagined in a way that did not disturb the social structures whose reproduction necessitated that oppression in the first place. This is precisely the rhetoric espoused by the Brazilian military regime of 1964–85. Defenders of the economic model of the regime claimed that mixed economies like their own needed to grant equal opportunities to the state and private enterprise, and this meant accepting foreign investment. As a result, economic and productive growth would trickle down in the form of expanded domestic markets, employment and opportunities for the poor (Costa 1971).

There are a number of reasons this discussion is important. The hegemonic narrative of human rights history has long been told from the Euro- or Western-centric perspective, built on the assumption that human rights are both individual and universal. The global human rights movement of the 1970s generated greater awareness of and attention to human rights abuses in Latin America through diverse activism, advocacy, diplomacy and solidarity (Moyn 2010; Sikkink 2022; Stites Mor 2013), as well as the beginning of an acknowledgement by regional organisations such as the Inter-American Commission on Human Rights (Torelly 2019). Nonetheless, liberal-democratic narratives persist. Pressure to establish group- or identity-based rights has demonstrated the ability of universal human rights to address pressing issues in the Global North, such as gender, ethnicity or health, without disturbing the neoliberal order or de-prioritising individual rights. At the same time, by representing Global South claims about rights through Western concepts uncritically, it claims agency over the development of collective or group-based rights while also excluding critical voices of the Global South that have long offered – both in theory and in practice – alternatives to universalist interpretations of human rights. Liberation theology has critical insights here. In a world of increasing inequality, seeing human rights as rights of the most impoverished and marginalised offers huge potential for rethinking global ethics (see Aldunate 1994). As such, an analysis emerges of liberation theology not simply as a critic of human rights but as itself pioneering the development of a critical, liberationist human rights perspective.

The objective of taking a closer look at the dialogue between Latin American liberation theology and Western human rights is twofold. On the one hand, this chapter seeks to highlight the agency of one of the many underrepresented protagonists of human rights theory and practice through the contribution of Latin America as a region of the Global

South. On the other hand, the chapter provides a more nuanced historical account of how the relationship between liberation theology and the political category of human rights developed. Looking past the more well-known canons of liberation theology literature to understand the liberationist position on Western human rights, I examine transnational spaces of solidarity as a basis for understanding how, through everyday activities and conversations, liberationists were brought into direct contact with definitions and practices of human rights in Western Europe.

Developing the rights of the poor

In his influential essay, Engler proposed an important periodisation of the responses liberation theologians had to human rights in the latter half of the twentieth century. Drawing from the first major works of the late 1960s and early 1970s, Engler notes a distinct lack of engagement with the concept of human rights. In this context of deep intellectual reformation within the radical Latin American Left, key figures such as Gustavo Gutiérrez, Hugo Assmann, José Míguez Bonino and Juan Luis Segundo presented liberationism as a means for creating a 'new society'; one that would break from the capitalist model that had birthed the individualism that marked the Universal Declaration of Human Rights and other Western initiatives. These early years were thus a time for liberation theologians to establish their own position within Latin America's political and ontological landscape, not to generate dialogue with Western human rights.

The second period was one of critique. Within some of the more well-established narratives of human rights history, the later 1970s are sometimes heralded as a turning point for global human rights (Eckel and Moyn 2015). Famously, 1977 was the year that Amnesty International was awarded the Nobel Peace Prize, and US President Jimmy Carter announced human rights as a component of US foreign policy. For liberation theologians, human rights thus became a means through which to critique US imperialism, liberal individualism and the aforementioned 'four dangers', regarding the practical implementation of human rights. A significant marker of this turn was the publication of *Carter y la lógica del imperialismo*, edited by Brazilian theologian Hugo Assmann (1978).

The third phase of Engler's periodisation is marked by a 'shift to appropriation' (2000, 350). This pragmatic turn was concerned not with the inherent elitist biases existing within mainstream conceptualisations of rights but with the potential for human rights as a conceptual framework to render liberationist value systems more readable. It was here that mainstream Latin American liberationists began speaking of marginalised groups' oppression in terms of rights: rights of the poor, rights to equality and other minority rights. By way of example, Engler points to the publication by José Aldunate of *Derechos humanos, derechos de los pobres* (Aldunate 1993). Elsewhere, I have shown that this also manifested in liberationists' appeals to the human rights language of internationally established documents and institutions, such as the UN (Grimaldi 2023, 35, 152).

These are not discrete chronological stages. They blur and overlap in parts, and the 'turns' to rejection, critique and appropriation do not necessarily mean a total overhaul of older ideas and attitudes to human rights. Likewise, it is also important to consider the spaces in which these debates were taking place: established through major published works and national and regional conferences, they represent a particular cohort of voices that emerged as the most prominent. Early debates were inward-looking and reflective; they sought to self-define, self-critique and self-promote. At the same time, many liberationist works were not translated or published in English or French on any significant scale until the early 1970s.

In the undercurrent of these more official and mainstream debates, every day on-the-ground interactions between liberationists, human rights advocates and solidarity activists were also taking place. An important figure often recognised for contributing to the third period (appropriation) was El Salvador's Óscar Romero, who in 1978 was nominated for the Nobel Peace Prize and in 2018 granted sainthood. In particular, Romero is known for disseminating a liberationist defence of human rights which addressed the structural socio-economic inequalities generated by the globalised neoliberal order from the murder of his Jesuit colleague Rutilio Grande, in 1977, until his own assassination in 1980 (Cangemi 2019; Lantigua 2020). Some years before Romero's 1977 turn towards liberation theology, from the early 1960s, exchanges and debates about rights were already taking place between liberationists of the Southern Cone of Latin America, in particular Brazil, and groups in the Global North. Taking a transnational approach, I turn to the specific event of Brazil's military dictatorship of 1964–85, during which some of the first transnational solidarity networks between Latin American groups and supporters in Western Europe were established to oppose the wave of military and authoritarian regimes sweeping across the region.

Drawing on the concepts of structural violence and oppression, liberationist voices from Brazil focused on the global economic order as the root of human suffering and rights violations, arguing that those who bear the brunt of economic policies are the primary victims. Interferences in union leadership and activity, limiting wages and other benefits, and establishing minimum wages that cannot cover the basic costs of living were all common themes discussed in these communications. The agricultural sector also featured regularly with attention drawn to the lack of access to land, seasonal and informal work that leaves farmers in a perpetual situation of precarity and insecurity, illiteracy and ill-health, homelessness, and the lack of even the most basic benefits of formal waged labour. Solidarity and exile publications amalgamated these data and testimonies to inform local audiences. One pamphlet, from 1974, argued that 'behind [the] façade of Brazil's economic growth there lies a situation of under-development and misery amongst a great majority of people', indicating that 'the most basic human rights are being violated and crimes against the individual are the norm' (cited in Grimaldi 2023, 78–9).

These arguments also drew from dependency theory to underline how the global economic order and the relationship between Brazil as a peripheral country and the Global North lay at the core of these individual human rights violations (Cardoso and Faletto 1971). Solidarity materials thus focused on dispelling Brazil's so-called 'economic miracle', highlighting Brazil's low exports vis-à-vis their increasing imports, the unfavourable terms of trade the country accepts, the increasing proportion of profits that either leave the country or contribute to growing domestic inequality, and, more generally, the dependence on US and other foreign firms. In the liberationists' eyes, keeping this system in place not only required the repression of workers through economic and social policy but also made it necessary to silence the opposition by limiting political freedoms and speech through censorship and imprisonment. In this analysis of the country's problems, the dictatorship was not presented as the principal or sole perpetrator of human rights violations through the arrest and torture of political activists, nor were political prisoners seen as the principal victims. Rather, the state was interpreted as a vessel of structural global oppression, through which individual political and civil rights violations were just the tip of the iceberg.

In what follows, I analyse three important ways in which Latin American liberation theology came into contact and dialogue with Western human rights during this time. The first is through what I call the friends and networks of the liberationist mission: Western European Christian clergy and laity sympathetic to and supportive of the cause of Latin American liberation theologians. The second, I refer to as the incidental exile of liberation theology: the fragments and strands of liberation theology that travelled to Western Europe through political exiles. Finally, I emphasise the direct encounter between the well-known Brazilian liberation theologian Dom Hélder Câmara and his public addresses and media appearances in Europe. It was through these channels, I argue, that Latin American liberation theology sat at the table with Western human rights and began a provocative debate about the rights of workers, Indigenous people, the rural and urban poor, and, more broadly, the marginalised and oppressed of the world.

Friends and networks of the liberationist mission

Liberation theology as a school of thought is made up not only of a small central circle of clergymen, intellectuals and academics but also the many individuals and organisations who ensure its theories are turned into practice. In the context of the Brazilian dictatorship, both groups include an international component – friends and networks of the thinkers, writers, leaders and practitioners of liberation theology in Latin America. This section looks at how some of the first networks were formed, as well as some of the ways they began to bring Latin America's liberation theology into contact with Western conceptualisations of human rights.

European Catholic Action of the early twentieth century is widely acknowledged as an important point of reference for many Latin American liberation theologians. Through the concepts of 'see, judge, act', Catholic Action established that its responsibility was to critically and actively engage with the social injustices around them. Catholic Action developed around the issues of child labour, trade unions, and youth and worker movements (Horn 2008). In Brazil, the concept of 'see, judge, act' was instead more relevant to local struggles faced not only by waged workers but by peasants, farmers, informal workers and the urban poor. The Catholic University of Louvain, in Belgium, stands out as one of the most important spaces through which Latin American and European theologians exchanged and shaped each other's ideas. Key figures from the liberationist circle, such as Peru's Gustavo Gutiérrez, Uruguay's Juan Luis Segundo, Colombia's Camilo Torres and Brazil's Clodovis Boff, all studied at Louvain starting in the early 1950s (Berryman 1987; Cleary 1985).

It was in Belgium that these Latin Americans were introduced to the work of organisations such as the *Jeunesse Ouvrière Chrétienne* (JOC) – or Young Christian Workers, in English – a group founded in 1912, which in 1957 became an international organisation. The JOC had an intimate relationship with the University of Louvain, for whom the former vice-rector Cardinal León-Joseph Suenens was a respected advocate (Grimaldi 2023, 15). Following the Brazilian military coup of 1964, which ushered in a dictatorship that would last twenty-one years, Cardinal Suenens and the broader JOC would host some of the continent's first public campaigns against the military regime. While Latin Americans came to Belgium to develop ideas about liberationism, Western European theologians were drawn to Latin America for the same reasons. Well-known activists, such as François Jentel, Jean Cardonnell, Jan Talpe, Charles Antoine and Georges Casalis, made their way to Brazil to carry out missionary work alongside local liberationists, teach in local universities, exchange knowledge with theologians, or even to join local revolutionary resistance movements (Gildea, Mark and Pas 2011; Grimaldi 2023).

All of the above laid the groundwork for some of the first encounters between Latin American liberation theology and Western human rights. European clergymen and representatives of Christian organisations who came up against the Brazilian regime and suffered persecution as a result generated significant attention among European audiences, who saw this repression as an attack on their own national citizens. As a result, the Latin American struggles that European clergymen came to support through missionary work – including those of Indigenous peoples, landless peasants, workers or the urban poor – would gain attention through awareness campaigns as well as national and international press coverage.

While many Brazilians did not explicitly discuss their troubles and struggles in terms of 'human rights', the international network of the JOC certainly did. The JOC had maintained regular correspondence with its Brazilian branch since before the 1964 coup, yet it was during the regime that letters from Brazilian members to the international headquarters of the JOC began to act as records of repression, harassment, torture and disappearance. Correspondence included notes and summaries of JOC meetings in Brazil, as well as transcripts of speeches and motions from important members of the Catholic hierarchy, such as the National Conference of Brazilian Bishops (*Conferência Nacional dos Bispos do Brasil*, the CNBB) or Archbishop Dom Hélder Câmara. Letters also provided detailed evidence on the targeting and arrest of JOC members, as well as the continued social and economic inequalities and other hardships faced by workers and marginalised groups across the country. Through global solidarity activists and advocates of liberationism, therefore, Brazil's human indignities were communicated to international audiences in terms of human rights. By January 1969, the JOC had set in motion a global solidarity campaign for Brazil. As part of the campaign, open letters and press releases were sent to the Brazilian president at the time, General Castelo Branco, as well as the general secretary of the UN, and the general secretary and president of the General Conference of the International Labour Organization (ILO). In these communications, the JOC were careful to 'translate' the situation in Brazil into human rights terms by making direct references to specific resolutions of the UN Economic and Social Council and the ILO, as well as the UN Universal Declaration of Human Rights:

> The International [JOC] declares [. . .] that the awakening of awareness amongst young workers of their inherent dignity as human persons, which enables them to assume responsibility in society towards the ideal of free human beings enjoying various freedoms and freedom from fear and want, is in accordance with the universal declaration of Human Rights.[1]

The JOC was predominantly concerned with the plight of traditional waged labourers in urban and suburban areas. Others worked more explicitly to raise the profile of the urban and rural poor of Brazil, including Indigenous peoples and peasants. Father François Jentel was one such individual. A priest from France, Jentel first arrived in Brazil in 1954 to carry out missionary work with the Tipirapé Indigenous people. The Tipirapé first gained widespread attention among European audiences when, in 1977, Professor Charles Wagley published *Welcome of Tears*, a work based on almost thirty years of anthropological fieldwork with the group.

Jentel first appeared in national news in September 1972, when his missionary work with peasants and Indigenous peoples and their defence against development projects captured the attention of Marcel Niedergang, a journalist for French newspapers *Le Monde* and *France-Soir*, who regularly investigated inequality in Latin America. In May 1973, Jentel was arrested in Brazil and sentenced to ten years' imprisonment for fighting back against illegal harassment taking place in the context of a development project in Araguaia, in the State of Mato Grosso. The dispute was between locals and the Development Company of Araguaia (*Companhia de Desenvolvimento do Araguaia*, CODEARA), a private company that had begun repurposing agricultural land through the illegal sale of public rural and urban landholdings.

Jentel's arrest once again made national headlines, both in *Le Monde* and *La Croix*, two major French newspapers.[2] Sparking the outrage was a public letter addressed to the Brazilian Ambassador in Paris, which was received by *Le Monde* with 1,895 signatures. Given Jentel's intentions to settle the dispute legally and pacifically, the letter argued: 'We therefore do not understand how a case with legal standing can today lead to the condemnation of Father François Jentel, who has only helped the peasants to defend their rights, which until now have been recognised by the Brazilian Constitution'.[3]

As a result of these international outcries and other underground diplomatic negotiations, Jentel was eventually released and returned to

France (Serbin 2001). Not long after, he re-entered Brazil to continue his work, only to be expelled again in 1975. Jentel eventually settled back in France, where he began working with the *Comité de Solidarité France-Brésil*, another organisation that campaigned against a variety of human rights abuses in Brazil.

Jentel and many like him would appear once again in the context of human rights debates in 1974, when the Bertrand Russell Tribunal for Brazil and Latin America investigated human rights violations carried out by states across the region. One of the testimonies they received was from Suzanne Robin, a French woman who had worked with Jentel in the late 1960s. Discussing missionary work in the state of Mato Grosso in central-west Brazil, Robin focused her accusation of human rights violations not only on the arrest and torture of missionary clergymen like Jentel but also on the local victims of large-scale development and modernisation projects.

The Bertrand Russell Tribunal also welcomed the support and input of other European liberationist missionaries who had spent time in Brazil. On the organising committee, for example, was the French Jean Cardonnell, who had been decommissioned as a priest in 1954 following his public criticisms of the Church and their treatment of workers. Cardonnell taught as a professor of theology in Rio de Janeiro, but was forced to leave in 1968. The tribunal committee also included the French liberation theologian Georges Casalis, who had worked with Brazilian liberationist Paulo Freire and spent his final years serving Nicaragua's Sandinista government.

Both the Bertrand Russell Tribunal and the JOC formed part of a broader network of Western European Christian solidarity groups and campaigns, including *Justitia et Paix*, the Christian Worker Movement (MOC), the General Council for the Apostolate of the Laity (CGAL) and the Christian Movement for Peace (MCP), among many others. In 1973, these groups formed a coalition to run the *Non a Brésil Export* campaign. The campaign intended to boycott a Brazilian trade exposition being held in Brussels that November, and it aimed to raise awareness of the situation in Brazil and to draw attention to the compliance of Western European nations in the regime's repression. A motion organised by CGAL as part of the campaign reads as follows:

> The CGAL assembly is concerned with the respect for fundamental human rights in all countries, and the coming organisation, in Brussels, of 'Brazil Export', which aims to present the image of a Brazil that promotes the economic and social development of the people. It is also concerned with numerous testimonies, most notably those of various groups of Brazilian priests, which demonstrate:

That the 'Brazilian Miracle' does not benefit more than a property-owning minority of the people and exerts an ever-growing gap between rich and poor.

That the Brazilian government represses freedoms of political expression and unions and that political assassination and torture are practised in the country.[4]

Human rights in this instance are defined first and foremost in terms of social and economic inequalities, while the human rights violations linked to political repression and state violence are presented second. This framework clearly reflects that of Latin American liberationist analysis, which placed the global economic order – in this case, global trade – at the centre of debates surrounding human dignity and oppression. What in the Western tendency is seen as the fundamental component of rights – individual, civilian and political rights – are here presented as a consequence of said oppression, rather than the primary human rights violation ongoing in Brazil.

Friends and networks of Latin American liberation theology were some of the first to bring liberationism into dialogue with Western human rights. They were also some of the first to campaign on behalf of Brazilians, educating the broader public as to what was going on under the regime. The foundations for this dialogue were set well before the start of Brazil's military dictatorship in 1964 through intellectual and academic exchanges between Latin American and European theologians. In particular, the Catholic University of Louvain in Belgium stood out as an important point of encounter, where Latin American and European liberationists learned of each other's context-specific theories and practices.

These connections and curiosities brought Europeans directly to Brazil, where they worked as missionaries and teachers, experiencing first-hand Latin America's own liberation theology. Individuals like Father François Jentel, who worked with poor and Indigenous communities, drew significant attention to oppression in Brazil. What was perceived as the fundamental human rights component of Jentel's experience for European audiences was his arrest, a clear attack on political rights to freedom of speech, political action and constitutional and legal procedures. However, by drawing attention to Jentel, the international community also raised awareness of the social and economic plight of marginalised Brazilians, whose situation was inseparable from the violation of Jentel's individual rights.

Meanwhile, liberationist groups in Europe, such as the international JOC, rallied their own networks to support their colleagues and friends in

Brazil. Brazilian members of the JOC and the broader Christian community were individually targeted and subject to political repression such as imprisonment and intimidation, which was often justified on the grounds of their so-called 'socialist' or 'communist' project to raise social consciousness and action around inequality. News about these arrests, received through regular correspondence, came accompanied by detailed reports on the social and economic situation of marginalised groups in Brazil. Accordingly, when the JOC staged public protests and information campaigns and wrote open letters to human rights institutions such as the UN or ILO, they presented the violation of social, economic and political rights as inseparable.

This phenomenon was not limited to predominantly liberationist or even Christian groups. As seen through events such as the *Non a Brésil Export* campaign, or the Bertrand Russell Tribunal for Brazil and Latin America, European groups regularly engaged with liberationist conceptual and analytical frameworks to talk about human rights. At a time when political rights were perceived as the most basic and inalienable, the idea that human rights could also be social and economic and that the root of the problem might sit with transnational structures beyond the state represented a significant shift in discourse.

The incidental exile of liberation theology

While local organisations and public media introduced some of the building blocks of Latin American liberationism to European audiences, ideas drawn from Latin American liberation theology also travelled through Brazilian exiles who fled or were expelled by the regime. A critical examination of exile testimonies, interviews and autobiographies has revealed that, like liberation theologians themselves, many of the most politically active opposition to the Brazilian regime struggled with the Western concept of human rights (Grimaldi 2023). Following an initial period of 'rejection', many exiles would begin to appropriate the language of human rights as a way of appealing and relating to European audiences.

Brazilian exiles were well connected and organised; they published, coordinated media campaigns and participated in solidarity events to share testimonies and spread awareness of the situation in Brazil. They used their identities as victims and their experiences of political rights violations, imprisonment and torture to capture the attention of European audiences before relating their experiences to other, less visible victims of oppression and marginalisation. The intersection of exiles' political activism and liberation theology, ethics and philosophy – as analytical and conceptual frameworks – thus provides another transnational space within which Latin American liberation theology entered into debate with Western human rights.

I call this particular encounter 'incidental' because not all Brazilian political exiles and activists were liberationists. The key here lies in the fact that Latin America's liberation theology developed alongside parallel political movements and economic theories with which it shared multiple defining characteristics. Therefore, Latin American liberation theology cannot be understood without considering the ongoing academic movement towards dependency theory, nor the humanist, Marxist-inspired, radical and militant political theories that were also taking shape from the late 1950s. This is what Mario Osorio has called 'Latin American Theory', the combination of dependency theory, theology and philosophy of liberation, and popular pedagogies (Osorio 2009).

What connected Brazilian political activists and liberation theologians was the analytical framework they used to shape political demands and visions for the future, the same framework that understood global inequality as the ultimate violation of human dignity and justice. Beyond these intellectual connections, there were significant overlaps between networks of theologians and political activists, ranging from urban guerrilla groups in Brazil to exile communities in Paris. Brazilian exiles relied on their Catholic networks to settle and assimilate in destination countries, to exchange news with political activists and prisoners back home in Brazil, to connect with local Christian solidarity groups, and to gain access to important platforms such as national newspapers.

One of the most well-known exile publications of the time was the *Frente Brasileira de Informações*, the Brazilian Information Front. Founded in 1969, the bulletin was set up firstly to connect and update Brazilian political exiles on developments back home, and secondly to bypass press censorship and offer an alternative source of news for international audiences unaware of the extent of repression in Brazil. Broadly speaking, the *Frente Brasileira de Informações* was quick to begin using the language of human rights to engage with local audiences, and not only through its publications. The widely dispersed network of exiles also functioned to connect several other advocacy and solidarity groups across the world. This network included, among others, an alumnus of the Catholic University of Louvain, Jan Talpe, who had moved to Brazil in 1965 and become involved in the left-wing Christian group *Ação Popular*.

The *Frente Brasileira de Informações* covered numerous human rights issues. Beyond providing updates on political prisoners, testimonies of torture, disappearances and other forms of state violence exerted on members of the opposition to the regime, the bulletins also presented a more expansive conceptualisation of rights by addressing what liberationists understood as the structural violence of the global economic order. Further, they regularly reported on the regime's treatment of liberationist Catholic priests and laypersons involved in social justice activities, raising additional awareness around many of the groups with which they worked. In this context, *Frente Brasileira de Informações* articles discussed workers, the urban poor, inequality and Indigenous peoples, frequently referencing terms and concepts from international human rights institutions.

Other exiles more explicitly identified as liberationist, such as the Brazilian sculptor Guido Rocha. Rocha, a political exile, disseminated his own liberationist ideas internationally through artistic and cultural production. He had been an active member of the Brazilian Socialist Party, and as a result was first arrested in 1962 – even before the coup – for protesting against the military. He was arrested again in 1969 during one of his exhibitions, where the political nature of his work roused suspicion of subversion. His first attempt to flee Brazil landed him in a Bolivian detention centre for ten days, before he was returned to Brazil. In 1971, he was arrested once again and detained for eight months, during which he was frequently tortured.

'By some sort of irony', recounts Guido Rocha in a pamphlet accompanying one of his exhibitions, 'one of the torturers hid his identity behind the pseudonym "Jesus Christ"'. From then on, Rocha began to create sculptures that depicted the crucifixion of Christ. Interpreting the principles of Brazilian liberation theology, Guido's sculptures were of a Christ that sided with the oppressed: 'From that moment on, all the Christs I make have facial characteristics which simultaneously reflect the expressions of comrades that were murdered or tortured by the police, as well as the faces of poor peasants.'

Their bodies were shaped to resemble the marginalised masses of the country's dry northeastern backlands, while the material they were made from, burned plaster, represented the regime's use of electric shock torture on political prisoners. On the eve of an exhibition of these sculptures, Guido was warned that he was in danger, and so fled once again with his partner, this time for Chile. It was not long after his arrival that the Chilean coup of September 1973 took place, and Guido was captured standing in line to enter the Argentine Embassy before being detained and tortured for another forty days. Connections in Switzerland eventually helped him to secure a special scholarship at the *École des Beaux Artes*, funded by the Canton of Geneva, allowing him to enter the country as a refugee.

In exile in 1975, Guido produced one of his signature sculptures and donated it to the All Africa Council of Churches (AACC) in Nairobi.[5] In July that year, it appeared on a poster produced by the Swiss Committee of Defence for the Political Prisoners of Chile; in September, the image was displayed during a discussion on torture held at the Parish of Saint Germain in Gevera; and in November, a print of the photo was presented to the World Council of Churches as a gesture of gratitude on behalf of refugees helped by the church.

Guido Rocha's work merged the concepts of political human rights with those of marginalisation and oppression in a powerful way. His exile in Switzerland was not planned; his intention had initially been to remain politically active through his work in Brazil, if not Latin America. Ultimately, it was his connection within Christian circles that gained him his safety in Western Europe and allowed him to continue producing and disseminating his work. Importantly, these artworks engaged critically with liberation theology and its mission to side with the poor and oppressed – placing equal emphasis on peasants and political prisoners, thus creating a conversation between liberationist and Western notions of human rights.

Rocha's experience relates to a broader phenomenon of political exile from Brazil, which was the alignment between the political project of opposition to the military dictatorship and the social action being carried out by liberationists. This alignment, intellectual, ideological and practical, manifested in exiles' political activity overseas, such as through the publications of the *Frente Brasileira de Informações*. In this way, news about members of the Church, mostly liberationists, and the plight of Brazil's oppressed were presented alongside reports on human rights violations, including illegal imprisonment, political repression, censorship, torture, disappearances, social and economic inequality, workers' rights and Indigenous rights, among many others.

Dom Hélder Câmara's European tour

The final way in which Latin American liberation theology was brought into contact with Western human rights was through the independent public campaigns of Brazilian liberationists themselves. Within Brazil, liberationists provided support for victims of the regime in a number of ways, ranging from working with marginalised groups, to supporting militant student and guerrilla movements, to lobbying the Catholic Church hierarchy to speak out against the regime (see Dussel 1995; Serbin 2001). Elsewhere, liberationists used their platforms to directly engage a range of European publics. An important figure in this regard was Dom Hélder Câmara, then Archbishop of Olinda and Recife in Brazil. Câmara was well known internationally, regularly speaking to a range of audiences in the Global North to raise awareness about the plight of the underdeveloped world, and to do so in the terms of Latin American liberation theology. Brazil, just one of many victims of global oppression caused by the neoliberal economic order, was often used as an example. Through a speech delivered in Manchester and London in 1969, titled *Violence and Misery*, Câmara introduces the concept of a 'triple violence', made up of internal colonialism, violence from the developed world, and structural violence (Câmara 1969).

The first, internal colonialism, is defined as the violence exerted upon the marginalised masses in order to sustain the wealth of a small, privileged group. As an example, he points to the fact that, at the time of writing, 94 per cent of the country's rural properties were owned by 6 per cent of landowners, leaving smallholders, share-croppers and tenants in a state of misery and even a form of slavery. The second violence is conceptualised in terms of the relationship between the developed and underdeveloped world. Here, Câmara points to the global trade system, foreign policies and overseas aid programmes that were created to suit the needs of the developed world and which perpetuate the situation of underdevelopment of the Third World. Such a system, he explains, prevents poorer nations from owning and using 'what material resources they possess in their own interests and in their own way' (1969, 493). Finally, is structural and legally established violence, which targets democratic social movements and collective actions that attempt to challenge the social, economic and political structures of violence. Câmara points to the liberationist method of 'conscientisation', or *conscientizaçao*, drawn from the pedagogical work of Freire, which seeks to awaken social consciousness and action. Such methods, he points out, are often deemed socialist or communist in nature, and thus subject to the military containment methods supported by US intelligence services.

Neither *Violence and Misery* nor many of Câmara's later public and media addresses focus explicitly on human rights – after all, he is speaking from the position of a Latin American and by drawing from the conceptual framework of humanist liberation theology. In this way, he simultaneously provokes a critique of Western human rights and their contradictions, while also appropriating the terminology as a way of identifying with European audiences. In his words, the victims of this system are considered to be 'sub-human'; they do not have the most basic human rights and dignities, such as access to clothing, food, education, health and welfare. Likewise, the marginalised lack self-determination and the right to develop according to their own needs. The violation of these rights is upheld by the same global economic order that claims to promote human rights:

> Capitalism, despite its championing of the human and individual freedom is egotistic, selfish and cruel. It does not hesitate to crush human beings when profit demands it. Under the banner of saving the free world, it commits terrible atrocities against freedom. It speaks proudly of tradition and family but it does not create the right conditions for workers and small proprietors to rear their families. It makes much of religion when it supports its own interests, but it defies and persecutes it when it fights for the development of the whole man and of all men. In the name of individual initiative, it supports national and international trusts and combines. (Câmara 1969, 493)

Over the following years, Dom Hélder Câmara would continue to use his overseas prestige to disseminate the ideas and practices of Latin American liberation theology, appearing in newspapers, radio programmes, documentaries and conference halls across Western Europe. Within those spheres, he and those who wrote about him would regularly connect the liberationist analysis of global inequality and oppression with mainstream concepts of human rights and development.

The international campaigning of Brazilian liberation theologians was of course not limited to Dom Hélder Câmara. In a later issue of the *New Blackfriars*, a group of Dominican Friars imprisoned in São Paulo published a collective testimony ('Accusation from Prison' 1970). Despite being political prisoners themselves, the focus of their text was on the structural nature of oppression and the problem with dominant methods of addressing it:

> Today we know that the roots of poverty are not natural, and almsgiving, which fails to attack the roots, is a mere palliative. Poverty is conditioned by particular socio-economic and political systems and structures, and charity cannot blink this fact. Today Christian charity will be seen in attempts to change these systems and structures. Love today is political or it is nothing; charity must have a social and political dimension. (Câmara 1969, 495)

In other spheres, Brazilian liberationists made more explicit efforts to dialogue with the language of human rights. The year 1973 was the twenty-fifth anniversary of the Universal Declaration of Human Rights, as well as the tenth anniversary of the Papal encyclical *Pacem in Terris*. To mark the occasion, a group of religious elders from the northeast of Brazil produced a twenty-five-page manifesto titled 'I have heard the cry of my people'. The manifesto was released on 6 May that year and provided a detailed overview of underdevelopment in the northeast of the country. In the tradition of Latin American liberation theology, the text focuses on the most marginalised of society, the poor, the working class, peasants, children and, more specifically, on how these groups suffer the additional oppression of living in the most neglected parts of the country.

To replicate the authority and professionalism of the large international institutions they were attempting to appeal to, the priests and religious elders drew from official statistics and data to support their claims about the human rights situation in Brazil. Discussing the 23 per cent figure of unemployment in the northeast of the country, they cite the fundamental right to work and participate in the economic life of their country. Referring to the 60 per cent level of illiteracy for all persons over the age of five in the region, the document claims a violation of the right to education and professional training. The list of examples goes on, but ultimately the message is that social, economic and political marginalisation and oppression are all violations of fundamental rights.[6]

With this final example, I come full circle to where the chapter began. At the start of the Brazilian regime in 1964, a French priest named Father Charles Antoine moved to Brazil to undertake missionary work as part of a development project with the Second Vatican Council (1962–5). There, he became an active member of the France-Latin America Episcopal Committee (CEFAL) and was involved in the National Conference of Brazilian Bishops (CNBB). When he returned to France in 1971, he created the Diffusion of Information on Latin America (DIAL), the very same news bulletin that printed 'I have heard the cry of my people'.[7] Charles Antoine was a friend of Latin American liberation theology, and the creation of DIAL provided a point of reference for several journalists, human rights organisations and solidarity campaigns for Brazil and wider Latin America. DIAL also provided a platform for the northeastern clergymen and their manifesto as it was sent into exile to add to political resistance taking place in Western Europe, in this case, to the build-up to the *Non a Brésil Export* campaign.

Conclusion

In the major publications and conferences attended by well-known liberation theologians in Latin America, a clear trajectory has emerged. Early works of the late 1960s and early 1970s did not bother to engage with the Western notion of human rights, and when they did, by the later 1970s, it was to critique and set themselves apart from the liberal, individualist tendencies that upheld an oppressive global economic order. It was only later on that liberation theology in Latin America would demonstrate a mainstream attempt to take advantage of the language of human rights to further their own philosophical and ethical missions. By engaging the concept of the 'rights of the poor', liberation theologians could 'bring the principle of "partiality" to bear on the claims to "universality" that they previously found so problematic in human rights' (Engler 2000, 353). Writing twenty years later, McGeorch revisits liberationism's relationship to human rights through the so-called 'Pink Tide' governments of the 1990s and 2000s. He argues that 'Liberation Christianity has chosen to "defend democracy" and "uphold human rights" within the broader narratives of democracy and human rights, without specifying what kind of democracy and human rights it is seeking to defend and uphold, particularly in light of its "option for the poor"' (McGeorch 2020, 11).

The journey across these varying interpretations of rights can be drawn back to the mid-1960s, when, spurred by the Brazilian military dictatorship of 1964, transnational spaces of solidarity, activism and knowledge exchange pushed Latin American liberation theology and Western human rights into direct conversation with one another. Political repression and violence exerted by the Brazilian regime upon its citizens sparked outrage across the Global North, where individual political and civil freedoms were upheld as the most fundamental and sacred of human rights. Opening a window into Brazil, activists shed light on several other human injustices and structural forms of violence, in particular social and economic inequality and oppression. Liberationist champions of social justice, both Brazilian and European, directly and indirectly, appropriated the language of human rights to further awareness and support for opposition not only to the regime, but to the global economic structure that perpetuated oppression.

Therefore, what we see is that between Engler's 'neglectful' phase of the late 1960s (in which prominent theologians ignored the notion of human rights), and the 'critical' turn of the late 1970s (when they began to scrutinise them), Latin America's Theology of Liberation had already established a dialogue with the concept of human rights through alternative channels of advocacy and solidarity. This dialogue is not so easily interpreted in terms of distinct periods; rather, the presence and absence of explicit concepts of Western human rights shows that while there were some moments of neglect, simultaneously and equally present were moments of critique and appropriation.

By dominant European standards of the time, the violation of individual political and civil rights was the ultimate moral wrong a government could commit. By this logic, the arrest and repression of European missionaries and Brazilian liberationists more clearly fit into the mainstream understanding of rights in Western Europe than did the social justice projects they were pursuing. In places, this tendency was indeed reflected within European media and solidarity activism that emphasised the individual rights violations taking place against members of the Church. Gradually, with the input of activists, liberationist concepts of oppression, preferential rights and self-determination came to embed themselves in the global human rights discourse surrounding Brazil. What challenged the sole focus on political rights and the Brazilian regime's violation thereof was the distinct analytical approach and conceptual framework established and disseminated by Latin American liberationism. Through structural analysis, Latin American liberationists drew out the relationship between marginalisation, oppression, social and economic inequality and political repression on the one hand, and the global economic order on the other. Liberationists and their networks of solidarity and political exiles also forged an important dialogue with Western human rights by framing experiences and manifestations of oppression in terms of specific rights violations.

The 1970s are often cited as a breakthrough moment for human rights, the moment that the global community began using human rights as a way of pressuring foreign states to end state violence (Eckel and Moyn 2015). In the decades that followed, human rights came to incorporate values relating to solidarity, equality and new notions concerning minority rights (such as the Indigenous), environmental rights and rights of development. From above, powerful liberal-democratic states and organisations addressed these issues through global mechanisms of human rights governance, while, from below, transnational activists and organisations contributed new interpretations and practices. From a global historical perspective, the story of liberation theology – incorporating as it does a theology, an analytical framework, an ethical position and praxis – and its encounters with human rights were shaped by transnational social networks and organisational strategies in Western Europe. In my telling of this story, I expand on existing historiographical accounts of the period by moving beyond the text. As alternative windows into the past, I consider diverse sociological contexts, forms of knowledge exchange, acts of solidarity and media representations to illustrate the diversity and complexity of interactions between Latin American liberation theology and human rights.

Notes

1. Letter to all international members of JOC from Jack Salinas, January 1969 source: JOCI 03.3.1–8

2. To cite a few examples: 'Brésil', *Le Monde*, 20 February 1974; 'Le P. Jentel Toujours en Prison', *La Croix*, 2 March 1974; 'Le Prêtre Français François Jentel', *Le Monde*, 17 April 1974; 'L'affaire Jentel Toujours en Suspense', *La Croix*, 25 May 1974.

3. 'Un appel en faveur du Père Jentel', *Le Monde*, 18 July 1973.

4. CGAL Motion on the Brésil-Export protest. Letter attachment from CGAL sent on 20 September 1973 source: CIEX BR DFAN BSB Z4 REX IBR 25 16.

5. Sculpture by Guido Rocha, World Council of Churches Archive, Geneva, WCC 429.07.03 40. See an image of the sculpture here: https://developingeconomics.org/2021/12/13/constructing-a-global-history-of-human-rights-and-development/. Accessed 3 August 2024.

6. J'ai Entendu Les Cris de Mon Peuple. Document d'Evêques et de Supérieurs Religieux du Nord-Est, 6 May 1973. DIAL 99. https://www.alterinfos.org/archives/DIAL-99.pdf. Accessed 21 February 2022.

7. https://www.alterinfos.org/spip.php?article1377. Accessed 21 February 2022.

References

'Accusation from Prison'. *New Blackfriars* 51, no. 607 (1970): 549–55. http://www.jstor.org/stable/43245159.

Adiprasetya, Joas. 'Beyond Universality and Particularity: The Problem of the Human Rights Language in Liberation Theology', *Religion & Human Rights* 8, no. 2 (2013): 163–71.

Aldunate, José S. J. 'Human Rights as the Rights of the Poor: The Perspective from Liberation Theology', *Journal of Moral Education* 23, no. 3 (1994): 297–303.

Aldunate, José S. J., ed. *Derechos humanos, derechos de los pobres*. Santiago, Chile: Rehue, 1993.

Assmann, Hugo, ed. *Carter y la lógica del imperialismo. Tomo 1*. Editorial Universitaria Centro Americana, 1978.

Berryman, Phillip. *Liberation Theology*. New York: Pantheon Books, Random House, 1987.

Câmara, Dom Hélder. 'Violence and Misery', *New Blackfriars* 50, no. 589 (1969): 491–6.

Cangemi, Michael. 'Saint Óscar Romero, Liberation Theology, and Human Rights in El Salvador', *Oxford Research Encyclopedia of Latin American History*, 2019. doi:10.1093/acrefore/9780199366439.013.610.

Cardoso, Fernando Henrique, and Enzo Faletto. *Dependency and Development in Latin America*. Berkeley: University of California Press, 1971.

Cleary, Edward L. *Crisis and Change: The Church in Latin America Today*. Maryknoll, NY: Orbis Books, 1985.

Costa, Sérgio Corrêa da. 'Brazil: A Reply', *New Blackfriars* 52, no. 608 (1971): 5–9.

de Oliveira, Orlandina, and Bryan Roberts. 'Urban Growth and Urban Social Structure in Latin America, 1930–1990'. In *The Cambridge History of Latin America. Volume VI, Part 1: 1930 to the Present*, edited by Leslie Bethell, 251–324. Cambridge: Cambridge University Press, 1995.

Dussel, Enrique. 'The Catholic Church in Latin America since 1930'. In *The Cambridge History of Latin America. Volume VI, Part 1: 1930 to the Present*, edited by Leslie Bethell, 545–82. Cambridge: Cambridge University Press, 1995.

Eckel, Jan, and Samuel Moyn, eds. *The Breakthrough: Human Rights in the 1970s*. Philadelphia: University of Pennsylvania Press, 2015.

Engler, Mark. 'Toward the "Rights of the Poor": Human Rights in Liberation Theology', *Journal of Religious Ethics* 28, no. 3 (2000): 339–65.

Ffrench-Davis, Ricardo, Oscar Muñoz and José Gabriel Palma. 'The Latin American Economies, 1950–1990'. In *The Cambridge History of Latin America. Volume VI, Part 1: 1930 to the Present*, edited by Leslie Bethell, 159–250. Cambridge: Cambridge University Press, 1995.

Filho, José Carlos Moreira da Silva. 'Corporate Accountability for Involvement in Gross Human Rights Violations during the Brazilian Civil-Military Dictatorship: The Role of the Truth Commissions and the Case of Volkswagen Do Brasil', *Journal of White Collar and Corporate Crime* 4, no. 2 (2023): 124–38.

Furtado, Celso. *Economic Development of Latin America*, 2nd ed. Translated by Suzette Machado. Cambridge: Cambridge University Press, 1970.

Gildea, Robert, James Mark and Niek Pas. 'European Radicals and the "Third World"', *Cultural and Social History* 8, no. 4 (2011): 449–71.

Grimaldi, Anna. *Brazil and the Transnational Human Rights Movement, 1964–1985*. London: Anthem, 2023.

Horn, Gerd-Rainer. *Western European Liberation Theology: The First Wave (1924–1959)*. Oxford: University of Oxford Press, 2008.

Lantigua, David. 'Neoliberalism, Human Rights, and the Theology of Liberation in Latin America'. In *Christianity and Human Rights Reconsidered*, edited by Sarah Shortall and Daniel Steinmetz-Jenkins, 238–60. Cambridge: Cambridge University Press, 2020.

Mainwaring, Scott. 'Grassroots Catholic Groups and Politics in Brazil, 1964–1985', *Kellogg Institute Working Paper*, no. 89, 1987.

Marchesi, Aldo. *Latin America's Radical Left: Rebellion and Cold War in the Global 1960s*. New York and Cambridge: Cambridge University Press, 2018.

McGeorch, Graham. 'Liberation Theology: Problematizing the Historical Projects of Democracy and Human Rights'. *Sociedade e Cultura. Revista de Pesquisa e Debates em Ciências Sociais*, vol. 23, e59897, 2020. doi:10.5216/sec.v23i.59897.

Merrick, Thomas W. 'The Population of Latin America, 1930–1990'. In *The Cambridge History of Latin America. Volume VI, Part 1: 1930 to the Present*, edited by Leslie Bethell, 1–62. Cambridge: Cambridge University Press, 1995.

Moreira Alves, Maria Helena. *State and Opposition in Military Brazil*. Austin: University of Texas Press, 1985.

Moyn, Samuel. *The Last Utopia: Human Rights in History*. Cambridge, MA: The Belknap Press of Harvard University Press, 2010.

Nagle, Robin. 'Liberation Theology's Rise and Fall'. In *The Brazil Reader: History, Culture, Politics*, edited by Robert M. Levine and John M. Crocitti, 462–7. Durham, NC: Duke University Press, 1999.

Osorio, Mario F. M. 'Praxis and Liberation in the Context of Latin American Theory'. In *Psychology of Liberation*, edited by Christopher Sonn and Maritza Montero, 11–36. New York: Springer, 2009.

Serbin, Kenneth P. *Dialogos Na Sombra: Bispos e Militares, Tortura e Justiça Social na Ditadura*. São Paulo: Companhia das Letras, 2001.

Sikkink, Katherine. *The Justice Cascade: How Human Rights Prosecutions Are Changing World Politics*. New York: WW Norton & Company, 2011.

Stites Mor, Jessica, ed. *Human Rights and Transnational Solidarity in Cold War Latin America*. Madison: University of Wisconsin Press, 2013.

Taffet, Jeffrey F. *Foreign Aid as Foreign Policy: The Alliance for Progress in Latin America*. New York: Routledge, 2007.

Torelly, Marcelo. 'From Compliance to Engagement: Assessing the Impact of the Inter-American Court of Human Rights Law in Latin America'. In *The Inter-American Human Rights System*, edited by P. Engstrom, 115–42. London: Palgrave Macmillan, 2019.

Wagley, Charles. *Welcome of Tears: The Tapirapé Indians of Central Brazil*. Oxford: Oxford University Press, 1977.

Chapter 6

'Women, the key to liberation?': A feminist theology of liberation at the Catholic women's conference at Puebla[1]

Natalie Gasparowicz

Introduction

'It is our conviction that the church, once conscious of the profound roots of its domination of women ... will be able to convert itself into the strongest support of those in search of their liberation and of our whole continent', spoke activist Itziar Lozano Urbieta in Puebla, Mexico, in 1979 at the little-known *Mujeres para el Diálogo* (MPD) conference (Espino Armendáriz 2022, 1749; Lozano Urbieta 1979).[2] A former woman religious of Basque origin, Lozano Urbieta's words were directed at the Roman Catholic Church at large, and specifically, the meeting of bishops and theologians that was happening at the same time: the Third Conference of Latin American Bishops (*Consejo Episcopal Latinoamericano y Caribeño*, CELAM III). As her words indicate, Lozano Urbieta believed that if she and the other Catholic women at the MPD conference could make those bishops aware of how the Church participated in the 'domination of women', the Church could become the biggest supporters of those seeking the liberation of the Latin American continent (Lozano Urbieta 1979, 53). As Catholic women and as adherents of liberation theology, the MPD conference attendees believed that the bishops were failing to address the obstacles they faced as women.

To ensure that what was discussed at the MPD conference would reach inside the *Seminario Palafoxiano*, where CELAM III was held, the MPD conference participants passed copies of Lozano Urbieta's piece 'Women, The Key to Liberation?' to allied bishops and theologians (Ruether 1979, 182). As Lozano argued, a true liberation of the continent meant addressing the exploitation of Latin American women. These few bishops and theologians read Lozano's compelling analysis of the obstacles Latin American women faced in labour, education, family, the Church and the economy. A controversial topic included in Lozano's pamphlet that was at the intersection of many of these issues – Church, economy, family and education – was the question of the birth control pill and family planning. As Catholics, as women and as liberationists, how did Lozano and other MPD conference attendees view the pill? To answer this question, I offer a close reading of one of the only sources that gives insight into the MPD conference, an English-language publication produced by American attendees who decided to publish the conference proceedings for audiences in the United States.[3]

Because the MPD conference participants imagined a theology of liberation that placed Latin American women at the centre, I argue that they had imagined a *feminist* theology of liberation. This is most evident in the question of the birth control pill. Unlike male liberationists before them, these Catholic women rejected the pill as a simple solution to poverty. Instead of focusing on the right to abortion, as did many feminists in and outside of Mexico, the MPD conference participants wanted Catholic women to make informed choices about their body, outside of Church and state pressures. Their multi-pronged critique of economic, cultural and religious structures – as exemplified in Lozano's excerpt – *made* their feminism.

To make such an argument is an opportunity to revisit Saba Mahmood's famous thesis and to reconsider the assumptions about what makes a feminist subject. The MPD conference provides a window into the emergence of a new feminist subject who placed women at the centre of their vision of liberation. By placing the under-studied MPD conference at the centre of my study, I merge scholarship on liberation theology and feminist activism. In this revised narrative, the CELAM III conference at Puebla becomes a catalyst for Catholic women's organising, the further development of feminist liberation theology, as well as the birth of a feminist subject invested in critiquing Church and state structures.

Literature review

'There is a scarcity of historical (rather than theological) studies of the affinities among these three [black, Latin American, and feminist] streams of liberation theology', writes scholar Lilian Calles Barger (2018, 9) in her intellectual history of the development of liberation theology in the Americas. As Calles Barger articulates so well in her work, Latin American liberation theology is primarily associated with male liberationists. In this paper, I place the contents of this under-studied MPD conference at the centre of my study and argue that these women imagined a feminist theology of liberation. To make this argument, I ask: what makes these women feminist subjects and their theology of liberation feminist?

My work builds on recent scholarship that considers questions of gender and sexuality in the study of liberation theology. Specifically, I build on the work of historians who have considered the role of Catholicism, including liberation theology, in family planning, notably the work of Raúl Necochea López.[4] In his analysis of Jesuit priests who justified the pill in Peru, Necochea López argues that the decision can be explained due to their 'double commitment' to the Vatican and to 'denouncing injustice', which he credits to the influence of liberation theology (Necochea López 2008, 54). I expand upon Necochea López's study by asking: what happens when we consider these conference participants as liberationists and when we consider their commitment to gender? I follow in the footsteps of Calles Barger (2018), whose work decentres Latin American male liberationists and traces the development of diverse liberation theologies across the Americas.[5] My study suggests that the MPD conference was a success, a catalyst for feminist liberation theology, thus revising how scholarship of liberation theology has portrayed CELAM III at Puebla.[6]

While scholars of liberation theology have omitted the MPD conference, scholars of feminist activism, on the other hand, have at least included it (Jaiven 2011, 168; Peña 2007; Sánchez Olvera 2002). Historian Saúl Espino Armendáriz's recent work offers a corrective to scholars' brief treatment of Catholics in feminist activism. His brilliant research moves beyond focusing solely on the MPD conference, and traces the development of transnational and heterogenous feminist dissent inside the Latin American Catholic Church.[7] To borrow his words, by analysing the MPD conference along with other 'previously ignored individual and collective actors', his work offers a 'new narrative about Catholicism and feminism in Latin America', bridging literatures that have otherwise been separate (Espino Armendáriz 2022, 1725).[8] I expand on Espino Armendáriz's research – that the MPD conference and subsequent meetings were an 'articulation of a dissidence' (2019, 176–7) – and argue that the MPD conference reveals the emergence of a new feminist subject.[9] Scholars have well documented Catholic women's activism in Mexico throughout the twentieth century, showing how, for example, anti-state Catholic Action members tried to make their country, their lives and their families Catholic.[10] Unlike her predecessors, this new feminist subject, as a Catholic and as a woman, called on the state *and* her Church to abandon its patriarchal norms so that liberation could be achieved for all. Saba Mahmood's work on feminist subject formation reminds us that agency cannot be conflated with resisting patriarchal norms. In her ethnographic study of the Egyptian mosque movement, Mahmood argues that agency can be found in the 'multiple ways in which one *inhabits* norms' even if it would appear to be 'deplorable passivity and docility from a progressivist point of view' (2005, 15).[11] Therefore, I argue that these women are feminist subjects in light of their commitment to the Catholic faith and their omission of abortion, a central concern of second-wave feminists in Mexico at the time.

Background

When the Preparatory Document for CELAM III was released in 1977 (consisting of a schema of what was to be discussed), Catholic women, among them activist Betsie Hollants, of Belgian origin and US-educated, were disappointed by how little it addressed women's concerns. To remedy this, Hollants began organising the MPD conference. As the leader of CIDHAL (*Comunicación, Intercambio y Desarrollo Humano en América Latina*), an organisation in Cuernavaca, Mexico, based just outside of Mexico City, Hollants had been networking and mobilising Catholic women throughout the 1970s. For instance, Itziar Lozano Urbieta had been working as a Psychology professor in Mexico City when she became involved with CIDHAL (Espino Armendáriz 2022, 1729–30 and 1744–8).[12] CIDHAL members – Hollants included – had attended and organised discussions during the 1975 United Nations Conference on Women and even organised their own preliminary meeting (Espino Armendáriz 2019, 130–38). To build contacts, Hollants even attended the US Women's Ordination Conference (WOC) in Baltimore in 1978 (Espino Armendáriz 2019, 169–72).[13] The work of CIDHAL throughout the 1970s in Cuernavaca, Mexico, had set the stage for the MPD conference in 1979. As much as this was a cosmopolitan meeting of women from across the Americas and Europe, it was also very much a Mexican project.

Hollants organised the conference in two parts. First, about a dozen of North American women and Latin American women met in Cuernavaca and began to discuss and prep for the conference (Espino Armendáriz 2019, 177–82). Then, they drove over to Puebla in a 'bus' to hold the second half of conferences (Fitzpatrick 1979, iii). Anywhere from thirty to 100 participants attended five public seminars (Isasi-Díaz 1979, 297). According to the few published statements by participants, the MPD seminars covered the following topics: 'exploitation of women within their homes', 'family planning and sexual ethics', women religious, women as 'subject of theology' and women as part of theology of liberation (Isasi-Díaz 1979, 297–9). While the official CELAM conference was held at the *Seminario Palafoxiano*, MPD initially held their conferences at the Museo de Antropología downtown (Espino Armendáriz 2019, 179; 2022, 1745–6; Isasi-Díaz 1979, 298; Ruether 1979, 177). Then, MPD became one of the many conferences organised by José Álvarez Icaza and his organisation, CENCOS (*Centro Nacional de Comunicación Social*), which had provided a forum for voices (Espino Armendáriz 2019, 178).

The Latin American woman as subject

As evident in the title of her piece, 'Women, The Key to Liberation?', Itziar Lozano Urbieta, and the other MPD conference participants, placed 'women' at the centre of their vision of liberation. Although these speakers did not use the term 'feminist' when problematising the exploitation and inequalities of women in Latin America, their critiques overlapped with existing feminist discourses. The absence of the term 'feminist' from the publication suggests an ambiguous relationship to feminism.

Throughout the 1970s, as second-wave feminist movements emerged in Mexico and other parts of the world, the term 'feminist' was contested and scrutinised. The term 'feminist' quickly became associated with a set of white, middle-class feminists based in the Global North. For instance, at the 1975 United Nations' International Women's Year Conference, the 'feminists' were the 'white, North American women' according to Peggy Antrobus, then-director for the Women's Bureau of the Jamaican Prime Minister (Olcott 2017, 244). At this time, Mexican liberal and socialist feminists organised around a cluster of issues: abortion, rape and domestic labour (Aceves Sepúlveda 2019, 44; Sánchez Olvera 2002, 113–31). The absence of the term 'feminist' in the MPD publication is noteworthy.

Unsurprisingly, the only time 'feminist' appears in the text is by one of the American editors. In her foreword, Ruth Fitzpatrick, who had coordinated the translation of the pieces from Spanish into English, uses the term 'feminist' to describe their mission. Specifically, Fitzpatrick (1979, iii) asks two questions she believes readers in North America must hear. First, 'What does Liberation Theology have to say to the Church in North

America?' She adds: 'What does that feminist perspective have to say?' For Fitzpatrick, this publication offered a 'feminist perspective' of liberation theology. This usage contrasts with the other pieces.

Of Peruvian origin, MPD conference participant Carmen Laure de Amesz directly inserted women into liberation theology. She engaged the works of preeminent Peruvian liberation theologian, Gustavo Gutiérrez.[14] Citing Gutiérrez's works, such as the famous 1971 *The Theology of Liberation* and the 1978 *The Power of the Poor in History*, de Amesz (1979, 1) explains theology of liberation as 'an effort of reflection and comprehension of a living faith personified in a concrete historic form, like faith is always lived'. While de Amesz draws on Gutiérrez's ideas of praxis, or how to live out faith, where she diverges from Gutiérrez is by reflecting explicitly on women. To argue that woman 'has affected and is affecting liberating praxis of the people', de Amesz points to the precedents set by the Bible. The Bible established women as 'participant(s) in the story of Salvation', as sexually differentiated persons, as members of the Christian community, and as participants in the history of the Church (de Amesz 1979, 2–5). Liberation hinged upon a poor woman's 'totality as a human being', her belonging to a collective experience, and her feminine identity (de Amesz 1979, 6). de Amesz's highlighting of women as 'sexually differentiated' and their particular 'feminine identity' suggests she was distancing herself from what has been called 'feminism of equity'.[15] She even explicitly shares: 'The women of our continent are not fighting for "equal rights"' (de Amesz 1979, 6). Feminism of equity called for the equality of men and women, whereas feminism of difference underscored how differences between men and women were a source of inequality (Aceves Sepúlveda 2019, 44). These differences between men and women were 'not limitations, on the contrary they are put to the service of the liberation of the people of God' (de Amesz 1979, 4). In other words, what set women apart from men was what made them special and essential to the liberation of the continent.

Although many speakers reflected on how economic, familial and Church structures exploited and oppressed women, only Sister Aída Concha, a nun from Mexico, addressed how these structures affected Indigenous women. She affirmed that 'liberation cannot be understood outside the general context of the oppression which the Indigenous groups suffer – their men, their women, their children' (Concha 1979, 12). In her analysis of the family and labour relations among Indigenous communities, Concha points out how 'the greater participation in work does not bring greater liberation for the individual woman, as it does for the woman in the city whose work makes her more independent and more capable of making decisions' (Concha 1979, 9). In other words, more work did not promise liberation for the Indigenous woman, something that was perhaps true for women in the city. Concha includes extreme examples of the working and living conditions among Indigenous women of Venezuela and Mexico to shatter the romantic image anthropologists have built of Indigenous life, 'as the model to which humankind should return' (Concha 1979, 11). Ultimately, Concha argues that the liberation of 'our people' rests in the 'Indian woman' (Concha 1979, 12).

In her compelling analysis, Itziar Lozano Urbieta spends the most time on women's work, the labour of women inside and outside of the home. Citing data from a range of countries (including El Salvador, Venezuela, Guatemala, Argentina, Brazil, Bolivia, Colombia and Mexico), Lozano Urbieta problematised the issue of wages. These critiques echo the patriarchal critiques of Marxist feminists. For example, since 1972, the Wages for Housework collective had been organising globally to advocate for the recognition of women's unpaid labour inside the household. In Mexico, activist Marta Acevedo had organised a Wages for Housework chapter in Mexico City (Toupin 2018, 96).[16] Even when women did not sympathise with the Wages for Housework initiative, what many of these women identified – like Urbieta – was that women's work was not recognised.[17] Ultimately, Urbieta asks: 'If the economic system, by reason of its vested interests is not going to change to meet the demands concerning the family and the exploitation of women – from where will change be able to come?' (1979, 62). The answer was educating women and raising their consciousness.

These pieces exemplify how the MPD conference imagined 'woman' as a subject of history, therefore making the Latin American woman key to liberation. And despite the many intersections with feminist discourses, these women chose not to identify with the contested terrain of feminism. This woman, a historical subject, had many attributes: poor, human, laborious, Indigenous and sexually distinct. Most importantly, she was an agent – a participant in history – who, if aware of her condition, could effect change.

Population politics, the pill and the future of liberation

The MPD conference placed Latin American women at the centre of its theology of liberation and, therefore, interrogated the pill and its accompanying population politics.[18] They critically interrogated how various actors – states and the Roman Catholic Church included – had used these population politics to further oppress poor Latin American women. Together, these women argued that liberation of the Latin American continent could be achieved if women were aware of their conditions and the obstacles they faced.

One of the ways that the Roman Catholic Church had participated in population politics was by upholding its prohibition of contraception, including the newly invented birth control pill. In 1968, Pope Paul VI released his encyclical, or letter to the people, *Humanae vitae*, after evaluating the Birth Control Commission's reports. The Majority Report, which reflected a majority of the commission, argued for the acceptance of the birth control pill for married Catholics. On the other hand, the Minority Report rejected it. In late July 1968, Pope Paul VI sided with the Minority Report and rejected the pill in *Humanae vitae*. Because both Majority and Minority Reports had already been published in the press, many Catholics thought the Pope would align with the Majority Report.[19] The final document encouraged couples to practice 'responsible parenthood' by avoiding sex when a woman was fertile according to her monthly cycle, otherwise known as the rhythm method (Paul VI 1968). Unsurprisingly, eleven years after the release of the document, MPD participant Marina Lessa was troubled by *Humanae vitae* and its lofty expectations.

Brazilian contributor for *Concilium* magazine and advocate for women's rights in the Church, Marina Lessa (1976, 103) explicitly critiqued *Humanae vitae*.[20] Lessa called on the Church to consider the fragility of human relationships (1979, 50). Research indicated that 'couples are indifferent or defiant' of this teaching and how priests in confessions, when advising people, 'search for other ways of escape, when confronting impossibilities' (Lessa 1979, 50). In other words, Lessa suggested that couples struggled to implement *Humanae vitae* and priests struggled to advise these struggling couples. Lessa was also concerned with how this was affecting the faith of Catholics. In an uncertain world, Catholics needed a faith that acknowledged their lived realities, one that was 'compatible' with the modern world in which they lived. Ultimately, Lessa urged the Church to 'adopt an attitude in touch with reality on human problems' (Lessa 1979, 46).

The Church was not the only actor participating in these population politics. Martha Sanchez Gonzalez, an expert on family planning who gave a similar speech at the symposium in Tijuana just the year before, laid out the terms of the debate (Sanchez Gonzalez 1980, 55–62). The ideas of 'family planning' and 'responsible parenthood' had taken the world by storm, and varied in meaning depending on who employed these concepts (Sanchez Gonzalez 1979, 110). For Gonzalez, 'family planning' entailed having the full information to make informed decisions about family, while 'responsible parenthood' was that and more – 'committing themselves [meaning parents] to raise them under the best possible material, educational and health conditions' (Sanchez Gonzalez 1979, 110). The distinction was that responsible parenthood ensured that children were born into the best conditions possible. Gonzalez writes that policies have been created in the world with 'these concepts in mind', and that 'even constitutional rights have been modified in some third world countries' (Sanchez Gonzalez 1979, 110). Although Gonzalez does not explicitly cite the Mexican state, she is likely referring to it.

One of the first countries in the world to add family planning into its constitution was Mexico. This decision overturned the pronatalist policy that had characterised the state's approach for most of the twentieth century. In 1974, President Echeverría created CONAPO (Consejo Nacional de Población), or the National Population Council. President Echeverría even added an amendment that guaranteed that 'every person had the right to decide in a free, responsible and informed manner on the number and spacing of their children'.[21] According to feminists, President Echeverría had strategically used this amendment to make Mexico suitable to host the UN International Women's Year Conference in 1975 (Olcott 2017, 54–9). By the late 1980s, Mexico's state-sanctioned family planning campaign even served as a model for other countries to follow (Soto Laveaga 2007, 27).

Central to the critique of these population politics were the concerns of poor women. In Mexico and across the rest of Latin America, many people had migrated from the countryside to the cities between the 1940s and the 1960s. The populations of cities increased and so did the visibility of poverty (Necochea López 2014; Soto Laveaga 2007, 20). According to Sanchez Gonzalez (1979, 111), the women who most often participated in debates regarding family planning were middle class. Yet, poor women were harmed at the expense of these interests. These middle-class women 'have within their reach the possibility of reducing the size of their families, and among men of wealth, power with class interests which are opposed to those of the women affected' (Sanchez Gonzalez 1979, 111). In other words, the interests of middle-class women disregarded poor women.

Lozano Urbieta and Sanchez Gonzalez identified the conditions of poor women that made them vulnerable to harm. Lozano Urbieta describes how poor women across the Americas faced 'numerous health problems', and 'inadequate birth control methods' (1979, 59). Most likely, 'inadequate birth control methods' refer to insufficient knowledge about preventing pregnancy or even rudimentary forms of birth control. Sanchez Gonzalez describes how poor Mexican women had 'more children than' their income allowed (1979, 110). Their bodies suffered from bearing multiple children. Most importantly, they both highlighted the violence that often accompanied these family planning policies and how poor women were disproportionately targeted.

Although in name the concepts 'family planning' and 'responsible parenthood' might connote ideal and lofty goals, in practice, these initiatives involved violence. Sanchez Gonzalez argues that policies of family planning and responsible parenthood 'hide an enforced policy of birth control' (1979, 110). Furthermore, Lozano Urbieta describes how poor women had been the victims of 'involuntary sterilizations' (1979, 59). Lozano Urbieta highlights how medical trials to test the birth control pill had been imposed upon women in not only Puerto Rico but also Guatemala and in the United States, among Chicana and Native American populations (1979, 59). Lozano Urbieta shares an alarming statistic: 'more than 35% of all the women of puberty age in Puerto Rico have been sterilized, the majority of them without their consent' (1979, 59). To execute her outline of the violence conducted against women of Puerto Rico, Sanchez Gonzalez cited the research of anti-imperial feminist Bonnie Mass.

Like Bonnie Mass, Lozano Urbieta located imperialism in the global project of managing population growth. For Lozano Urbieta, family planning was a project enforced by advanced capitalist countries upon Third-World countries and the 'lucrative projects' conducted by international pharmaceutical companies (1979, 60). Similarly, Bonnie Mass's *Population Target* (1976) outlined how First World countries implemented these campaigns, an imperialist endeavor to prevent the births of Brown and Black bodies. The case of Puerto Rico in particular was of grave concern. American doctors and scientists had used Puerto Rico as a 'laboratory', conducting trials of the pill on women and, in some cases, even sterilised women against their will, as indicated in Mass's work (Briggs 2002, 110).[22] This was very much a global story as well, which went beyond Puerto Rico.[23]

Part of the problem was also the 'unequal distribution of resources' (Sanchez Gonzalez 1979, 112).[24] Employing a critique that echoed dependency theory, a lens of analysis used by liberation theologians like Gustavo Gutiérrez, Martha Sanchez Gonzalez acknowledges the history of extraction of the region's resources by 'foreign powers' (likely referring to former colonial powers, Spain, Portugal, the UK and, in more recent history, the United States). In a sense, this had made Latin America dependent upon countries of the First World, where also 'coincidentally are those that are most interested in imposing family planning' (1979, 112). Controlling demographic growth was not going to change these systems in place.

Nor was it going to solve poverty or hunger. Marina Lessa argued that 'world hunger' had a more profound origin (1979, 52). Martha Sanchez Gonzalez rejected population control initiatives as the solution. She shares that the 'answer to the problem of hunger is found not in introducing global policies controlling demographic growth in poor countries, but distributing wealth in a more equal way' (Sanchez Gonzalez 1979, 112). Sanchez Gonzalez did note the relief contraception might offer to the 'situation of individual families, but it has no influence upon the equal distribution of richness, land, employment, income, health and benefits of education' (1979, 114). Ultimately, population control treated the symptoms of the disease, instead of eradicating it from the entire body, or system.

The question of whether the pill could help alleviate poverty or 'the problem of hunger' was a question taken up by Catholic actors previously. When the Pope rejected the pill in *Humanae vitae*, some asked whether this was dismissive of issues like poverty and global hunger. For example, the Jesuits working in Peru, under the influence of liberation theology, had administered the pill to married couples in the name of justice (Necochea López 2008; 2014). In the early 1970s, contributor Joaquín Herrera Díaz published an article in *Juventud*, a monthly published by the Association of Young Mexican Women Catholics (Juventud Católica Femenina Mexicana, or JCFM), where he asks: 'could family planning be a response to the problem of hunger?' (Herrera Díaz 1970).[25] While he echoes the arguments of the Jesuits in the article, however, he never answers the question he posed. Because the MPD participants placed women at the centre of their theology of liberation, they rejected the pill as a way to alleviate poverty and hunger.

The MPD conference participants imagined solutions and proposals for the liberation of the American continent. Sanchez Gonzalez 'denounce[d] official family planning programs' and accepted the pill as a 'limited solution insofar as the medical assistance that it may offer to millions of needy women, and we must devote ourselves to clarify the *real* causes of the misery of our people' (Sanchez Gonzalez 1979, 114).[26] The pill alone was not the answer. Sanchez Gonzalez called on others to work together to address the 'real causes' of poverty (1979, 114). On the other hand, Marina Lessa (1979, 51) argued a true responsible parenthood meant an informed choice by the couple, despite any pressures exerted by the government, and as people responsible to each other, their family and their community. Lozano Urbieta's proposition was even more ambitious.

Lozano Urbieta declared: 'it is also necessary to de-ideologize the woman's body' (1979, 60). Specifically, Lozano Urbieta explained that '[a woman's] body does not belong to the family, not to the husband, nor to the state. It belongs to the woman herself' (1979, 60). Lozano Urbieta argued that women should have control over their own bodies, not the states, husbands and pharmaceutical companies that tried to make decisions for them. Urbieta explains that a woman 'must be her own owner' regarding decisions 'to use or not to use the methods of birth control, to be sterilized or not, to have or not to have sexual relations' (1979, 60). Lozano Urbieta's call for the de-ideologization of the woman's body in many ways echoed what feminists were advocating for in Mexico and the rest of the Americas.

Lozano Urbieta wanted to de-ideologise the woman's body but did not explicitly cite the right to abortion. The right to abortion had become one of the demands of feminists in Mexico. By the mid-1970s, the *Coalición de Mujeres Feministas* (Coalition of Women Feminists) had formed. This group called for 'maternidad voluntaria', or voluntary motherhood and the elimination of sexual violence (Lamas 2011, 183). Voluntary motherhood placed women at the centre of reproductive decision-making. It gave women the right to use contraception (controlling when someone decided to get pregnant) and the right to abortion.[27] In 1976, the *Coalición de Mujeres Feministas* submitted a bill by the name of 'Voluntary Motherhood' for the *Cámara de Diputados* in Mexico City to consider (Lamas 2011, 183). That same year, CONAPO organized a group of more than eighty experts to study the problem of abortion (Lamas 2011, 184). The commission's recommendation was to make abortion legal when it was a woman's voluntary decision. However, President Echeverría ignored this advice and prohibited the group from disclosing their findings. Still, feminist groups continued to organise conferences about abortion and protests into the late 1970s (Lamas 2001; 2011, 184).

Yet, abortion was absent in the MPD publication. Martha Sanchez Gonzalez mentioned abortion only once and in the context of birth control.[28] Throughout the 1970s, the organisation CIDHAL and its leader, Betsie Hollants – a key organiser of the MPD conference – saw abortion more as a tragedy rather than a right (Espino Armendáriz 2019, 214). This is reflected in the MPD publication. Their distance to the term 'abortion' perhaps explains why they did not necessarily use the term feminist to describe themselves. Or, perhaps, they were thinking of their audience – the bishops inside the *Seminario Palafoxiano* – and suspected abortion would be too isolating. It is even possible that when it came to abortion, they believed in the Catholic position, and, therefore, that is why they reflected more broadly on a woman's freedom to make decisions about her reproductive life. Regardless of the reason for this ambiguous relationship to abortion, this was what composed their feminist theology of liberation.

To successfully de-ideologise the woman's body, or achieve these other goals, many of the MPD conference attendees reflected on what was most important – raising consciousness. In the words of Lozano Urbieta, for instance, 'de-ideologization [of the woman's body] is intimately linked with the active promotion of the consciousness of her rights' (1979, 50). Martha Sanchez Gonzalez reflected on how 'ignorance' kept women away from their liberation (1979, 114). When discussing the condition of the Indigenous woman, scholar Leonor Aida Concha echoed the same (1979, 12). And indeed, when considering the impact of the conference, a few attendees reflected on its effectiveness, primarily because it raised the consciousness of women.

Theologian Ada María Isasi-Díaz reflected on how there was an 'effective feminine presence' at Puebla, citing how the final document of CELAM III had borrowed concepts and language from their own documents (1979, 296). Professor and theologian Rosemary Radford Ruether reflects on the 'consciousness-raising work' that Puebla accomplished (1979). In the feminist, Mexico City-based, *Fem* magazine, Lozano Urbieta commented on how women refused to be silent and made their voices heard (1978).[29] These few recollections – including the ones shared by the collaborators of the publication – indicate that this conference was productive for these women. The work had begun.

Conclusion

At the next MPD meeting in October of 1979, Sister Leonor Aída Concha reflected on the impact of the Puebla meeting earlier that year (Espino Armendáriz 2019, 183–4; 2022, 1752). At that meeting, she shared that the MPD conference was 'the first occasion in which Christian women ... offer a space in the struggle, recognizing the historic role they can play' (Mujeres para el Diálogo 1981, 78).[30] Decades later, Sister Concha echoed the same. In an interview for historian Milagros Peña, Sister Concha argued that the 1979 MPD Conference was a key turning point and shared: 'We gave the [Christian feminist] women's movement a political character which did not exist at the same time' (Peña 2007, 110). That is, Sister Concha saw that the MPD conference had helped make, in her words, a Christian feminism visible and political. She relayed to the interviewer that 'the first thing that happened [at the Puebla meeting] ... was developing a gender consciousness' (Peña 2007, 110). And, indeed, these women of MPD and other Catholic feminists continued to organise. They participated in the regional feminist meetings of the *Encuentro Feminista Latinoamericano y del Caribe* (EFLAC), which had begun in

1981, and even in the parallel conference that emerged in 1985, centring on feminist theology (Espino Armendáriz 2019, 185–6; 2022, 1754). It was in this flourishing landscape of exchange that a Catholic feminism emerged invested in the right to abortion. Among these women was Itziar Lozano Urbieta.

Once Itziar Lozano Urbieta became head of CIDHAL in the 1980s, CIDHAL began publishing explicitly on the right to abortion (Espino Armendáriz 2019, 214–15 and 294). According to historian Saúl Espino Armendáriz (2019, 212 and 214), a generational gap existed among CIDHAL collaborators. Betsie Hollants, the key organiser behind MPD, exemplified an older generation of Catholic women who emphasised birth control to prevent the tragedy of abortion. On the other hand, Lozano Urbieta represented a younger generation of Catholic women who saw abortion as a right (Espino Armendáriz 2019, 221). This helps explain the ambiguous relationship to abortion at MPD – the women themselves likely varied in opinion. More importantly, where the beliefs of MPD participants converged was their vision of liberation. They wanted a world where women could make informed decisions about having children, which meant dismantling the systems in place that exacerbated the harms done to the poor women of Latin America. By the time Lozano Urbieta stepped down from serving as the head of CIDHAL in 1992, *Católicas por el Derecho a Decidir* (Catholics for Choice), a Catholic organisation dedicated to reproductive rights, opened their first office in Mexico City (Espino Armendáriz 2019, 227).

And so, the women that had emerged from the MPD conference continued to organise as women, Catholics and liberationists. She may not have identified as 'feminist', but deeply cared about the conditions of her fellow women in Latin America. Some, like Lozano Urbieta, helped develop a Catholic feminism devoted to the right to abortion. This paper has begun to explore the role of the MPD conference in forming this new Catholic feminist subject. Still, more research is necessary to learn and understand feminist subject formation in this diverse, flourishing landscape of feminisms and liberation theologies in the 1980s.

Notes

1. With 'Women, The Key to Liberation?', I use the title that appears In Lozano Urbieta (1979, 53), which is closer to the Spanish translation. See Espino Armendáriz (2019, 215). Special thanks to historian Saúl Espino Armendáriz, whose ground-breaking work directed me to the MPD conference. Thank you to Pablo Bradbury and Niall Geraghty for inviting me to join this volume, and for organising the November 2020 conference from which this project began. Thank you to the archivists of the Ada

María Isasi-Díaz Papers, 1966–2007, Archives of Women in Theological Scholarship, The Burke Library at Union Theological Seminary, Columbia University Libraries (hereafter AMIDP) for digitally sharing materials with me during the pandemic, and to the reviewers of this volume. Thank you to the participants of the February 2021 Duke Gender, Sexuality, Feminist Studies Colloquium, as well as my discussant, Espino Armendáriz, for sharing such thoughtful, rich comments on an earlier version of this paper. I also presented a version of this paper at the 2022 CLAH meeting. I am especially grateful to my advisor, Jocelyn Olcott, as well as Martha Espinosa, Avrati Bhatnagar and Travis Knoll.

2. See also Espino Armendáriz (2019, 178, 214 and 294).

3. This team collected and translated speeches into English. The editors intentionally excluded any speeches given by North American women, in particular, the seminar given by theologian and professor Rosemary Radford Ruether in English. See *Women in Dialogue* (1979, 53).

4. See chapter 6 in Necochea López (2015) and Necochea López (2008). For other works in family planning that consider the complexity of Church actors see Lopera López (2016), Felitti (2012) and Mooney (2009).

5. See also the upcoming work of historian Mariana Gómez Villanueva, who explores the role of women liberationists in Mexico.

6. Scholars and historical actors alike have debated the role of CELAM III in the wider development of liberation theology, and to what extent it affirmed/rejected it. See a range of works, including Dussel (1981), Cleary (1985), Smith (1991) and Blancarte (1992). More recently, see Espino Armendáriz (2019).

7. Espino Armendáriz (2022) explores the exchanges between activists in the US and Mexico, and the role of the women's ordination movement in the development of this feminist dissent inside the Catholic Church. His 'Feminismo católico en México' (2019) offers a broader account of the transnational development of Catholic feminism.

8. Translation my own.

9. I am influenced by scholar Jocelyn Olcott's (2017) use of Alain Badiou to think through the birth of a subject.

10. Some notable examples include Boylan (2006) and Andes (2019). Recently, Sanders (2020) has argued that the Catholic Action's moralisation campaign in the mid-twentieth century embraced modernity, challenging, for example, the role of women as envisioned by Soledad Loaeza (2005).

11. Italics appears in original text.

12. For a fuller account, see Espino Armendáriz (2019, 178, 214 and 294).

13. For more on the exchange between US and Latin American Catholic activists, regarding feminism and women's ordination, see Espino Armendáriz (2022).

14. Gutiérrez's 1971 publication of *The Theology of Liberation* launched liberation theology on the continent.

15. See Aceves Sepúlveda (2019, 44).

16. Acevedo is often credited for initiating the second-wave feminist movement in Mexico at the start of the 1970s.

17. For example, historian Jocelyn Olcott describes how some Mexican feminists actually 'paid someone else to perform this labor' (2017, 58 and 143).

18. I loosely define 'population politics' in the words of Connelly (2008, 152).

19. For accounts of the Birth Control Commission, see Kaiser (1987) and McClory (1995).

20. Thank you to Travis Knoll for finding this article.
21. Found in Soto Laveaga (2007, 23).
22. See chapter 5 of Briggs (2002). See Connelly (2008, 175).
23. For a global account of population control, see Connelly (2008).
24. Marina Lessa (1979, 52) describes this as 'an unequal distribution of income' and Lozano Urbieta (1979, 60) shares 'the poor are not poor because there are so many of them, but because riches are badly distributed'.
25. Translation my own.
26. Italics my own.
27. For more on Mexican second-wave feminism and the right to abortion, Espino Armendáriz (2019), Nelson (2022), Nelson (2019), Jaiven (2011), Ortiz-Ortega and Barquet (2010), Sánchez Olvera (2002) and Lamas (2001). For more on abortion politics broadly, see, for example, Ortiz-Ortega (2005).
28. The potential of abortion, as she puts it, is limited in a 'capitalist country'. Demanding birth control and the legalisation of abortion must be part of the 'struggle of women towards a more just society'. See Martha Sanchez (1979, 113).
29. See also Espino Armendáriz (2022, 181).
30. Translation my own.

References

Primary Sources

Archives of Women in Theological Scholarship, The Burke Library at Union Theological Seminary, Columbia University Libraries (AMIDP).

Concha, Leonor Aída. 'The Indigenous Woman in Latin America'. In *Women in Dialogue: Inter-American Meeting*. Notre Dame, In: Catholic Committee on Urban Ministry, 1979. Series 2, Box 1, Folder 5, AMIDP.

de Amesz, Carmen Laure. 'The Theology of Woman and Liberation'. In *Women in Dialogue: Inter-American Meeting*. Notre Dame, In: Catholic Committee on Urban Ministry, 1979. Series 2, Box 1, Folder 5, AMIDP.

Fitzpatrick, Ruth. 'Foreword'. In *Women in Dialogue: Inter-American Meeting*. Notre Dame, In: Catholic Committee on Urban Ministry, 1979. Series 2, Box 1, Folder 5, AMIDP.

Herrera Díaz, Joaquín. '¿La planeación familiar, una repuesta al problema del hambre?', *Juventud* (Mexico City: Mexico), March 1970, Universidad Iberoamericana, Colección de Acción Católica, Caja 86.

Isasi-Díaz, Ada María. 'Silent Women Will Never Be Heard', *Missiology* 7, no. 3 (1979/07/01): 295–301. doi:10.1177/009182967900700303.

Lessa, Marina. 'La mujer en los movimientos eclesiales en Latinoamérica', *Concilium: Revista Internacional de Teología*, no. 111 (1976): 132–5.

Lessa, Marina. 'The Family and the Church'. In *Women in Dialogue: Inter-American Meeting*. Notre Dame, In: Catholic Committee on Urban Ministry, 1979. Series 2, Box 1, Folder 5, AMIDP.

Lozano Urbieta, Itziar. 'La presencia de las no invitadas', *Fem* 2, no. 8 (September 1978): 44–9. https://archivos-feministas.cieg.unam.mx/publicaciones/fem.html#autor.

Lozano Urbieta, Itziar. 'Women, The Key to Liberation?'. In *Women in Dialogue: Inter-American Meeting*. Notre Dame, In: Catholic Committee on Urban Ministry, 1979. Series 2, Box 1, Folder 5, AMIDP.

Mujeres para el Diálogo. *Mujer latinoamericana: Iglesia y teología*. Mexico City: s.n., 1981.

Paul VI. *Humanae Vitae*, July 25, 1968. http://www.vatican.va/content/paul-vi/en/encyclicals/documents/hf_p-vi_enc_25071968_humanae-vitae.html. Accessed 20 January 2021.

Ruether, Rosemary. 'Theology and the Social Sciences: The Issues at Puebla – Consciousness-Raising at Puebla: The Women's Project at CELAM III'. *Proceedings of the Catholic Theological Society of America* (1979).

Sanchez Gonzalez, Martha. 'Woman and Family Planning'. In *Women in Dialogue: Inter-American Meeting*. Notre Dame, In: Catholic Committee on Urban Ministry, 1979. Series 2, Box 1, Folder 5, AMIDP.
Sanchez Gonzalez, Martha. 'La mujer y la planificación familiar'. In *Mujer y sociedad en América Latina*, edited by Lucía Guerra-Cunningham, 55–62. Irvine; Santiago, Chile: Universidad de California; Editorial del Pacífico, 1980.
Women in Dialogue: Inter-American Meeting. Notre Dame, In: Catholic Committee on Urban Ministry, 1979. Series 2, Box 1, Folder 5, AMIDP.

Secondary Sources

Aceves Sepúlveda, Gabriela. *Women Made Visible: Feminist Art and Media in Post-1968 Mexico City*. Lincoln: University of Nebraska Press, 2019.
Andes, Stephen. *The Mysterious Sofía: One Woman's Mission to Save Catholicism in Twentieth-Century Mexico*. Lincoln: University of Nebraska Press, 2019.
Blancarte, Roberto. *Historia de la Iglesia Católica en México*. Mexico: Colegio Mexiquense; Fondo de Cultura Económica, 1992.
Boylan, Kristina A. 'Gendering the Faith and Altering the Nation: Mexican Catholic Women's Activism, 1917–1940'. In *Sex in Revolution: Gender, Politics, and Power in Modern Mexico*, edited by Jocelyn Olcott, Mary Kay Vaughan and Gabriela Cano, 199–222. Durham, NC: Duke University Press, 2006.
Briggs, Laura. *Reproducing Empire: Race, Sex, Science, and U.S. Imperialism in Puerto Rico*. Berkeley: University of California Press, 2002.
Calles Barger, Lilian. *The World Come of Age: An Intellectual History of Liberation Theology*. New York, NY: Oxford University Press, 2018.
Cleary, Edward L. *Crisis and Change: The Church in Latin America Today*. Maryknoll, NY: Orbis Books, 1985.
Connelly, Mathew James. *Fatal Misconception: The Struggle to Control World Population*. Cambridge, MA: Belknap Press of Harvard University Press, 2008.
Dussel, Enrique D. *A History of the Church in Latin America: Colonialism to Liberation (1492–1979)*. Grand Rapids, MI: Eerdmans, 1981.
Espino Armendáriz, Saúl. 'Feminismo católico en México: La historia del CIDHAL y sus redes transnacionales (c. 1960–1990)'. PhD diss., El Colegio de México, 2019.
Espino Armendáriz, Saúl. 'Disidencias feministas en la Iglesia católica mexicana: El movimiento para la ordenación de mujeres durante los

años setenta del siglo XX', *Historia Mexicana* 71, no. 4 (284) (2022): 1723–64. doi:10.24201/HM.V71I4.4373.

Felitti, Karina. 'Planificación familiar en la Argentina de las décadas 1960 y 1970: ¿Un caso original en América Latina?', *Estudios Demográficos y Urbanos*, 79th ser., 27, no. 1 (2012): 153–88.

Jaiven, Ana Lau. 'Emergencia y trascendencia el neofemenismo'. In *Un fantasma recorre el siglo: Luchas feministas en México 1910–2010*, edited by Gisela Espinosa Damián and Ana Lau Jaiven, 151–82. Mexico City: Universidad Autónoma Metropolitana, Unidad Xochimilco, 2011.

Kaiser, Robert Blair. *The Encyclical That Never Was: The Story of the Pontifical Commission on Population, Family and Birth, 1964–1966*. London: Sheed & Ward, 1987.

Lamas, Marta. *Política y reproducción: Aborto, la frontera del derecho a decidir*. Mexico City: Plaza & Janés, 2001.

Lamas, Marta. 'Cuerpo y política: La batalla por despenalizar el aborto'. In *Un fantasma recorre el siglo: Luchas feministas en México 1910–2010*, edited by Gisela Espinosa Damián and Ana Lau Jaiven, 183–212. México, D.F.: Universidad Autónoma Metropolitana, Unidad Xochimilco, 2011.

Loaeza, Soledad. 'Mexico in the Fifties: Women and Church in Holy Alliance', *Women's Quarterly* 33(3–4) (2005): 138–60.

Lopera López, Juan Alejandro. 'Paternidad o procreación responsable: Iglesia católica, Acción Cultural Popular y control de la natalidad en Colombia (1964–1978)', *Historia y Sociedad* 31 (2016): 235–67.

Mahmood, Saba. *Politics of Piety: The Islamic Revival and the Feminist Subject*. Princeton, NJ: Princeton University Press, 2005.

Mass, Bonnie. *Population Target: The Political Economy of Population Control in Latin America*. Brampton, Ont: Charters Publ, 1976.

McClory, Robert. *Turning Point: The inside Story of the Papal Birth Control Commission, and How Humanae Vitae Changed the Life of Patty Crowley and the Future of the Church*. New York: Crossroad, 1995.

Mooney, Jadwiga E. Pieper. *The Politics of Motherhood: Maternity and Women's Rights in Twentieth-Century Chile*. Pittsburgh, PA: University of Pittsburgh Press, 2009.

Necochea López, Raúl. 'Priests and Pills: Catholic Family Planning in Peru, 1967–1976', *Latin American Research Review* 43, no. 2 (2008): 34–56. doi:10.1353/lar.0.0025.

Necochea López, Raúl. *A History of Family Planning in Twentieth-Century Peru*. Chapel Hill, NC: University of North Carolina Press, 2014.

Nelson, Jennifer. 'Feminism, Human Rights, and Abortion Debates in Mexico', *Journal of Women's History* 34, no. 2 (2022): 119–40.

Nelson, Jennifer. 'Transnational Reproductive Politics: Abortion Rights and Human Rights in Mexico'. In *Reproductive Justice and Sexual Rights: Transnational Perspectives*, edited by Tanya Saroj Bakhru, 125–44. New York: Routledge, 2019.

Olcott, Jocelyn. *International Women's Year: The Greatest Consciousness-Raising Event in History*. New York, NY: Oxford University Press, 2017.

Ortiz-Ortega, Adriana. 'The Politics of Abortion in Mexico: The Paradox of the Doble Discurso'. In *Where Human Rights Begin: Health, Sexuality, and Women in the New Millennium*, edited by Wendy Chavkin and Ellen Chelser, 154–79. New Brunswick, NJ: Rutgers University Press, 2005.

Ortiz-Ortega, Adriana and Mercedes Barquet. 'Gendering Transition to Democracy in Mexico', *Latin American Research Review* 45 (2010): 108–37. http://www.jstor.org/stable/27919216.

Peña, Milagros. *Latina Activists across Borders: Women's Grassroots Organizing in Mexico and Texas*. Durham, NC: Duke University Press, 2007.

Sánchez Olvera, Alma Rosa. *El feminismo mexicano ante el movimiento urbano popular: Dos expresiones de lucha de género, 1970–1985*. Mexico City: Universidad Nacional Autónoma de México, Campus Acatlán: Plaza y Valdés, 2002.

Sanders, Nichole. 'Women, Sex, and the 1950s Acción Católica's Campaña Nacional de Moralización Del Ambiente', *Mexican Studies* 36, no. 1–2 (2020): 270–97. doi:10.1525/msem.2020.36.1–2.270.

Smith, Christian. *The Emergence of Liberation Theology: Radical Religion and Social Movement Theory*. Chicago: University of Chicago Press, 1991.

Soto Laveaga, Gabriela. '"Let's Become Fewer": Soap Operas, Contraception, and Nationalizing the Mexican Family in an Overpopulated World', *Sexuality Research & Social Policy* 4, no. 3 (2007). doi:10.1525/srsp.2007.4.3.19.

Toupin, Louise. *Wages for Housework: A History of an International Feminist Movement, 1972–1977*. Vancouver, BC, and London: UBC Press and Pluto Press, 2018.

Chapter 7

Towards the possibility of an ecofeminist political theology: The case of the *Con-spirando* collective[1]

Ely Orrego Torres

The question of political theology is a recent topic in the study of political philosophy, political theory and political science. In continental philosophy and contemporary Italian thought, political theology had an intellectual boom in the 1990s, with the emergence of re-readings of Carl Schmitt and Walter Benjamin by the international academy, and the publication of a renowned international journal on the subject, *Political Theology*, in the late 1990s and early 2000s. Among the aforementioned re-readings, a notable event was the publication of the *Homo Sacer* series by the Italian Giorgio Agamben. In particular, the publication of *Homo Sacer: Il potere sovrano e la nuda vita/Homo Sacer: Sovereign Power and Bare Life* (1995) posed an explicit critique of the Schmittian idea of sovereignty.

In Latin America the reception of political theology also grew in the late 1990s and became fully established in the 2000s with Jorge Dotti (2000; Dotti and Pinto 2002) and Luis Oro's (2005; 2013) readings of Schmitt; and the interpretation of Benjamin in connection with the critique of culture in the work of Chilean philosophers such as Nelly Richard (1994; 1999), Willy Thayer (2007; 2010), Pablo Oyarzún, and Elizabeth Collingwood-Selby (1997; 2009), who disseminated many of his ideas in the now defunct *Revista de Crítica Cultural*.[2] However, it was only after the arrival of the Spanish translations and dissemination of Agamben's *Homo sacer* that the dissemination of new understandings of political theology became more relevant in the region.[3] In the case of Chile, the work of Rodrigo Karmy (2011; 2014; 2018) and Miguel Vatter

(2004; 2009; 2011a; 2011b; 2011c; 2012; 2013; 2016; 2019a) on the concept of biopolitics has increased interest in the intersections between these two lines of thought. Other intellectual efforts to make visible the critical debate on the concept of political theology have been presented in the journals *Deus Mortalis* and *Revista Pléyade*.[4]

As someone who has followed the political theology debate closely, especially since the emergence of Agamben's texts, I suggest that it has tended to be situated on an axis of geographical and gender domination. That is to say, the main currents are written and thought from the northern hemisphere, or in terms of authors belonging to that region. Likewise, approaches to political theology tend to be androcentric, with little room for interpretation from a gender perspective. Furthermore, the anthropocentric drift of its statements raises questions about the place that ecology or other non-human beings can occupy in the worldview of political theology. For this reason, one of the questions that arises and motivates this chapter is the possibility of proposing a feminist, ecological and southern hemisphere-based political theology. That is to say that the relevant questions become: can political theology expand its boundaries and open up new understandings of the world and sovereignty in a post-secular world?[5] How would an ecofeminist perspective allow for a different approach to what has been understood and posited as political theology, particularly in terms of its political implications?

To respond to these questions, I will focus on the work of women ecofeminist theologians whose work has been developed in Latin America and explicitly influenced by liberation theology, such as Ivone Gebara and Mary Judith Ress, who have theorised new possibilities for politically experiencing the body in community with other women. As I note, these theologians emerged from within the liberation theological tradition but gradually came to critique and challenge what they identified as the retention of a patriarchal anthropology and cosmology within that same tradition. By assuming the notion of holistic ecofeminism, this chapter seeks to sketch out a new understanding of political theology in a postsecular world. To help with this task, the specific case of the group *Con-spirando* will also be addressed as an alternative of resistance and sisterhood in the context of new forms of spirituality and politics.

Women's bodies and Radical Evil

When, in 1994, the Brazilian and Catholic ecofeminist theologian Ivone Gebara declared her support for abortion rights, she never imagined that her 'punishment' by the Vatican would be having to repeat her theological studies and maintain a long silence. Gebara – who was influenced by liberation theology and denounced gender injustices from a feminist perspective – was not only censured by the Vatican but also had to repeat her doctoral studies at the Catholic University of Louvain and accept the punishment of thoughtful silence.

Her period of silence and censorship gave birth to her doctoral thesis, published in English as *Out of the Depths: Women's Experience of Evil and Salvation* in 2002 and considered one of the most important works in her career. In this book, Gebara offers a novel and innovative interpretation of the problem of God and evil from a feminist perspective, including 'not the evil we do personally, but the evil that we undergo, that we suffer or endure, something not chosen, the kind of evil present in institutions and social structures that accommodate it, even facilitate it' (2002, 1). In other words, Gebara replied to her experience of 'punishment' and envisioned it as a possibility to speak for women through their experiences of bodily control and oppression.

Clearly, the body is a crucial term in feminist theology, as in other feminisms, to understand patriarchal domination and structures in society. In this regard, it is important to keep in mind that mainstream political theology also relies on the function of the body and its relationship with sovereignty. Indeed, in 1995, Giorgio Agamben's concept of *homo sacer* emerged from reflection on the power exercised over the body: 'The very body of *homo sacer* is, in its capacity to be killed but not sacrificed, a living pledge to his subjection to a power of death. And yet this pledge is, nevertheless, absolute and unconditional, and not the fulfillment of a consecration' (1995, 61). From this, one can deduce that the condition of *homo sacer* is defined by the ambivalence between the sacrificable and the non-sacrificable, as by that between his consecration to the gods and the mortal power over his body.[6] Agamben's *homo sacer* is thus not only defined by the character of exception portrayed by Carl Schmitt but also Ernst Kantorowitz's notion of sovereignty depicting the king's two bodies (1981), whose definition of political theology has been broadly discussed in political philosophy and political theory.

However, what is the role of the body in the case of feminist theology? How does it seek to reinterpret women's bodies from the perspective of spirituality and religious institutions? First, feminist theology has found its place in images and in the resignification of the divine. The question of God the father and the deconstruction of God the father, as well as of the Judeo-Christian tradition as a whole, have been constant themes in its discussion.[7]

To provide a brief summary: within the Judeo-Christian tradition women have, since ancient times, been burdened with the myth of Eve and her guilt, as well as the invisibility of other women in biblical history, with the exception of the figure of the Virgin Mary. Women have been labelled as a source of lust, temptation and sinfulness for men, leading to a primary distinction in how evil has been treated in theology and the sacrifice to be made by women. As Gebara argues, this living on the basis of the sacrifice of obeying the father God has been translated into obedience to men who hold certain social and religious power, such as husbands, brothers and priests (2002, 88). The problem would not only be this absolute obedience to the male figure since our childhood but also how women's lives have meant a renunciation of pleasure, of their own thoughts, dreams and of their own will, that is, a renunciation of their body in order to put themselves at the service of others or to live according to what others say about them (2002).

From this sacrifice and women's potential guilt for not complying with the expected canons, women would assume a behaviour of bearing and accepting suffering as part of the fear that is reproduced from our childhood. Thus, from a series of testimonies, Gebara develops her understanding of the primary female experience of evil as women's 'lack of ownership', 'lack of power', 'lack of education', 'lack of worth' and the experience of 'the evil attributed to skin colour' (2002, 17–41). In addition, Gebara argues that women's bodies are subjected to cultural and physical violence because they are *women's* bodies. And, over time, women internalise this violence and reproduce these evils, especially in the domestic space. As Gebara states, it is women who ultimately reproduce the patriarchal model in the most fundamental social structures such as the home, the school and the church (2002, 98). A similar logic operates in the public sphere with the entry of women into a mainly male space and where they act oppressively towards other women, thus reproducing patriarchy.

Although the so-called 'women's evils' denounced by Gebara are a reality experienced by women whether they are Christians or not, the deconstruction of the image of the divine provides one answer as to how to live in another possible way. According to feminist theology, one of the great discoveries of women who experience their spirituality through feminism is that overcoming the figure of the Judeo-Christian male God makes way for a love of the divine within themselves. In that sense, it means opening up to the symbolism of the Goddess as an affirmation of women's power, women's bodies, women's will and women's bonds and inheritance.[8] Or as Carol P. Christ asks: 'Is the spiritual dimension of feminism a passing diversion, an escape from the difficult but necessary political work, or will this emergence of the Goddess symbol among women have significant political and psychological implications for the feminist movement?' (1994, 159). In other words, what feminist women theologians raised at that time not only refers to a reinterpretation of biblical readings, but also to new ways of understanding the divine that would have consequences for their actions and understanding of being a woman in the context of the Christian church.

With the spread of Christianity, female figures have taken a secondary role. An exceptional case has been Mary, as the mother of the Messiah and a virgin, who acquires her importance through her role as a mother and the extraordinary gift of being conceived without sin. However, of the other women disciples such as Mary Magdalene or Martha, we know only what tradition has taken care to disseminate: Mary Magdalene is frequently understood to be a prostitute and sinner who finds salvation, while Martha is the hostess of the house ultimately distracted by housework in the presence of Jesus, and chastised for that same distraction (Luke 10: 38–42). This invisibilisation would have cost women the subjugation of their bodies and a 'disposition of mind to trust in male salvific power and distrust of female power in herself and other women, considering it inferior and dangerous' (Christ 1994, 161). In this sense, it is a disposition that would be transformed into a motivation that becomes a social and political reality, especially in institutions and the public sphere.[9] Therefore, the significance of the Goddess *within* women contemplates an affirmation of their bodies, as it is from there the cycle of life emanates, as opposed to the taboos that women have been burdened with in life such as menstruation, childbirth and menopause (1994, 165). What is interesting about this image of the Goddess is that she does not need an external image, nor a temple or dogmas under which much of the Christian tradition has been built, but the Goddess is in each woman, she lives and conceives her as such as she experiences a connection with her body and with others in community.

In one way or another, this vision of feminist theology breaks with the foundations of a traditional political theology based on the notion of the sovereign, which legitimises the concept of authority and hierarchy characteristic of monotheistic religions. Although this is a first approach to what could be called a new form of feminist political theology, it is necessary to introduce the concept of ecofeminism and its drift from resistance in order to understand its potential in a post-secular understanding.

Ecofeminist answers to a post-secular world

The critical theologies of Latin America that began to develop from the 1960s onwards have undergone an evolution from that moment until the present day. As a result of a new way of thinking about theology in dialogue with Latin American reality and the option for the poor, liberation theology emerged from the work of theologians such as Gustavo Gutiérrez, Leonardo Boff and Rubem Alves. In this context of criticism of ecclesiastical authority and based on a grassroots Christianity, feminist theology was born in Latin America with representatives such as Elsa Tamez, Ivone Gebara and Mary Judith Ress. Its development can be broadly divided into three stages: an initial stage (1970s) involving the identification of women biblical scholars and theologians with the methods and practices of liberation theology, where they saw themselves and other women as subjects of history and protagonists of liberation. A second stage (1980s) involving a growing awareness that liberation theology contained a patriarchal mentality that made them uncomfortable, which led them to produce theological resources creatively expressed in liturgy, art and poetry, as well as beginning to dialogue with other women's movements in the region and with feminist theologians in the First World.[10] And finally, a third stage (1990s to the present) that challenges the model of patriarchal anthropology and the cosmology of liberation theology by calling for a reconstruction of theology from a feminist perspective. In other words, what Ivone Gebara has called a 'holistic ecofeminism' (cited in Ress 2012, 15–20).

It is from this notion of holistic ecofeminism that we will trace what I would view as a new understanding of political theology in a post-secular world. This concept of holistic ecofeminism has meant a very radical – and even post-Christian – restructuring, which is, nonetheless, a source of both great significance for poor Latin American women, and of passion and joy (Ress 2012, 120). However, how does this critical drift emerge, in turn, from a critical interpretation that in itself was constituted within liberation theology? According to Gebara, as summarised by Ress, although liberation theology questioned the hunger, injustice, dictatorships and destruction of entire peoples in Latin America in the 1960s and 1970s, it had not challenged the anthropology and patriarchal cosmology of Christianity (2012, 121). In addition to the situation of dictatorships in the region, ecofeminism emerged as a response to feminist and ecological movements that were beginning to develop in the wider world.[11] Such movements would begin to challenge the so-called 'hegemony of the patriarchal empire' (Gebara 2000, 17), although there are intellectuals and women who oppose linking feminism and ecology as common struggles.

But what is ecofeminism? In Gebara's words:

> Ecofeminism as a thought and social movement basically refers to the ideological connection between the exploitation of nature and the

exploitation of women within the hierarchical-patriarchal system. From a philosophical and theological point of view, ecofeminism can be seen as a wisdom relegated by the patriarchal system, and particularly by modernity, to being a force of labour reproduction – 'blessed wombs' – as nature became an object of domination for the growth of capital. As Carolyn Merchant rightly recalls, modernity – even if historians do not talk about it – begins with the torture of witches and the establishment of a new scientific method. Witches were seen not only as symbols of evil, but also of the violence of nature, capable of causing storms and disease, of killing children. The association between women and nature was clear. That is why unruly women and nature was clear. That is why unruly women and nature in disorder needed to be controlled. (Gebara 2000, 18)

From this quotation we can rescue several elements that will allow us to define the outline of holistic ecofeminism. First, the basis of ecofeminist thought is related to a cosmology linked to nature. It is not by chance that ecofeminism alludes to Mother Earth as that mother – and even Goddess – whose connection transcends the earthly, reaching a new spirituality. Along these lines, ecofeminism also questions modern rationality, the expression of which has been capitalism, which oppresses not only humanity, but also nature itself, that is, the mother. This is why Gebara's critique of liberation theology itself alludes to the reconsideration of a holistic cosmology. In other words, a critique of capitalism and an option for the poor is not enough if there is no critique of the androcentrism and anthropocentrism inherent in the system in question. And finally, it brings us back to what was discussed in the previous section about the 'evil of women' and its expression in the witches, where they were responsible for the damage caused by nature, due to their intimate connection. That said, Gebara's assertion that women have been made the bearers of guilt and are condemned as being responsible for evil in the world is, once again, confirmed.

At this point it is necessary to highlight the specificity of ecofeminist thought. Unlike liberation theology, which focused on the preferential option for the poor as a socio-economic condition, ecofeminism alludes to the triple discrimination of being a woman in a Latin American context, incorporating gender, class and racial discrimination. While Gebara developed her ideas within the liberation theology tradition, she questions the extent to which liberation theology promotes a new epistemology that breaks away from the dualist tradition of Christian theology.

According to Gebara, epistemology in Christian theology (particularly within the Catholic Church) relies on natural reason as promoted by the philosophy of Aristotle and Thomas Aquinas: 'While natural reason can prove the existence of God, it cannot demonstrate the existence of the Trinity, the Incarnation, and the Resurrection. Those truths of the faith can only be learned through revelations from the Bible' (2000, 63). Considering this epistemology, Gebara continues, the Catholic Church opposed modernism and a dialogue with issues from this world. Thus, the problem with this epistemology is that Christian theology cannot formulate human values differently to the 'unquestionable truth' proposed by natural reason. In other words, Gebara writes that the dualist perspective is still rooted in 'eternal truths', which makes it impossible to introduce the feminist reflection on that perspective based on the experience of women (2000, 65).

Although the Second Vatican Council opened the Church to the real problems of the world, the dualist epistemology did not change. Instead, following Gebara, liberation theology proposed the conciliation of an antique and medieval epistemology with a modern one. However, there is no new epistemological proposal. As Gebara continues, there is, instead, an attempt to 'harmonize two epistemological universes without removing either of them' (2000, 66). In her work *Intuiciones ecofeministas*, Gebara acknowledges the contributions of liberation theology in introducing the perspective of the poor into theological foundations and birthing a new spirituality rooted in liberation from various oppressions. Similarly, she recognises that liberation theology also championed the historical figure of Jesus and addressed social injustices in Latin America (2000, 65). However, as she argues, the core of liberation theology is still rooted in an anthropological and androcentric perspective:

> It is about God in the history of men, a God who ultimately remains the Creator and the Lord. From there, all Thomistic tradition about God, about the Incarnation, is, in a way, reclaimed. There is no need to revisit the cosmological and anthropological foundations of the formulation of the Christian faith (2000, 67–8).

Continuing her critique, Gebara highlights that the ethical stance of authors like Gustavo Gutiérrez remains grounded in an Aristotelian-Thomistic epistemology that ecofeminism opposes.

In essence, ecofeminism seeks to broaden the epistemological perspective beyond the Aristotelian-Thomistic binary and formulates a theology that recognises new epistemologies beyond traditional dogmatisms. One of these is the private aspect of politics. To liberate everyone unconditionally implies acknowledging the public and private as theological elements. For example, as van Andel notes (2021, 58), Gebara introduces new topics dismissed by the first generation of liberation theology, such as the division of labour, informal economy, domestic violence and sexual ethics. She also brings visibility to Gebara's epistemic contributions by focusing on the bodies, emotions and rationality of women in their quest for liberation as poor and Christian women. In other words, Gebara challenges the taboo of Christian epistemology by acknowledging essential aspects of theological reflection in relation to personal and socio-political analysis.

Nevertheless its emphasis is on the condition of being a woman. Gebara insists that liberation and new understanding has to occur equally in men and women within the cosmos in order to reconstruct notions of divinity. In that sense, re-situating individuals within – not above – the universe and calling for a new relationality that, in Gebara's words, 'is the basic reality of all that is or can exist. It is the underlying fabric that is in continuous movement within the vital process in which we are immersed' (cited in Ress 2012, 123). In other words, it advances an ethical possibility of opening up spaces of relationship between humanity and nature.

This ethical response would oppose the notion of a hierarchy of power that Christianity has taught us about the individual relationship with the divine. This is why woman and nature have always been approached from a vision of subjugation and domination that begins in Genesis, where rational man is above the world. In other words, man is presented as a god. It is striking that this notion of man's power is seen as a power of subjugation to another, insofar as it is an external power that needs to be exemplified by hierarchies and authority, that is, by the need to manifest this sovereignty. However, when we refer to power relations in ecofeminism, we find a notion that does not require such a manifestation. According to Primavesi, when speaking of ecofeminism and ecology, we find other forms of power: power-from-inside and power-with, bringing together spirit and body, humanity and nature, God and world (1994, 478). In this way, a sovereign would not be needed for its possibility, but rather the relationship with oneself, with others and with nature. In this way, we return to the importance of the personal body and its connection to the earth. In saying that there is a power-from-inside, this is often unknown or repressed by women themselves. It is part of a spirituality that needs a connection with the earth and with the meaning of the body for women, which is given by the natural cycle of life. One of its expressions is through dances and rituals that allow women to connect with this little-explored aspect. To speak from this spirituality means to loosen the Goddess that is within each one of us through creation, symbols and rituals. However, it is a path that is made in community with others, where women can relate and share experiences as well as new spiritualities. A good example of this and of how ecofeminism has influenced Latin American women is the *Con-spirando* collective, which emerged as an alternative and possible source of resistance to traditional political theologies.

The case of the *Con-spirando* collective: an ecofeminist alternative in a post-secular world

The *Con-spirando* collective was born in the early 1990s in Chile as an alternative space for feminist women in search of new visions in the fields of spirituality, feminist theology and ecofeminism. According to Mary Judith Ress, the women who participated in the collective in those years were strongly influenced by liberation theology, only later identifying themselves as 'ecofeminists' (2006, xi). Regardless, from the beginning they have been called together by politics, the universe, the body, culture and everyday life. They consider themselves part of the feminist and other social movements.[12]

In Gebara's words, there are five contributions of the collective to women's development and a new spirituality:

> 1. Faith is in the wisdom of our bodies and the priority of knowing through our corporeality in relationship [. . .]; 2. Efforts to seek non-hierarchical ways of being that model 'power with' rather than 'power over'; 3. The sharing of new ways of celebrating, new rituals that nourish our emerging spiritualities and our commitments; 4. The re-examination of those foundational myths on which Western Christian culture is based, in order to revitalise them and to seek new myths that can nourish our emerging spiritualities, theologies and ethics; 5. Everyone is my kin, from the people in the neighbourhood to the animals, to the mountains, to the rivers. (cited in Ress 2012, 131–2)

The first of these contributions demonstrates another dimension of ecofeminism in Latin America: the interconnectedness between Christian and Indigenous cosmologies in comprehending the role of women. As I have argued in an article co-authored with Diego Rossello (forthcoming), Latin American Ecofeminist Political Theologies and Ecocriticism (LAEPT) underscore the importance of ecological spiritualities rooted in Indigenous and Afro-descendant cosmologies. LAEPT redefines the connection to the earth, incorporating new concepts such as the planetary, cosmos, common home and Pachamama, which accentuate the distinctions between LAEPT and Christian anthropology. In this regard, Sofía Chipana (2019), an Aymara theologian from Bolivia, contends that colonisers dismissed the knowledge and spiritualities associated with the cycles of the cosmos in the Americas, imposing a dominant hegemonic religion that persists today. Chipana introduces the concept of 'cosmopraxis', revealing novel forms of relational practices characterised by co-participation with and in the world. In this worldview, 'everything possesses life and a place in the Cosmos, where humanity is an integral part of the vast community of interrelations that mutually and complementarily foster life' (2019, 62). In other words, there is no ecofeminism without the connection between body and the cosmos, as Indigenous cosmologies assert.

In several interviews between 2018 and 2020, Ress, one of the founders of *Con-spirando*, shared with me that the motivations of *Con-spirando* included participants getting to know themselves through their bodies, changing the prevailing epistemology of the hierarchical and patriarchal Christian tradition, as well as empowering themselves as women through celebration. This last aspect is particularly relevant because the cause of rediscovering themselves as women was to change the concept of evil that had been attributed to them in the past, and instead of responding with rage, it had to be done through celebration. This celebration did not imply changing faith or churches, which most of the participating women attended, but rather creating new meanings through rites referring to the cycles of nature, the seasons of the year and meetings with their sisters. In this sense, *Con-spirando* began to constitute itself as a space of resistance and an alternative to the rites offered to them in their traditional ecclesiastical spaces. If in the temple they were forbidden to dance, in the rites they danced; if in the liturgies there were hierarchical and established structures, in the rites there were no structures and they danced in circles; if in the church they did not speak of the Goddess, in the rites they began to celebrate her. In other words, these spaces signified what women longed for and dreamed of, a place of spirituality that gave women a voice and meaning. In a certain sense, they were breaking with the system without knowing that they were doing so. And that breaking with the system implies a change in culture and relationship to the body, as discussed in the second part of this article, as there is no liberation without a paradigm shift. This is why the work of *Con-spirando* has meant denouncing theological violence towards women, renaming and re-signifying the sacred, developing new methodologies and working with the body, as well as the ecofeminist theological contribution through the magazine *Con-spirando*, which has published some sixty editions.

In this regard, it seems pertinent to allude to the pedagogical proposal that a collective such as *Con-spirando* contributes to new understandings of a critical political theology today. Feminist authors such as Saba

Mahmood (2005) and Chandra Talpade Mohanty (2003) have questioned the category of 'Third World women', mainly because of the implication that they are ignorant, poor, religious and family-oriented (Mohanty 2003, 40). However, that they have managed to build and form communities based on solidarity and religious practices are aspects that both Mohanty and Mahmood have highlighted in their research with women from the so-called 'Global South' or 'Two-Thirds' of the world. In this sense, both highlight the role of a critical pedagogy, based on rethinking the position of being a woman in the world and in a particular context. In the case of Mahmood, she highlights the importance of rituals in Islam and body postures as a space for learning with other women (2005, 40–117). This learning would open up spaces for linking knowledge, social responsibility and collective struggle in order to challenge spaces of domination and create more equitable public spaces (Mohanty 2003, 201). Although Mohanty makes this proposal in the context of North American universities and academia, her analysis is relevant to the case of a critical, horizontal pedagogy that questions notions of authority and the divine, as proposed by *Con-spirando*.

Historically, Latin American women have struggled with pejorative notions of being women, especially because of an 'apparent' religiosity and lack of questioning of ecclesiastical authorities. However, *Con-spirando*'s proposal challenges these notions. First, it questions liberation theology as androcentric and anthropocentric. Second, it rethinks a worldview of the divine insofar as it excludes women and the cosmos from full participation in the sovereign body. In other words, the deconstruction of the divine proposed by *Con-spirando* and ecofeminist theologies is about reinterpreting women's bodies. And along with this reinterpretation of the body, they also allude to a questioning of the concept of power. As the notion of theological-political sovereignty has argued, 'power over' has determined the way politics is done. However, 'power within' challenges this notion of sovereignty by locating it in the body of each individual and re-signifying it, in that common pathways and collectivities based on solidarities and sororities are constructed in religious space.

Despite these contributions, there is no doubt that the greatest impact has been expressed in the testimonies of the many women in Latin America who have been touched, encouraged and empowered by the *Con-spirando* collective.[13] Not only finding a welcoming space of joy but also one within which sadness and lament can be shared, and even one in which dreaming of new possible worlds and aligning themselves politically with the new feminist movements that are taking shape in Chile today, is possible. And although its founders worry about the renewal of the collective in the future, they write with hope:

Instead of the predominant 'power over', the seed suggests 'power within'. The seed lies dormant, breaks, sprouts, blossoms, flowers, bears fruit, matures, dries up and falls to the ground again. It will be what it is meant to be. We too are seeds, called to be what we are meant to be. And so is *Con-spirando*. Let it be what it is meant to be – nothing more, nothing less. (Ress 2012, 144)

Final reflections

It is my belief that Schmitt was not wrong when he stated that 'all the central concepts of modern state theory are secularised theological concepts' (2009, 37). However, in writing about political theology and liberation theology, I was troubled by the idea of presenting sovereignty or 'power over' as an unquestioned category. New studies on political theologies resist and challenge the mainstream accounts of Schmitt's idea of power and sovereignty (Orrego Torres 2024, forthcoming; Orrego Torres and Rossello, forthcoming; Rossello 2019; Vatter 2021; Yelle 2022).

Just as we find in theology the foundations for domination and violence, we also find the possibility for redemption and liberation of the oppressed. And in speaking of the oppressed, unlike liberation theology, which can at times seem like it spoke exclusively in terms of socio-economic status, I situate myself with those who suffer exclusion and oppression because of their gender, race, caste and other forms of discrimination today. We could even speak of domination over species and nature, as ecofeminist theology puts it. And we can, moreover, ask whether such an ecofeminist theology is a continuation of, or a break from, liberation theology, especially given the development of both feminist and ecological liberation theologies in Latin America.

The configuration of new understandings of relationships between human beings and towards nature are key to giving meaning to the understanding of political theology and liberation theology today. The challenges refer to living ecofeminism not exclusively in the private sphere of spirituality but as a way of living politically. Ecofeminism invites us to change the paradigm of how we relate not only to other human beings but also to nature. And, today, with the news alerting us to climate change and the consequences of the Anthropocene (which reflects the impact of humans on the earth) and the Technozoic era (focused on the exploitation of resources and the planet through techno-science) it is becoming increasingly difficult to move towards an Ecozoic era (where ecology is the axis) and thus diminish the ongoing devastation. And, for this, the commitment of governments and their authorities is not enough, but the commitment of all through a 'power-with' and 'power-from-within', as Primavesi put it, provides a way to find ourselves again in community with others, but also with ourselves, with the knowledge of our bodies and the connection with nature.

An ecofeminist approach would allow us to reformulate and broaden known notions of political theology. First, the focus would not be exclusively on state sovereignty. It would make it possible to question the idea of power and authority, situating it in the relationship with the cosmos and new ways of thinking about power. Second, women's experiences have reaffirmed the importance of re-signifying the role of bodies. In this sense, a body appropriated by women for their own pleasure, as well as for the performance of rituals. Both terms, which in a theological-political understanding of sovereignty have been appropriated by the state or the Church, from an ecofeminist point of view make visible the importance of connecting with oneself through the power-from-inside or the so-called Goddess. Third, the example of *Con-spirando*, in its desire to constitute an alternative space, promotes what Mohanty calls 'pedagogies of dissent'. That is, as a space that challenges spaces of domination – such as anthropocentrism and androcentrism – in order to dispute democratic and inclusive gender spaces from an ecofeminist perspective.

This is why, in a post-secular world, overcoming anthropocentric and androcentric notions should be at the heart of the new proposals for political theologies and their readings. Only in this way will we be able to speak of a political theology that not only resists the notion of sovereignty but also integrates those voices and positions that are not incorporated into the discussion and understanding of political theology. In this sense, understanding political theology as an approach that is not necessarily dominant but, rather, one that proposes alternatives from the periphery and rebellion.

In this chapter, the intention is to show a possibility of this, through the discussion, visibility and reading of authors who write from the experience and knowledge of Latin America. But also, from the particular experience of *Con-spirando* as an example of the politics of 'dissidence' from an ecofeminist perspective. However, this knowledge is not yet widely disseminated in academic circles. Therefore, to echo Mohanty (2003, 170), the academy as a public space for dialogue, engagement and vision of democracy and justice needs feminism as a political and pedagogical project. But not only that. Doing political theology from the South or from the Two-Thirds would mean making sense of these discourses for an understanding of our socio-political reality and of the approach to new ways of what power and knowledge of our bodies means. As I have argued (Orrego Torres, forthcoming), it is crucial to underscore the significance of recognising religious and spiritual practices originating from ecofeminist perspectives in Latin America. In this context, the global transnational influence of feminism and ecofeminist theology has the potential to decentralise the prevailing notion of political theology, presenting it as a viable political and ethical possibility. On the other hand, it is an invitation to those who read feminism and environmentalism as two separate paths without finding a point of union, since there are more paths that unite than those that distance us.

Notes

1. Many thanks to the editors and the anonymous reviewers for their feedback and suggestions. I am grateful for the generous, moving and insightful conversations about ecofeminism with Judith Ress and Arianne van Andel. A previous version of this paper was first published in Spanish as 'Hacia la posibilidad de una teología política ecofeminista' in *Síntesis. Revista de Filosofía* 2, no. 2 (2019): 114–41. Translated by Pablo Bradbury.

2. Oyarzún translated works by Benjamin into Spanish.

3. Antonio Gimeno Cuspinera translated the texts for Editorial Pre-textos and Flavia Costa, Edgardo Castro, Mercedes Ruvituso and Rodrigo Molina-Zavalía for Editorial Adriana Hidalgo.

4. Jorge Dotti served as editor of *Deus Mortalis* until his death in 2018. One of the pioneering editions on the subject in *Revista Pléyade* in Chile was published in 2011. See: https://www.revistapleyade.cl/index.php/OJS/issue/view/21.

5. The term post-secular has been widely debated in political theory as a category that questions the 'apparent' secularisation of the modern era. Some of its proponents have been Jürgen Habermas (2008), Charles Taylor (2007) and José Casanova (1994). In general terms, it is a concept that alludes to rethinking the categories of religion and politics, considering that religion has not been abolished from the public sphere, as liberalism would have suggested. For a critical positioning from the notions of biopolitics and Italian political thought, see the recent article by Vatter (2019b). Despite these initial considerations, my position is aligned with that proposed by Saba Mahmood (2005) and Joan Wallach Scott (2018).

6. On the relationship between the unsacrificable and divine violence, see Orrego Torres (2008).

7. See the anthology edited by Mary Judith Ress, Ute Seibert and Lene Sjørup entitled *From Heaven to Earth* (1994).

8. There are accounts of the creation of the world in the Near and Middle East that allude to female deities. Certain ancient civilisations to this day keep vestiges of temples dedicated to the goddesses of the earth and fertility, among others. One of the most emblematic is Ashtoreth, considered a 'pagan' goddess in the Old Testament, but known in Canaan as the Queen of Heaven. See Stone (1994).

9. As a response to this 'historical debt' to female figures in early Christianity, see the recent book by Kateusz (2019), focusing on a new historical interpretation of Mary and other women.

10. Within this schema, it is interesting to note that Natalie Gasparowicz's chapter in the present volume analyses an important event that stands at the transition from the first to the second stage, pp. 159–78.

11. According to Mies and Shiva, the concept of ecofeminism refers to 'a new term for an old wisdom' that was introduced in the late 1970s and early 1980s. As they note, Françoise D'Eaubonne first used the term in the context of social movements and protests against the environmental disasters of the time (2014, 13).

12. More information about the collective can be found on their website: http://www.conspirando.cl.

13. Chapter 4 of Mary Judith Ress's book (2012) offers a series of reflections on the experiences of Latin American women in relation to ecofeminism.

References

Agamben, Giorgio. *Homo sacer. Il potere sovrano e la nuda vita*. Torino: Einaudi, 1995.

Andel, Arianne van. *Teología en movimiento: Ensayos eco-teológicos y feministas para tiempos de cambio*. Miami: JUANUNO1 Ediciones, 2021.

Casanova, José. *Public Religions in the Modern World*. Chicago: University of Chicago, 1994.

Chipana Quispe, Sofía. 'Relational Wisdom and Spiritualities in Abya Yala'. In *Decolonial Theology: Violence, Resistance and Spiritualities*, edited by Carlos Mendoza-Álvarez and Thierry-Marie Courau, 59–68. London: SCM Press, 2019.

Christ, Carol P. 'Por qué las mujeres necesitan a la Diosa: Reflexiones fenomenológicas, sicológicas y políticas'. In *Del cielo a la tierra. Una antología de teología feminista*, edited by Mary Judith Ress, Ute Seibert and Lene Sjørup, 159–73. Santiago: Sello Azul, 1994.

Collingwood-Selby, Elizabeth. *Walter Benjamin. La lengua del exilio*. Santiago: LOM, 1997.

Collingwood-Selby, Elizabeth. *El filo fotográfico de la historia. Walter Benjamin y el olvido de lo inolvidable*. Santiago: Ediciones Metales Pesados, 2009.

Dotti, Jorge. *Carl Schmitt en Argentina*. Rosario: Homo sapiens editores, 2000.

Dotti, Jorge, and Julio Pinto, eds. *Carl Schmitt, su época y pensamiento*. Buenos Aires: Eudeba, 2002.

Gebara, Ivone. *Intuiciones ecofeministas. Ensayo para repensar el conocimiento y la religión*. Madrid: Trotta, 2000.

Gebara, Ivone. *Out of the Depths: Women's Experience of Evil and Salvation*. Minneapolis: Fortress Press, 2002.

Habermas, Jürgen. 'Secularism's Crisis of Faith: Notes on Post-Secular Society', *New Perspectives Quarterly* 25 (2008): 17–29.

Kantorowitz, Ernst H. *The King's Two Bodies: A Study in Medieval Political Theology*. Princeton, NJ: Princeton University Press, 1981.

Karmy, Rodrigo, ed. *Políticas de la interrupción. Ensayos sobre Giorgio Agamben*. Santiago: Editorial Escaparate, 2011.

Karmy, Rodrigo. *Políticas de la ex-carnación. Para una genealogía teológica de la biopolítica*. Buenos Aires: Editorial UNIPE, 2014.

Karmy, Rodrigo, and Luna Follegati, eds. *Estudios en Gubernamentalidad. Ensayos sobre poder, vida y neoliberalismo*. Viña del Mar: Ediciones Comunes, 2018.

Kateusz, Ally. *Mary and Early Christian Women: Hidden Leadership*. London: Palgrave MacMillan, 2019.
Mahmood, Saba. *Politics of Piety: The Islamic Revival and the Feminist Subject*. Princeton, NJ: Princeton University Press, 2005.
Mohanty, Chandra Talpade. *Feminism without Borders: Decolonizing Theory, Practicing Solidarity*. Durham, NC: Duke University Press, 2003.
Oro, Luis. 'Crítica de Schmitt al liberalismo', *Estudios Públicos* 98 (2005): 171–87.
Oro, Luis. *El concepto de realismo político*. Santiago: RIL Editores, 2013.
Orrego Torres, Ely. 'Hacia la posibilidad de una teología política ecofeminista', *Síntesis. Revista de Filosofía* 2, no. 2 (2019): 114–31.
Orrego Torres, Ely. 'Exploring Democratic Turns in Political Theologies after Schmitt', *Ethics & Politics* 26 (2024): 295–307.
Orrego Torres, Ely. 'Beyond Boundaries: Exploring Transnational Ecofeminist Political Theologies and Solidarities in Latin America', *Philosophy and Global Affairs* (forthcoming).
Orrego Torres, Ely, and Diego Rossello. 'Imagining Ecopolis: Visions of Ecofeminist Political Theology and Ecocriticism in Latin America', *Social Compass* (forthcoming).
Primavesi, Anne. 'Poder jerárquico y poder ecológico'. In *Del cielo a la tierra. Una antología de teología feminista*, edited by Mary Judith Ress, Ute Seibert and Lene Sjørup, 455–79. Santiago: Sello Azul, 1994.
Ress, Mary Judith, Ute Seibert and Lene Sjørup, eds. *Del cielo a la tierra. Una antología de teología feminista*. Santiago: Sello Azul, 1994.
Ress, Mary Judith. *Ecofeminism in Latin America*. New York: Orbis Books, Maryknoll, 2006.
Ress, Mary Judith. *Sin visiones nos perdemos. Reflexiones sobre Teología Ecofeminista Latinoamericana*. Santiago: Colectivo Con-spirando, 2012.
Richard, Nelly. 'Roturas, memoria y discontinuidades (en homenaje a W. Benjamin)'. In *La insubordinación de los signos*, edited by Richard Nelly, 13–36. Santiago de Chile: Cuarto Propio, 1994.
Richard, Nelly. 'Memoria del arte y traza fotográfica', *Revista Teoría del Arte* (1999): 37–46.
Rossello, Diego. 'Pluralizando la teología política. Nuevas agendas en torno a un antiguo problema', *Síntesis. Revista de Filosofía* 2, no. 2 (2019): 1–8. doi:10.15691/0718-5448Vol2Iss2a286.
Schmitt, Carl. *Teología política*. Madrid: Trotta, 2009.
Scott, Joan Wallach. *Sex and Secularism*. Princeton, NJ: Princeton University Press, 2018.

Shiva, Vandana, and Maria Mies. *Ecofeminism*. London and New York: Zed Books, 2014.

Stone, Merlin. 'Cuando Dios era mujer'. In *Del cielo a la tierra. Una antología de teología feminista*, edited by Mary Judith Ress, Ute Seibert and Lene Sjørup, 175–84. Santiago: Sello Azul, 1994.

Taylor, Charles. *A Secular Age*. Cambridge, MA: Belknap of Harvard University Press, 2007.

Thayer, Willy. 'El giro barroco. De G. Deleuze a W. Benjamin', *Archivos. Revista de Filosofía* 2/3 (2007): 93–119.

Thayer, Willy. *Tecnologías de la crítica: Entre Walter Benjamin y Gilles Deleuze*. Santiago: Ediciones Metales Pesados, 2010.

Vatter, Miguel. 'Strauss and Schmitt as Readers of Hobbes and Spinoza: On the Relation between Liberalism and Political Theology', *The New Centennial Review* 4, no. 3 (2004): 161–214.

Vatter, Miguel. 'Political Theology without Sovereignty: Some 20th Century Examples (Voegelin, Maritain, Badiou)', 26 August 2009. https://bit.ly/2WWnfBi. Accessed 22/11/2024.

Vatter, Miguel, ed. *Crediting God: Sovereignty & Religion in the Age of Global Capitalism*. New York: Fordham University Press, 2011a.

Vatter, Miguel. 'Habermas between Athens and Jerusalem: Public Reason and Atheistic Theology', *Interpretation: A Journal of Political Philosophy* 28, no. 3 (2011b): 243–61.

Vatter, Miguel. 'Pensar la política desde la teología política (entrevistado por Ely Orrego)', *Revista Pléyade* 8 (2011c): 185–98.

Vatter, Miguel. *Constitución y resistencia. Ensayos de teoría democrática radical*. Santiago: Ediciones Universidad Diego Portales, 2012.

Vatter, Miguel. 'Politico-Theological Foundations of Human Rights: The Case of Maritain', *Social Research: An International Quarterly* 80, no. 1 (2013): 233–60.

Vatter, Miguel. 'Cosmopolitan Political Theology in Cohen and Rosenzweig', *Philosophy Today* 60, no. 2 (2016): 295–324.

Vatter, Miguel. '"Only a God Can Resist a God" Political Theology between Polytheism and Gnosticism', *Political Theology* (2019a). doi:10.1080/1462317X.2019.1618597.

Vatter, Miguel. 'Civil Religion and the Pursuit of Happiness from Machiavelli to Italian Theory', *Giornale Critico Di Storia Delle Idee* 1 (2019b): 75–89.

Yelle, Robert A. 'The Sovereign Remains'. *Religious Studies Review* 48 no.4 (2022): 525–7.

Afterword

Contemporary witnesses to life and liberation: The persistent and evolving reality of Latin American martyrdom

Elizabeth O'Donnell Gandolfo

Sr. Dorothy Stang, Brazil, 2005
Isaura Alves Muniz and Family, Brazil, 2006
Valmir 'Keno' Mota de Oliveira, Brazil, 2007
Raimundo Agnaldo Dourado de Almeida, Brazil, 2008
Marcelo Rivera, Ramiro Rivera Gómez, Felícita Echeverría,
Dora Alicia Recinos Sorto, El Salvador, 2009
Alberta 'Bety' Cariño Trujillo and Jyri Antero Jaakkola, Mexico, 2010
Juan Francisco Durán Ayala, El Salvador, 2011
Adenilson Kirixi Munduruku, Brazil, 2012
Juan Pablo Jiménez, Argentina, 2013
Faustino Acevedo Gaitán, Colombia, 2014
Raimundo dos Santos Rodrigues, Brazil, 2015
Berta Cáceres, Honduras, 2016
Carlos Maaz Coc, Guatemala, 2017
Marielle Franco and Anderson Gomes, Brazil, 2018
Dilma Ferreira Silva, Brazil, 2019
Roberto Carlos Pacheco, Peru, 2020
Fernando dos Santos Araújo, Brazil, 2021
Luz Marina Arteaga, Colombia, 2022
Manuel 'Tortuguita' Paez Terán, USA, 2023
Ludivia Galindez, Colombia, 2024[1]

Around the turn of the twenty-first century, Latin American liberation theology began to go out of fashion in the theological academy of the North Atlantic world.[2] With the decline in its marketability to white theologians, a widespread assumption took hold that liberation theology had also declined in Latin America (or even that it was 'dead'), which rendered continued engagement with it and with the communities from which it emerged 'nostalgic'. This theological development in the North Atlantic world also coincided with the decline in European and North American solidarity with Latin American liberation movements after the end of the dictatorships, their so-called 'dirty wars', and their death squads of the late twentieth century. The handful of theologians in the Global North who have continued to engage Latin American liberation theology over the past two decades have resisted this trend with beautiful work plumbing the depths both of first-generation liberation theologies – for example, of Gustavo Gutiérrez and Jon Sobrino – and, even more notably, of the lives and commitments of the martyrs of the 1970s and 1980s, such as Fr. Rutilio Grande, Monseñor Óscar Arnulfo Romero and Fr. Ignacio Ellacuría. Indeed, Gutiérrez and Sobrino themselves insist that liberation theology emerged in Latin America from the blood-soaked ground where these martyrs and so many others committed their lives to the liberation of their people and were consequently murdered by agents of the state and the wealthy elite. In the beginning, liberation theology was steeped in this day-to-day reality and spirituality of martyrdom. Martha Zechmeister's foreword to this volume rightly calls on contemporary liberation theologies to remain rooted in the blood-soaked soils of the places and struggles where so many lives have been sacrificed to the gods of empire.

In recent years, the Church has officially begun to recognise this form of martyrdom in which committed Christians have been crucified as a consequence of their solidarity with the crucified people. With the canonisation of San Romero and the beatification of several other 'martyrs of solidarity',[3] Pope Francis has 'rehabilitated' liberatory forms of Christian faith, and the contemporary relevance of Latin American liberation theology is being reconsidered in both the Church and the theological academy around the world. At the same time, popular movements for liberation in Latin America have proliferated and diversified over the past several decades, carrying on the legacies of these martyrs and responding in their own particular contexts to more multidimensional experiences and understandings of the signs of the times. Feminist and ecofeminist, Indigenous, Black and queer theologies have emerged from Christian engagement with popular movements of these communities in the region, such that the term liberation theologies 'came to be used in the plural because what was once only the so-called liberation theology opened the way to a plurality of theological perspectives that came to claim place and emancipated voices' (Pacheco 2017). Far from a trajectory of decline, liberation theologies and spiritualities are flourishing in a diversity of contexts and expressions across the continent. What is the place of martyrdom in relation to these new waves of liberatory faith and theological reflection? Is the relationship between liberation theology and martyrdom 'as it was in the beginning'?

Latin American martyrdom: as it was in the beginning?

When I first began to study liberation theologies in the late 1990s, and then lived and worked with the ecclesial base communities (*Comunidades Eclesiales de Base*, CEBs) of El Salvador in the early 2000s, Latin American memory of martyrs who had been murdered during the revolutionary years of the late twentieth century was fresh, the wounds of war and political repression still gaping. As a privileged, white student of liberation theology in the North Atlantic world, though, the rhetoric of liberation theology's decline gave the impression that the days of self-styled 'dirty wars', armed conflict and martyrdom in Latin America were over. I naively relegated the era of martyrdom to the 1970s and 1980s, although I knew that Monseñor Juan José Gerardi had been murdered for his prophetic commitment to speaking the truth about the Guatemalan genocide just three short years before I studied Spanish in his homeland. Even when Sr. Dorothy Stang was murdered in 2005 for her defence of subsistence farmers' land rights and the preservation of the Amazon, I jumped to the conclusion that this was an aberration. And so, when I published my first academic article on women and martyrdom in El Salvador in 2007 (Gandolfo 2007, 26–53), I wrote and reflected as if martyrdom was a thing of the past, from which liberation theology had been born, but which was now present in contemporary praxis of historical memory and collective resurrection, not in continued persecution and death. The above litany of human rights and environmental defenders murdered in the past twenty years indicates that I could not have been more wrong. This blind spot in my own work is not surprising, given my social location in the United States and my theological formation at a time Latin America was no longer 'trending' in the theological academy or in the praxis of solidarity more broadly.

If we care enough to pay attention, though, it becomes obvious that martyrdom in Latin America was not and is not a thing of the past, but rather a very real and present experience, taking on new and complex forms, yet just as persistent a reality as it was in the beginning of both liberation theology and the history of Latin America more broadly. In fact, it is from the blood-soaked grounds of martyrdom that new and diverse expressions of liberation theology have emerged and proliferated across the continent. Zechmeister invites readers to lean into the 'productive asynchronicity' that exists between theological reflection, memory of historical martyrdom and memory of Jesus' own concrete practices of healing, liberation and communion.[4] However, the productive asynchronicity of liberation movements with the historical memory of martyrdom is too often met with the destructive asynchronicity of powerful forces that repeatedly respond with violence, time and time again, when oppressed and marginalised communities rise up to demand justice and freedom. These perpetual cycles of violence thus require a creative synchronicity between contemporary liberation theologies and the challenges that contemporary martyrdom poses to the praxis of and affective commitment to liberation.

The persistence of Latin American martyrdom: from origins to contemporary reality

In the beginning was the sword. When Iberian conquistadors invaded and colonised the lands that would later be designated as the *Américas*, the extractivist imagination that they brought with them required that they violently seek possession and total control of land, labour, religion and culture, in order to amass untold wealth and global dominance. In the face of this new reality, the original peoples of these lands resisted the extractivist evils of enslavement, land theft, cultural annihilation and genocide. When European agents of human trafficking captured Africans and transported them across the Atlantic Ocean to serve as forced labourers in the Americas, enslaved peoples resisted, fleeing to the forests to form autonomous Maroon communities and *quilombos*. In both cases, colonisers responded to the defiance of those they sought to colonise with further violence, meeting uprisings and opposition with acts of war, ethnic cleansing and political executions. For example, in the Caribbean, the Indigenous Taíno Cacique Hatuey is remembered as one who valiantly resisted the Spanish invasion and was burned at the stake for his rebellion, refusing baptism with the famous statement that he wanted nothing to do with a heaven where the Spanish would be present.[5] In Brazil, the *quilombola* king Zumbi dos Palmares, who is remembered for his resistance to the enslavement of his people and his refusal to submit to Portuguese rule, was executed and decapitated to disprove his perceived immortality.[6] But, like so many martyrs of liberation, these men represented untold masses who were also killed. And, moreover, popular memory of Hatuey, Zumbi and other martyrs has not silenced their witness but rather has multiplied their impact across time and space. Just as the Inca-descendant revolutionary Tupac Amaru II prophesied for himself before his own execution, these martyrs have returned and have become millions.[7]

Refusal to submit to colonisation, oppression and exploitation in Latin America did not begin or end with the revolutionary popular movements from which liberation theology was born in the mid- to late twentieth century. As the previous examples indicate, the liberationist experience of Latin American martyrdom did not originate at this time either, for the peoples of Latin America have repeatedly sought freedom, faced violent defeat and risen again from the ashes over the course of more than 500 years. A key difference in the experience of martyrdom during the early years of twentieth-century liberation theology was that a significant number of public religious leaders, including archbishops, stood in solidarity with the poor and oppressed in their struggles for liberation and therefore suffered 'the same fate as the poor'.[8] What was new was not the resistance of colonised and impoverished peoples, but the response of certain sectors of the Church to their resistance, and the violence that was meted out on those ecclesial sectors in return. This perpetual cycle of extractivism, oppression and violence is abhorrent, but it should not be surprising that liberation struggles continue to face violent repression in the Americas today. Indeed, there are places in contemporary Latin America where solidarity with collective struggles for human rights and social and ecological liberation is a perilous endeavor that too often leads to violent persecution by powerful proxies of global capital and local agents and beneficiaries of organised crime and political corruption.

In fact, since the turn of the century, thousands of human rights defenders have been slain across Latin America for their commitments to justice, peace, equality, truth, human rights, Indigenous autonomy and sustainable access to the social and ecological goods on which human life depends. Certain countries are particularly dangerous (such as Mexico, Honduras, Colombia and Brazil), and land and environmental defenders are especially at risk, with Indigenous peoples being the most disproportionately vulnerable population in the region. Advocates for gender justice and LGBTQ+ rights are also targeted with violence, and anti-racist organising is always risky, particularly for persons of African descent. Online databases of persecuted and murdered human rights and environmental defenders are replete with examples of violent repression, and these databases only document confirmed cases, which represent a much larger phenomenon in the region and around the world.[9]

The reality of contemporary martyrdom in Latin America is rooted in more complex social, economic and political networks of power and violence than it was during the 1970s and 1980s, and martyrdom is no longer as visibly tied to the Church, Christian commitment and public religious leadership as it was in the early years of liberation theology. Martyrdom for justice and liberation has always transcended the narrow confines of religious affiliation in Latin America, as the examples of Hatuey and Zumbi above make clear, but the late twentieth-century martyrs whose lives and legacies are most well known in the ecclesial communities and theological academy of the North Atlantic world are still male clerics and women religious, such as Monseñor Óscar Arnulfo Romero, the four North American churchwomen, the UCA (Universidad Centroamericana José Simeón Cañas) Jesuits and Sr. Dorothy Stang. Nevertheless, in more recent years, Latin American liberation theologians and ecclesial communities committed to a liberating faith have begun to engage more deeply with the witness of twenty-first-century martyrs – Christian or not – who have paid the ultimate price for embodied participation in their peoples' struggles for social and ecological liberation. As Zechmeister suggests, we must 'see – take the weight', and we must 'hear – and give space in our hearts to what we hear' in the witness of contemporary martyrs so that '[t]he theological word that our time demands' might not be taken as 'already given' but rather reborn from our encounters with their struggles. And so, it is right and just to conclude this volume by signalling how the lives and commitments of contemporary martyrs challenge us to deepen our analysis of what we 'see and hear' so that we can better 'take on the weight and give space in our hearts' to the witness of popular movements for liberation in our world today.

The theological challenge of contemporary martyrdom

In his extensive theological reflections on martyrdom, Jon Sobrino (1999) posits that martyrdom brings to theology a 'dialectical disposition' that challenges theology not only to announce the good news of grace, justice, truth and the living presence of God but also to denounce the historical realities of sin, injustice, falsehood and death. Contemporary persecution of human rights and environmental defenders is a clear revelation of how capitalism, racism, patriarchy and ecological destruction are violently entangled manifestations of sin in our world today. This dialectical disposition opens Christian theology in general and liberation theologies in particular to self-examination and self-critique in light of the witness of martyrs who have incorporated not only liberationist, but also intersectional, feminist, anti-racist, queer, environmental and decolonial modes of analysis into their struggles for justice, liberation and ecological well-being.

Take, for example, the case of Marielle Franco, a queer Black woman who was born in a Rio de Janeiro favela in 1979 and became a fierce opponent of racism, police brutality and economic exploitation, fighting for the rights and dignity of Afro-Brazilian and LGBTQ+ people, first as a community activist and then as a councilwoman.[10] She was especially astute in her analysis and vocal in her denunciation of the police and military violence in Black neighborhoods of Rio and Brazil more broadly, where police kill upwards of 6,000 people per year, with Black Brazilians accounting for 83 percent of the victims but 56 percent of the population (Carvalho and Costa 2023). Marielle's prophetic denunciation of this reality, coupled with her unapologetic existence as a queer Black woman, was such a threat to the ruling elite that she was assassinated by hitmen in Rio de Janeiro on March 14, 2018, along with her driver, Anderson Gomes. Liberation theologies are at their best when they elevate the witness of contemporary human rights defenders who, like Marielle, show us what it means to struggle against contemporary forms of oppression and injustice in Latin America, and throughout the Americas as a whole. Benedictine monk Marcelo Barros makes this connection clear by recognising Marielle as one of many martyrs who, Christian or not, challenge the Church to stand in solidarity with the poor, marginalised and oppressed, not as an 'appendage of faith', but as 'the fundamental core of what it means to follow Jesus' (Barros 2022). Furthermore, in his response to the murders of Marielle and Anderson, Leonardo Boff (2019) calls on white Brazilians to deepen their critical reflection on the ever-present and rising discrimination not only against the poor, but against LGBTQ+ folks, *quilombolas*, Indigenous communities and especially the Black community, which makes up over half of the Brazilian population. The CEBs of Brazil include Marielle in their litany of martyrs, and her witness is a touchstone for a new generation of Black theological reflection emerging in Brazil, including that of Ronilso Pacheco (n.d.), who coordinated the publication of a book on Jesus and human rights in the same year that Marielle was murdered. Marielle's commitments to economic, racial, gender and LGBTQ+ justice point us toward intersectional analyses of oppression and an appreciation for how the fullness of liberation is multidimensional and universal – it cannot privilege one identity, form of oppression or expression of liberation over others. In the words of Fannie Lou Hamer (2010, 134–9), 'nobody's free until everybody's free'.

Similarly, the witness of Berta Cáceres, who was murdered on March 2, 2016, illuminates the intersectionality of oppressions and the multidimensionality of what decolonial scholars today call the 'colonial matrix of power'.[11] Berta was an Indigenous Lenca woman organizing among her people in the mountainous region of southwestern Honduras. At the time of her death, she and the Civic Council of Popular and Indigenous Organizations of Honduras (COPINH), which she co-founded and directed, were fighting to protect the sacred waters of the Gualcarque River and surrounding communities from social and ecological devastation by the internationally financed Agua Zarca hydroelectric dam project. Berta herself was inspired by the legacy of historical and contemporary martyrs, and dedicated the prestigious Goldman Environmental Prize that she was awarded in 2015 to all the rebels out there, including the martyrs who have been slain for defending the goods of the natural world. In the analysis of Berta and COPINH, defence of the natural world and the liberation of human communities are intertwined, with both processes requiring multi-pronged resistance to not only projects of capitalist extractivism that devastate local ecosystems and marginalised human communities, but also the patriarchal and racist structures that fuel these extractivist projects with the bodies of women, *campesinos*, Indigenous peoples and Afro-descendant communities. Berta's Goldman Prize acceptance speech states the matter succinctly:

> Wake up! Wake up, humanity! We are out of time. We must shake ourselves free of the rapacious capitalism, racism and patriarchy that will only assure our self-destruction. The Gualcarque River has called upon us, as have all the rivers that are seriously threatened in our world. We must answer the call. Our Mother Earth – militarised, fenced in, poisoned, where basic rights are systematically violated – demands that we take action. (Cáceres 2015)

With these words and the witness of her life, Berta teaches us that the struggle for liberation, and ultimately for the future of human life and the planet itself, must be anti-capitalist, anti-racist and anti-patriarchal. As ecofeminist and ecowomanist activists and scholars have been arguing for decades, there is no reducing the struggle to one of these logics of domination, for they are all inextricably interconnected.

As with Marielle, ecclesial communities and liberation theologies have embraced Berta's witness with love, rage and courage for carrying on her legacy. María José Caram (2017, 123–4) names Berta as one of the 'crucified people' whose 'death provides a glimpse of the intricate challenges facing those who have committed their lives to the cause of justice today'. On the fourth anniversary of Berta's assassination, Radio Progreso, the community radio station run by the Jesuits in Honduras, offered an extensive theological reflection on the meaning of martyrdom, the brutality of the violence that precipitates it, the depth of the loss that it occasions, and the ways in which the martyrdom of persons like Berta 'dignifies' all those who struggle for life and the life of creation as a whole. This broadcast named Berta's martyrial significance as equal to that of San Romero:

> Berta is also our Monseñor Romero in our Honduras, although it may sound blasphemous to certain clergy who are well-situated. And if it doesn't seem that way to them, then we are saying it wrong because Jesus was assassinated with the approval of those who were religiously well-situated in his time. (Radio Progreso 2020)[12]

Berta has since become a subversive symbol for ecologically conscientious communities and environmental justice movements throughout the Americas, including in Honduras' neighbouring country El Salvador, where ecclesial base communities emblazon her image on banners and reverently place it on altars alongside the images of Romero and other Salvadoran martyrs of liberation. The symbolism of her martyrdom is *hecho realidad* and the seed that was planted when she died has multiplied in the concrete praxis of all those who carry on her struggle.[13]

A comprehensive commitment to socio-environmental justice has led many human rights defenders to deepen and broaden their understanding of how the *coloniaje* of the current world system is designed to privilege an elite minority at the expense of the colonised peoples and the earth itself. As we have seen, the analysis and praxis of Berta Cáceres reminds us that the *anti-reino* against which martyrs of liberation stand as dialectical witnesses is not only structured by capitalism but by the extractivist and colonial ravages of racism and patriarchy. Liberation theologies have begun to take these intersectional and decolonial critiques into account in their attempts to formulate a dialectical understanding of how the sinful dynamics of anti-social and anti-ecological imaginaries operate in complex interconnected webs of violence and oppression. Just as the elements and energies that give life to the cosmos are interconnected, so, too, are the human systems that produce the cries of the earth and the cries of the poor.[14] These cries intersect with the cries of Indigenous peoples and people of African descent, women (especially women of color), immigrants and refugees, LGBTQ+ folks, persons with disabilities, the elderly and all those whom society dismisses as disposable. First-generation liberation theologians were not fully equipped to engage the fullness of these intersections of oppression and liberation all that well, even as they attempted to expand the category of the poor to include race and gender. Pope Francis' integral ecology gestures toward the intersections of multiple systems of oppression, but his contributions require significant correction in terms of his omission of an explicit analysis of racism and his reaffirmation of binary and essentialist thinking around gender and sexuality. Nevertheless, the proliferation of feminist, ecofeminist, Black, Indigenous and queer theologies across the Americas has moved the analyses of liberation theologies toward synchronicity with the struggles of contemporary martyrs for the fullness of liberation in all of its multidimensional forms.

It bears mentioning here that another dimension of the dialectical disposition that engagement with contemporary martyrdom can cultivate in liberation theologies has to do with the dangers of Christian supremacy and the need to cultivate a culture of interreligious encounter characterised by humility and solidarity. The murder of human rights and environmental defenders is a worldwide phenomenon that claims the lives of many more non-Christians than Christians, especially Indigenous and Afro-descendant peoples, many of whom adhere to their own ancestral cosmovisions, lifeways and spiritualities. Remembering that Latin American martyrdom embraces and transcends many religious and spiritual traditions can challenge liberation theologies to an internal critique of the barriers to encountering non-Christian communities in a dialogical spirit of genuine respect and collaboration. Given the history and current legacy of Christian complicity with colonialism's extractivist legacy of neoliberal capitalism, racism and patriarchy, Christian churches have much to learn from this dialogue.

Creative synchronicity with the 'living martyrs' of today

In his tribute to Marielle Franco on the first anniversary of her death, Marcelo Barros recalls sentiments expressed by the CEBs of Brazil at their sixth national meeting in 1986: '*Nós queremos nossos mártires vivos e não mortos.*' We want our martyrs alive, not dead! Witnessing to the sacred interconnectedness of human life and the life of our earth community, our common home, should not lead to unjust and early death. It should not provoke persecution, criminalisation, defamation, torture or imprisonment. It should not lead to death threats, nor should it end in the violent theft of human lives. To be a witness to the integrity of creation and to human dignity, justice and peace is an option for life, albeit in the face of death. Indeed, as Barros (2022) puts it,

> the journey of the popular church and its immersion in struggles for liberation teach us that martyrdom is not only a way of dying; it is above all a way of living. We [in the popular church] are witnesses that there is redemption in this world and that, despite all the forces of evil, we will continue on this journey.

Similarly, all freedom fighters and land and environmental defenders in the Americas and around the world continue on this journey of life, witnessing to their own particular wellsprings of love for humanity and the earth as one interconnected community. In their continued social and ecological struggles, in their persistent praxis of love and liberation, they make present and honour the resurrection and legacy of those witnesses who have fallen, not only in historical liberation struggles but in their own contemporary popular movements. Those whom Barros names as 'living martyrs' continue to bear witness to the realities for which historical and contemporary martyrs have died, refusing to be silent in the face of violence and continuing to build an alternative world in which many worlds are free to co-exist,[15] a world that resembles, at least in part, the reality named by Christians as the reign or kin-dom of God.[16] Scholars and practitioners of liberation theology are therefore faced with the task of seeking creative synchronicity with contemporary martyrs – both the living witnesses who face persecution and those who have died and risen in the struggles of their people – such that we all might participate in the incarnation of the divine dream of life in the face of death and destruction.

Notes

1. This litany of contemporary Latin American martyrs has been drawn from the following online databases and reports on the persecution and assassination of human rights and environmental defenders: Organization of American States, www.oas.org; Human Rights Defenders Memorial, www.hrdmemorial.org; Front Line Defenders, www.frontlinedefenders.org; Amnesty International, www.amnesty.org; Global Witness, www.globalwitness.org.

2. For an incisive critique of liberation theology's marketability and decline in European theological circles, see Althaus-Reid (2000, 23–33).

3. This is how Michael E. Lee (2018) describes martyrs who have been murdered as a result of their solidarity with the poor and oppressed.

4. Martha Zechmeister's keynote address at the November 2020 conference, 'As It Was in the Beginning? Liberation Theology and Praxis in Contemporary Latin America', on which her foreword to this volume is based, was originally titled 'The

Productive Asynchronicity of Liberation Theology: Theology in the Footsteps of the Martyrs'.

5. See Lucas (2004, 36). All translations from original Spanish and Portuguese sources are mine unless otherwise noted.

6. See Lucas (2004, 77–82).

7. See Lucas (2004, 95–8).

8. In one of his final homilies in 1980, Archbishop Romero made this observation: 'Christ tells us not to fear persecution. Because – believe me, sisters and brothers – those who commit themselves to the poor must experience the same fate as the poor. And in El Salvador we know what the fate of the poor is: being disappeared, being tortured, being arrested, being found dead' (Romero 1980). Martyred Maryknoll Sister Ita Ford is said to have quoted these words soon before she and three other North American churchwomen were murdered later that year. See Noone (1984).

9. For an extensive analysis of ecological martyrdom in Latin America, see Gandolfo (2023).

10. See Erdos (2018).

11. For an introduction to decolonial scholarship, see the series of essays under the topic 'Globalization and the De-Colonial Option' in *Cultural Studies* (Mignolo and Escobar 2007).

12. Full English translation available in Gandolfo (2023, 232–6).

13. Among those who carry on Berta's legacy, it is often said that 'Berta did not die, she multiplied.' See, for example, the poem by Berta's daughter Laura Zúniga featured on COPINH's Facebook page at https://m.facebook.com/copinh.intibuca/posts/2856494517957642?locale2=ar_AR.

14. See Boff (1997).

15. This is the language used by the Zapatistas of Chiapas, Mexico, to describe the world that they envisioned in their 1994 uprising and continue to embody in their construction of an autonomous Indigenous homeland and a world in which all people are free to fully exist. 'The world that we desire is one in which many worlds fit. The Homeland that we are building is one in which all peoples and their languages fit, that is traversed by all paths, that all may enjoy, that is made to dawn by all' (Comité Clandestino Revolucionario Indígena-Comandancia General del Ejército Zapatista de Liberación Nacional 1996).

16. See Ada María Isasi-Díaz's (1990, 34) use of 'kin-dom' language for the reign of God. See also Isasi-Díaz (1996; 2004).

References

Althaus-Reid, Marcela. *Indecent Theology: Theological Perversions in Sex, Gender, and Politics*. New York: Routledge, 2000.

Barros, Marcelo. 'Queremos nossos mártires vivos', Brasil de Fato Website, March 25, 2022. https://www.brasildefatope.com.br/2019/03/25/queremos-nossos-martires-vivos. Accessed 22/11/2024.

Boff, Leonardo. *Cry of the Earth, Cry of the Poor*. Maryknoll, NY: Orbis Books, 1997.

Boff, Leonardo. 'Elogio aos afrodescendentes no seu dia 20 de novembro', November 20, 2019. https://leonardoboff.org/2019/11/20/elogio-aos-afrodescendentes-no-seu-dia-20-de-novembro/. Accessed 22/11/2024.

Cáceres, Berta. 'Goldman Environmental Prize Acceptance Speech', April 22, 2015. https://youtu.be/AR1kwx8boms. Accessed 22/11/2024.

Caram, María José. 'El amor en un mundo de opresión: Aportes de la Teología de la Liberación a la reflexión sobre las relaciones entre justicia y misericordia', *Anuario Iberoamericano Derecho Internacional Penal* 5, no. 5 (May 2017): 123–4.

Carvalho, Andrea, and Fernanda Costa. 'UN Experts Call on Brazil to End "Brutal" Police Violence', Human Rights Watch Website, December 15, 2023. https://www.hrw.org/news/2023/12/15/un-experts-call-brazil-end-brutal-police-violence. Accessed 22/11/2024.

Comité Clandestino Revolucionario Indígena-Comandancia General del Ejército Zapatista de Liberación Nacional. 'Cuarta Declaración de la Selva Lacandona', January 1, 1996. enlacezapatista.ezln.org.mx.

Erdos, Fábio. 'Marielle and Monica: The LGBT Activists Resisting Bolsonaro's Brazil', Documentary Film. *The Guardian*, December 28, 2018. https://www.theguardian.com/world/video/2018/dec/28/marielle-and-monica-the-lgbt-activists-resisting-bolsonaros-brazil-video. Accessed 22/11/2024.

Gandolfo, Elizabeth O'Donnell. 'Women and Martyrdom: Feminist Liberation Theology in Dialogue with a Latin American Paradigm', *Horizons* 34, no. 1 (2007): 26–53.

Gandolfo, Elizabeth O'Donnell. *Ecomartyrdom in the Americas: Living and Dying for Our Common Home*. Maryknoll, NY: Orbis Books, 2023.

Hamer, Fannie Lou. 'Nobody's Free Until Everybody's Free'. In *Speeches of Fannie Lou Hamer: To Tell It Like It Is*, edited by Maegan Parker Brooks and David W. Houck, 134–9. Jackson, MS: University Press of Mississippi, 2010.

Isasi-Díaz, Ada María. 'Solidarity: Love of Neighbors in the 1980s'. In *Lift Every Voice: Constructing Christian Theologies from the Underside,* edited by Susan Brooks Thistlethwaite and Mary Potter Engel, 31–40. San Francisco, CA: Harper & Row, 1990.

Isasi-Díaz, Ada María. *Mujerista Theology: A Theology for the Twenty-First Century*. Maryknoll, NY: Orbis Books, 1996.

Isasi-Díaz, Ada María. *En La Lucha: Elaborating a Mujerista Theology*, 10th Anniversary Edition. Minneapolis, MN: Fortress Press, 2004.

Lee, Michael E. *Revolutionary Saint: The Theological Vision of Óscar Romero*. Maryknoll, NY: Orbis Books, 2018.

Lucas, Kintto. *Rebeliones indígenas y negras en América Latina: Entre viento y fuego*. Quincenario Tintají, 2004.

Mignolo, Walter D., and Arturo Escobar, eds. 'Globalization and the De-Colonial Option', *Cultural Studies* 21, no. 2–3 (2007): 155–523.

Noone, Judith M. *The Same Fate as the Poor*. Maryknoll, NY: Orbis Books, 1984.

Pacheco, Ronilso. 'Black Theology in Brazil: Decolonial and Marginal', *CrossCurrents* (March 2017): 55–72.

Pacheco, Ronilso. 'The Diaspora Will Be the Multiplication of Hope, Resistance and Memory', Alliance of Baptists, n.d. https://allianceofbaptists.org/the-diaspora-will-be-the-multiplication-of-hope-resistance-and-memory/. Accessed 22/11/2024.

Radio Progreso. 'Berta y el Martirio', Radio Progreso Website, March 5, 2020.

Romero, Óscar. Homily, February 17, 1980. http://www.romerotrust.org.uk/homilies-and-writings/homilies/poverty-beatitudes-force-true-liberation-people. Accessed 22/11/2024.

Sobrino, Jon. 'Los mártires jesuánicos en el tercer mundo', *Revista Latinoamericana de Teología* 16, no. 48 (1999): 237–55.

Index

A

abortion, 3, 16–17, 160, 162–3, 170, 172, 174n27–8, 180. *See also* birth control pill; *Católicas por el Derecho a Decidir*
abstraction, 14–15, 114–18, 120–24
Ação Popular, 146
acompañamiento / accompaniment, 13–14, 54–5, 57–8, 60, 62–72, 74–78
Afro-descendent communities, 6, 188, 202–3, 205–8
Agamben, Giorgio, 179–81
Aguilar, Mario I., 5, 17, 55, 59, 77, 78n1
Aldunate, José, 136, 138
alienation
   and ecclesial hierarchies, 11, 14, 25, 31, 33–34, 37
   and architecture, 114, 120–21
   religion as, 91
All Africa Council of Churches (AACC), 148
Allende, Salvador, 4
Alliance for Progress, 85, 119–20, 133
Althaus-Reid, Marcella, 6–8, 18n8, 209n2
Alvez, Rubem, 95–6
Amazon Synod, 3. *See also* ecology
Angelelli, Enrique, 3. *See also* martyrs / martyrdom
anthropocentrism, 10, 17, 180, 185, 190–92
Antoine, Charles, 141, 151
Antoncich, Ricardo, 59, 62
apostolic obedience, 13, 28–31, 34, 37, 43, 182
Aramburu, Juan Carlos, 29, 37
architecture, 15, 114, 116, 121, 123
architecture without architects, 114
Arquitetura Nova, 120–21
Assmann, Hugo, 137
Autogobierno, 121

B

Battista Alberti, Leon, 116, 121
Benítez, Hernán, 30
Benjamin, Walter, 88, 105n5, 179, 193n2
Bertrand Russell Tribunal, 143, 145. *See also* dictatorship, repression
Bidegaín, Ana María, 7
birth control pill, vii, 16, 160, 166–8, 170, 172, 173n19, 174n28. *See also* abortion
Black theology, 6, 102, 160–61, 200, 205, 208. *See also* ethnicity

Boff, Clodovis, 140
Boff, Leonardo, 2–3, 6, 9–11, 13, 24, 44, 113, 184, 205, 210n14
bogotazo, 84
Bolatti, Archbishop Guillermo, 28, 31
Bonavía, Pablo, 58–9, 61, 63–4, 66–8
Bonhoeffer, Dietrich, xi–xiii
Bonino, José Míguez, 18n8, 137
Brazilian Information Front. See *Frente Brasileira de Informações*
Brunelleschi, Filippo, 116
Bukele, Nayib (Salvadoran president), xii

C

Cáceres, Berta, 199, 206–7. *See also* martyrs / martyrdom
Caggiano, Antonio, 27–8, 33
Câmara, Dom Hélder, 16, 139, 141, 148–51
Cañales, 53–4, 56, 58, 60, 62, 68–70
capitalism, 3–4, 39, 55, 58, 114, 132, 150, 185, 204, 206–8
Carbone, Alberto, 40–42, 45n16–17
Cardenal, Ernesto, 2–3, 10
Cardonnell, Jean, 141, 143
Carter, Jimmy, 8–9, 137
cartoneros, 75
Casalis, George, 141, 143
Catholic Church, 1–2, 4, 11–12, 14, 16, 18n1, 55, 58, 61, 63, 77, 106n11, 114, 123, 143, 148, 153, 185–6
   in Argentina, 5, 13, 24–45
   and conservatism, 90, 133–4
   and women, 159–64, 166, 173n4, 173n7
   and martyrdom, 200, 203–5
Catholic humanism, 85
Catholic social teaching, 14, 56, 59, 62
Catholic University of Louvain, 93, 140, 144, 146, 181
Católicas por el Derecho a Decidir, 3, 172. *See also* abortion
Catholics for Choice. See *Católicas por el Derecho a Decidir*
celibacy, 13, 23–5, 38, 41–3
Centro Nacional de Comunicación Social (CENCOS), 163
charism, 56, 58
charity, 14, 31, 34, 55, 58–9, 63, 65–6, 71, 74, 78, 90, 136, 150
Chipana, Sofía, 188–9
Christ, xi–xiv, xvi, 10, 16, 31–2, 56–9, 65–6, 75, 147, 183, 210n8
   historical Jesus, xvi, 100, 186, 202, 205, 207

Christian Movement for Peace (MCP), 143
Christian Worker Movement (MOC), 143
CIA, 131, 133
Civic Council of Popular and Indigenous Organizations of Honduras (COPINH), 206, 210n13
civil war (El Salvador), xi–xii
clasificadores, 54, 63, 72, 74–6, 78n3
clericalism, 10–12
climate crisis, 8, 191. See also ecology, environment
Coalición de Mujeres Feministas, 170. See also feminism
Coalition of Women Feminists. See *Coalición de Mujeres Feministas*
Cold War, the, vii–viii, 3–4, 119, 133
colonialism / coloniality, 5–6, 8, 10, 15–16, 93, 115, 122, 149, 206, 208
Comisión Económica para América Latina / Economic Commission for Latin America (CEPAL), 119, 122, 132
Comisión Episcopal de Pastoral (COEPAL), 42, 45n18
Comité de Solidarité France-Brésil, 143
Companhia de Desenvolvimento do Araguaia (CODEARA), 142
Comunicación, Intercambio y Desarrollo Humano en América Latina (CIDHAL), 162, 170, 172
Comunidades Eclesiales de Base / *Comunidades Eclesiais de Base*, 4, 11, 24, 31, 57–8, 93, 97, 99, 101, 113, 123, 133, 201, 207
Concatti, Rolando, 39–40
Conferencia Episcopal Argentina (CEA), 27
Conferência Nacional dos Bispos do Brasil (CNBB), 141, 151
conquistadores / conquistadors, 116, 202
conscientizaçao / conscientisation / concientización, 149, 171
Consejo Episcopal Latinoamericano y Caribeño (CELAM)
 second meeting in Medellín, 1, 25–6, 29, 35, 58–9, 62, 93, 133
 third meeting in Puebla, 1–2, 7–8, 11, 16, 25, 42, 58, 159–63, 171, 173n6
Consejo Nacional de Población (CONAPO), 167, 170
Con-spirando, 180, 188–92
Cooperativa de Vivienda de Familias Unidas (COVIFU), 13, 53–78
cordobazo, 28, 38
corpus mysticum / mystical body of Christ, 11, 35
Cortés, Hernán, 118
cosmopraxis, 189

Cristianismo y Revolución, 27, 33, 43
Cristianos por el Socialismo, 4
Cross, Nigel, 115
crucified people, xii–xiv, 200, 206–7
crucifixion, xi, xiii, 10, 147
Cuban Revolution, 4, 91, 119
curas villeros (Argentina), 42–3

D

death, xii–xiii, xv, 122, 201, 204, 207–9
 powers of, xvi, 181
decolonisation / decoloniality / decolonial theory, vii–viii, 6, 14, 93, 117–18, 122, 205–7, 210n11. See also colonialism / coloniality
dependency, 4, 9, 16, 59, 70, 119, 132, 139, 146, 168. See also colonialism / coloniality
Descartes, Rene, 118, 122
design, 15, 114–16, 118, 121, 124–5
Development Company of Araguaia. See *Companhia de Desenvolvimento do Araguaia* (CODEARA)
devolución sistemática (systematic devolution), 99, 104. See also Fals Borda, Orlando
De Carlo, Giancarlo, 114
Dictatorship. See also Pinochet, General Augusto; Onganía, General Juan Carlos
 in Argentina, 5, 13, 18n1, 27–8, 38, 42–3
 in Brazil, 4, 16, 131, 134, 138–40, 144, 148, 152
 in Chile, 4
 in Uruguay, 55, 59–60, 62–3, 77, 78n1–2
Diffusion of Information on Latin America (DIAL), 151
Dirty War, 200–201
docetism, xi
Dominicans, 150
Dri, Rubén, 34, 40–41, 44, 45n1
Dussel, Enrique, 6, 24, 122

E

ecclesial base communities. See *Comunidades Eclesiales de Base* / *Comunidades Eclesiais de Base*
ecclesiology, 3, 11, 13, 24–5, 31, 35, 38, 44
 people of God, 13, 26, 28–9, 31–7, 39, 43–4, 58, 164
ecofeminism, 17, 180, 183–9, 191, 193n1, 194n11, 194n13
ecology, viii, 3, 5, 9–10, 17, 60, 76, 118, 122, 180, 184, 187–8, 191, 203–9, 210n9
Ecumenical Association of Third World Theologians (EATWOT), 12

ecumenism, 6, 12, 18n9, 40, 93, 100
Eisenman, Peter, 115
Ejército de Liberación Nacional (ELN), 92
Ellacuría, Ignacio, xi–xiv, 12, 200
Encuentro Feminista Latinoamericano y del Caribe (EFLAC), 171. *See also* feminism; gender; *Mujeres para el Diálogo* (MPD)
Engaged sociology, 83, 92–3, 97. *See also* Fals Borda, Orlando
environment, 3, 9–10, 18, 60, 118, 153, 193, 194n11, 201, 203–9, 209n1. *See also* ecology
Episcopal Commission of Pastoral Ministry. See *Comisión Episcopal de Pastoral* (COEPAL)
epistemology, 10, 12, 84–5, 97, 101–3, 115, 122, 185–7, 189
Erskine, Ralph, 115, 121
Escobar, Arturo, 118–19, 122
Escuela de Arquitectura, Universidad de Talca, 124–5
ethnicity, 5–7, 9, 136, 202. *See also* indigeneity; Indigenous people
Evangelii Gaudium, 3, 11
evangelisation, 5–6, 11, 42, 58, 103
exile, 6, 16, 120, 139, 145–8, 151, 153
Exodus, 58

F

Fals Borda, Orlando, vii, 14, 83–112. *See also devolución sistemática* (systematic devolution), engaged sociology, *La Rosca*, moral subversion, School of Sociology, National University of Colombia
analysis of *la Violencia*, 85–8, 101, 105n3
and the Presbyterian Church, 14, 83, 85, 94–5, 103
and revolutionary politics, 85, 88–90, 92, 94, 98, 101, 103
false binaries, 9, 90
Federación Uruguaya de Cooperativas de Vivienda por Ayuda Mutua (FUCVAM), 121
feminism, 6V8, 16–17, 18n6, 102, 160–74, 180–94, 200, 205–6, 208. *See also* Althuas-Reid, Marcela; Gebara, Ivone; gender; LGBTQ+ communities and theologies
France-Latin America Episcopal Committee (CEFAL), 151
Franciscans, 56, 58, 61, 63, 70, 78
Franco, Marielle, 199, 208. *See also* martyr / martyrdom
Freire, Paulo, 57, 59, 61, 97, 113, 119, 121–3, 133, 143, 149

Frente Brasileira de Informações, 146–8
Frente Unido (Colombia), 91
Fuerzas Armadas Peronistas (FAP), 36

G

García Elorrio, Juan, 27–8
Gebara, Ivone, 6, 17, 180–88
gender, 5, 6–9, 12, 16, 18, 18n6–7, 72, 136, 161, 171, 180–81, 185, 191–2, 203, 205, 208. *See also* Althuas-Reid, Marcela; feminism; Gebara, Ivone; LGBTQ+ communities and theology; sexuality; women's theology
General Council for the Apostolate of the Laity (CGAL), 143, 154n4
Gera, Lucio, 30, 42. *See also* theology of the people
God, xi–xii, xiv–xvi, 10, 13, 32, 58–60, 66, 93, 96, 181–2, 186–7, 204, 209, 210n16. *See also* people of God
Goddess, 182–3, 185, 187, 189, 192, 193n8. *See also* gender; feminism
Golconda, 11, 92, 106n11
Gospel, xvi, 40, 61, 93. *See also* Christ; God; People of God
Graeber, David, 65, 67–9
Grande, Rutilio, xi, 138, 200. *See also* martyrs / martyrdom
guerrilla, 14, 27, 38, 84, 86, 88, 91–2, 105n4, 146, 148
Guevara, Ernesto 'Che', 57, 88, 119
Gutiérrez, Gustavo, 1, 3, 5–6, 9–11, 93, 98, 101–2, 113, 137, 140, 164, 168, 173n14, 184, 186, 200

H

hermeneutics, xiii, 15, 59, 103
human rights, 3, 5, 15–16, 18n9, 78n2, 131–2, 134–53, 201, 203, 205, 207
liberationist conception of, 8–9, 12, 18n9, 131, 134–53
violations of, 3, 9, 18, 37, 201, 203–5, 208, 209n1
Humane Vitae, 166, 169

I

indigeneity, 5, 85, 117. *See also* colonialism / coloniality; decolonisation / decoloniality / decolonial theory; ethnicity; Indigenous people
Indigenous people, 5, 16, 94, 133, 140–2, 144, 147–8, 153, 164–5, 171, 188–9, 200, 202–3, 205–8, 210n15. *See also* colonialism / coloniality; decolonisation / decoloniality / decolonial theory; ethnicity; indigeneity
institutionalised violence, 4, 9, 93

Integral Educational Model. *See modelo educacional integral*
Inter-American Commission on Human Rights, 136. *See also* human rights
Inter-American Court of Human Rights, 9. *See also* human rights
inter-class relations, 55, 74, 77
international aid, 57, 133, 136, 149
International Labour Organisation (ILO), 141–2, 145
International Monetary Fund (IMF), 132
Irarrázaval, Diego, 5

J

Jentel, François, 141–4, 154n2, 154n3
Jesuit martyrs (El Salvador), xi, 2, 12, 138, 200, 204
Jesuits, ix, xi, 2, 56, 78n1, 123, 138, 161, 169, 204, 207
Jesus. *See* Christ
Jeunesse Ouvrière Chrétienne (JOC), 16, 28, 140–45, 154n1
Justice et Paix, 143
Juventud Católica Femenina Mexicana (JCFM), 169
Juventud Obrera Cristiana, see *Jeunesse Ouvrière Chrétienne* (JOC)

L

La Rosca, 93–5, 97–103. *See also* Fals Borda, Orlando
la Violencia, 85–7, 101, 105n3. *See also* Fals Borda, Orlando
laity, 1, 26, 28, 30–32, 35, 134, 139, 143
Latin American Bishops Conference. *See Consejo Episcopal Latinoamericano y Caribeño* (CELAM)
Laudato Si, 3, 10. *See also* Francis, Pope
LGBTQ+ communities and theologies, 6, 8, 200, 203, 205, 207–8
López Trujillo, Alfonso, 25
Löwy, Michael, 3, 24
Lutheran Church, xiii, 74

M

Marturet, Raúl, 33, 45n9
Marxism / Marxist, 1, 42, 44, 58, 60, 85, 88, 90, 92, 97–8, 101, 106n11, 114, 121, 133–5, 146, 165
Mary Magdalene, 183
martyrs / martyrdom, xi–xvii, 3, 5, 12, 18, 88, 199–210
Mayol, Alejandro, 33–4
Message of Third World Bishops (1967), 39
Metz, Johann Baptist, xiv

Mignolo, Walter, 118, 122
military coup. *See* dictatorship
Miranda, José Porfirio, 58–9
Moctezuma, 118
modelo educacional integral (MEI), 92
modernity, 10, 115, 122, 173n10, 185
Moral subversion, 83, 85, 88–9. *See also* Fals Borda, Orlando
Movimiento de Sacerdotes para el Tercer Mundo (MSTM), 5, 7, 11–13, 23–52. *See also* people of God
  celibacy, 23–5, 38, 41–3
  dispute with episcopal hierarchy, 25–38, 41, 43
  Peronism, 23–6, 36, 38–45
  socialism, 28, 39–40, 42, 44
Mugica, Carlos, 26, 37
Mujeres para el Diálogo (MPD), 16–17, 159–78

N

National Conference of Brazilian Bishops. *See Conferência Nacional dos Bispos do Brasil* (CNBB)
National Population Council. *See Consejo Nacional de Población* (CONAPO)
NATO, 131
neoliberalism, 4–5, 9, 55, 136, 138, 149, 208
New Christendom, 11, 35
nuns. *See* women religious

O

Onganía, General Juan Carlos, 27, 43. *See also* dictatorship
Organization of American States (OAS), 119, 132

P

Pacem in Terris, 8, 150. *See also* John XXIII
Padre Cacho, 14, 54–6, 60–61, 63–5, 69–71, 74–5, 77–8
Participatory Action Research (PAR), 14, 83–5, 101–4, 104n1. *See also* Fals Borda, Orlando
participatory design, 114–15, 118–23
peasant movement (Colombia), 83–4, 94–6, 100–101, 104, 104n1. *See also* Fals Borda, Orlando
Pentecostalism, 12, 55, 95
Peronism, 23–6, 36, 38–45
Peronismo de Base, 36, 40, 44
Peronist Armed Forces. *See Fuerzas Armadas Peronistas* (FAP)
Petrella, Iván, 3–4, 12, 14–15

Pinochet, General Augusto, 4. *See also* dictatorship
pluralism, 17, 90
Podestá, Jerónimo, 24, 35–6, 41
Political theology, ix, 17, 179–81, 183–4, 189, 191–3
Pope Francis, 2–3, 10, 18n6, 42, 75, 200, 208
  'throwaway society', 75
Pope John Paul II, 2, 11, 25
Pope John XXIII, 8
Pope Paul VI, 8, 31, 35, 37, 106n11, 166
popular religiosity, 11
Populorum Progressio, 8. *See also* Paul VI
praxis, 2–3, 8, 12–15, 17–18, 24, 36, 40, 44, 55–6, 59, 62–5, 70, 83–4, 96–102, 104, 113, 121, 124, 153, 164, 189, 201–2, 207, 209
preferential option for the poor, 12, 55, 58, 60, 62–3, 77, 113, 134, 185
prophet / prophetic / prophetism, 1, 4–5, 9, 39, 60, 100, 106n8, 201, 205
Protestantism, 6, 11–12, 40, 74–5, 85, 87, 93, 95–6, 100. *See also* Pentecostalism
Ptolemy, 116

Q

queer theology. *See* LGBTQ+ communities and theologies
Quijano, Aníbal, 118, 122

R

Ramondetti, Miguel, 39
refugees, 147–8, 207
repression, vii, xii, 2, 4–5, 29, 37, 59, 89, 134–5, 139, 141, 143–6, 148, 152–3, 201, 203–4
Ress, Mary Judith, 180, 184, 188–9, 193n1, 193n7
resurrection, xi, 186, 201, 209
Rocha, Guido, 147–8, 154n5
Romero, Oscar, xi–xii, xiv, 2–3, 56–7, 77, 138, 200, 204, 207, 210n8. *See also* Jesuit martyrs (El Salvador); martyrs / martyrdom
  canonisation, xii, 3, 200
Rudofsky, Bernard, 114

S

Saint Francis of Assisi, 10
Salesians, 53, 56, 58
salvation, xv, 10, 12, 100, 164, 181, 183
Sandinistas, 2, 143
Schmitt, Carl, 179, 181, 191

School of Sociology, National University of Colombia, 85, 93. *See also* Fals Borda, Orlando
Second Vatican Council, xiii, xvi, 26–9, 31, 58, 62, 93, 134, 151, 186
  Lumen Gentium, 13, 35
  Presbyterorum Ordinis, 31
security policy (El Salvador), xii
see-judge-act, xiv, 92, 97, 204
Segundo, Juan Luis, 25, 78n1, 113, 137, 140
sex / sexuality, vii, 6–8, 161, 163–6, 170, 187, 208. *See also* abortion; gender; LGBTQ+ communities and theologies
Shaull, Richard, 85, 94–5, 103
signs of the times, xiii, 200
sin, xi, xiii, 9, 12, 55, 59, 63, 65, 69, 71, 78, 135, 183, 204–5
Smith, Christian, 4–5, 24
Sobrino, Jon, xi, xv, 58, 200, 204
socialism, xv, 4, 13, 28, 34, 39–40, 42, 44, 85, 89–90, 105n6, 145, 147, 149, 163. *See also* Allende, Salvador; Cuban Revolution
socialist bloc, 2
Stang, Dorothy, 199, 201, 204
structural sin, xiii, 9, 12, 55, 59, 63, 65, 69, 71, 135, 204–5, 207
Suenens, Cardinal León-Joseph, 140–41

T

Tafuri, Manfredo, 114
Talpe, Jan, 141, 146
Tello, Rafael, 42, 44. *See also* theology of the people
Tenochtitlan, 118
Theology in the Americas' conference (1975), 6, 161
theology of the people, 25, 42–4, 45n4. *See also* Gera, Lucio; Tello, Rafael
Tierra Nueva (Argentina), 33
Tombs, David, 5, 17
Torres, Camilo, 14, 57, 83–5, 88–93, 106n10, 140
Tortolo, Archbishop Adolfo, 33–4, 37
Turner, John F. C., 114, 119–20

U

ubi, xi
UN Economic and Social Council, 142
United Nations, 120, 131
United Nations Conference on Women 1975, 162–3
United Nations Economic Commission for Latin America. *See Comisión Económica para América Latina* (CEPAL)

Universal Declaration of Human Rights, 131, 134, 137, 142, 150. *See also* human rights
Universidad Católica de Valparaíso, 113, 123–4
Universidad Centramericana José Simeón Cañas (UCA), xi, 2, 204
urbanism. See architecture, 113
Uruguayan Federation of Housing Cooperatives for Mutual Aid. *See Federación Uruguaya de Cooperativas de Vivienda por Ayuda Mutua (FUCVAM)*
utopia, viii, xv, 9, 14, 88, 90–91, 105n5, 105n7

V

Vatican, 2, 35, 43, 161, 181
Vicaría de la Solidaridad, 4
Vicariate of Solidarity. *See Vicaría de la Solidaridad*
victims, xi–xv, 4, 13, 138–9, 143, 145, 148–9, 168, 205. *See also* Jesuit martyrs (El Salvador); martyrs / martyrdom; repression
Virgin Mary, 27, 53, 182–3, 193n9

W

Wages for Housework (collective), 165
Weil, Simone, xiv
women religious, 6–7, 14, 18n3, 31, 33, 54, 56–8, 61, 63, 65, 70, 73, 75, 78, 92, 163–4, 204
women's theology, 3, 180, 184. *See also* Althaus-Reid, Marcella; Bidegaín, Ana María; feminism; Gebara, Ivone; gender; *Mujeres para el Diálogo* (MPD); Ress, Mary Judith; sex / sexuality
World Bank, 120, 122, 132
World Council of Churches, 6, 94, 148. *See also* ecumenism

Y

Young Christian Workers. *See Jeunesse Ouvrière Chrétienne* (JOC)
Young Mexican Women Catholics. *See Juventud Católica Femenina Mexicana* (JCFM)

Z

Zapatistas, 210n15
Zazpe, Archbishop Vicente, 37

www.ingramcontent.com/pod-product-compliance
Lightning Source LLC
Chambersburg PA
CBHW041656210625
28439CB00005B/9